D1413456

public personnel administration

public affairs and administration
(editor: James S. Bowman)
vol. 10

Garland reference library
of social science
vol. 170

the public affairs and administration series: James S. Bowman, editor

public personnel
administration
an annotated bibliography

Sarah Y. Bowman
Jay M. Shafritz

Garland Publishing, Inc. • New York & London
1985

Library of Congress Cataloging in Publication Data

Bowman, Sarah Y.
  Public personnel administration.

  (Public affairs and administration ; vol. 10)
(Garland reference library of social science ; vol. 170)
  Includes index.
    1. Civil service—United States—Personnel management
—Bibliography. 2. Administrative agencies—United
States—Personnel management—Bibliography. I. Shafritz,
Jay M. II. Title. III. Series: Public affairs and
administration series ; 10. IV. Series: Garland
reference library of social science ; v. 170.
Z7164.C6B68 1985   016.353001   82-49150
[JK765]
ISBN 0-8240-9151-5 (alk. paper)

Cover design by Laurence Walczak

Printed on acid-free, 250-year life paper
Manufactured in the United States of America

contents

series foreword

The twentieth century has seen public administration come of age as a field and practice. This decade, in fact, marks the one hundredth anniversary of the profession. As a result of the dramatic growth in government, and the accompanying information explosion, many individuals—managers, academicians and their students, researchers—in organizations feel that they do not have ready access to important information. In an increasingly complex world, more and more people need published material to help solve problems.

The scope of the field and the lack of a comprehensive information system has frustrated users, disseminators, and generators of knowledge in public administration. While there have been some initiatives in recent years, the documentation and control of the literature have been generally neglected. Indeed, major gaps in the development of the literature, the bibliographic structure of the discipline, have evolved.

Garland Publishing, Inc., has inaugurated the present series as an authoritative guide to information sources in public administration. It seeks to consolidate the gains made in the growth and maturation of the profession.

The Series consists of three tiers:
1. core volumes keyed to the major subfields in public administration such as personnel management, public budgeting, and intergovernmental relations;
2. bibliographies focusing on substantive areas of administration such as community health; and
3. titles on topical issues in the profession.

Each book will be compiled by one or more specialists in the area. The authors—practitioners and scholars—are selected in open competition from across the country. They design their work to include an introductory essay, a wide variety of bibliographic materials, and, where appropriate, an information resource section. Thus each contribution in the collection provides a systematic basis for managers and researchers to make informed judgments in the course of their work.

Since no single volume can adequately encompass such a broad, interdisciplinary subject, the Series is intended as a continuous project that will incorporate new bodies of literature as needed. The titles in preparation represent the initial building blocks in an operating information system for public affairs and administration. As an open-ended endeavor, it is hoped that not only will the Series serve to summarize knowledge in the field but also will contribute to its advancement.

This collection of book-length bibliographies is the product of considerable collaboration on the part of many people. Special appreciation is extended to the editors and staff of Garland Publishing, Inc., to the individual contributors in the Public Affairs and Administration Series, and to the anonymous reviewers of each of the volumes. Inquiries should be made to the Series Editor:

James S. Bowman
Tallahassee

preface

In this volume, Sarah Bowman and Jay Shafritz demonstrate that expertise in a subject area can lead to an artful bibliography that simultaneously provides basic references and defines a field of inquiry. The chapters of this book probe the essential topics that demarcate public personnel administration. They extend from the perennial concerns of the field, such as position classification, to more recent issues that have spawned conflict over its fundamental assumptions, such as equal employment opportunity. Considerable scope is also evident in the range of materials covered in each chapter. The book includes references found in such mainstream academic publications as *Administrative Science Quarterly* and the *Public Administration Review* while summarizing articles in journals oriented more toward practitioners such as *Personnel Management*. The annotated citations range from examinations of the philosophic underpinnings of a personnel decision arena to specific techniques useful in getting the job done. The citations not only encompass information, theories, and prescriptions focused on the particular problems of the public sector, they also address the more generic issues of personnel administration that surface in almost any complex organization.

Aside from pointing the way to publications appearing in books and journals, Bowman and Shafritz present references to major court cases. This step beyond the conventional focus of annotated bibliographies greatly heightens the value of their work. The emergence of the courts as major players in the personnel arena comprises one of the central developments of the last twenty years. Students and practitioners of personnel management need to be aware of these cases and become more accustomed to reading them.

Given its virtues, this volume should ultimately prove useful to several groups. First, teachers of public personnel administration in academic settings can draw on it in constructing syllabi for courses and comprehensive reading lists for graduate students. In many instances, indeed, it will help instructors discover publications that have escaped their attention. Second, those enrolled in courses or training sessions dealing with public personnel administration will find the volume useful in unearthing basic references for specialized papers. It will also help them grasp the boundaries of the field. Third, practitioners of public personnel management will value the book as a convenient way to acquaint themselves with some of the basic techniques and issues in a given area. The bibliography can become a useful means for cutting their information costs. Finally, those doing in-depth research in personnel will find this volume a useful place to start. It provides a foundation on which to build a more elaborate bank of knowledge.

In sum, the authors have fashioned a bibliography of impressive scope that can legitimately command the attention of those interested in public personnel management. Above all, it reflects choice. A bibliography in personnel administration needs to place the user on a balanced diet. It must avoid the dangers of excess, of simply trying to cite everything, for a surfeit of citations can paralyze the user or lead him or her to waste time reading excessively redundant materials. It can also put too much of the field's junk food on the table. Simultaneously, of course, a carefully constructed bibliography must take reasonable steps to avoid the other extreme, that is, an insufficient number of citations that will not provide intellectual nourishment. A little knowledge can indeed be a dangerous thing when it leads to the illusion of knowledge and an accompanying commitment to simplistic nostrums. In striking the needed balance, the expertise of Bowman and Shafritz looms large.

Frank J. Thompson
University of Georgia

introduction

Although the functions of personnel administration (recruitment, selection, placement, development, compensation) have not changed remarkably over time, times have changed. There is a movement in public personnel administration toward an emphasis on the effective use of human resources to achieve organizational goals and away from the negative, protective approach of the civil service reformers of the nineteenth century. A review of the literature reveals concern for such issues as:

> Representative bureaucracy through equal employment opportunity/affirmative action programs
> Protection of the constitutional rights of public employees
> Reform of the civil service system
> Strategic planning which integrates management strategies based on some anticipation of government's needs
> Amelioration of problems of position classification and pay administration through the application of management systems concepts
> Effective position-person matching systems
> Removal of productivity measures from the influence of politics
> Rationalization of training and development programs
> Linkage of appraisal to performance
> Creation of meaningful work

This annotated bibliography assembles selected citations dealing with these issues as well as the standard functions of personnel administration.

organization

The book represents the full range of personnel topics with the exception of labor-management relations which appears as a separate volume in this series (see page facing title page). While equal opportunity problems receive coverage here, another bibliography in this series focuses exclusively on that area. The annotated entries are organized into 10 chapters; chapter 11 is an unannotated list of texts and readers. Major emphasis is placed on recent publications although some classic readings are included. Entries are arranged alphabetically by author within each chapter and numbered consecutively throughout the book (1 to 684).

We began our search of the literature by pursuing the bibliographical entries listed in *Personnel Management in Government: Politics and Process,* second edition, by Shafritz, Hyde, and Rosenbloom(678). The sources cited were accepted as authoritative. This bibliography represents an update and expansion of that work; see page xxv for a list of the journals cited. We manually searched the libraries of the University of Colorado and the University of Denver, and all annotations were derived from the original source materials. Quotations used have been taken directly from the works being annotated.

Chapter Highlights

Civil Service Reform, Chapter 1, has two main thrusts. The first is historical. Histories are included to aid in understanding the pressures and influences which shaped the development of the civil service system. Pressures for reform date back to the era of Andrew Jackson. The history of the early civil service reformers and the formation of the National Civil Service Reform League is traced by Hoogenboom(26) and Stewart(57). A monograph by the U.S. Civil Service Commission(61) briefly presents the most significant events in the development of the civil service while Van Riper's history(64) is quite comprehensive. McBain(36) develops the history of patronage in New York; Murphy(41) presents a detailed account of the first civil service commission under President Grant; and Crenson(14) addresses the beginnings of bureaucracy. For a philosophical/cultural view of the development of public personnel management, see Mosher(40); for a more personal view of administrative arrangements in the federal government, examine Meriam(38) and Seidman(52); and for a view of the civil service reform movement within an international context, consult Fish(21) and Huddleston(27) as well as Huddleston's bibliography in this series.

The second thrust centers around the influences and pressures surrounding the passage and subsequent analyses of and reactions to the Civil Service Reform Act (CSRA) of 1978. Since the passage of the Pendleton Act in 1883 (An Act to Regulate and Improve the Civil Service of the United States) which created the U.S. Civil Service Commission, debate about the commission form of personnel administration has ensued. The commission has had its promoters and defenders; see Crouch(15), Harvey(24), and Meriam(38). However, pressure for reorganization eventually led to the passage of the CSRA of 1978. As early as 1952, Carpenter(9) advocated reorganization of the civil service, followed by Hall(23) and Rosenthal(50) in 1967. More recently others have recommended changes [e.g., Rosen(49)] and defended the 1978 legislation [Campbell(6,8)].

Since 1978, a plethora of articles has appeared in the literature examining and analyzing various provisions of the CSRA of 1978. The Senior Executive Service has been examined by Buchanan(5), Cohn and Fisher(10), Colby and Ingraham(11), Long(33), and Rosen(46). Performance appraisal provisions drew the attention of McCarthy(37), Siegel(55), and Thompson(59) (also see Chapter 9, Performance Appraisal). Kramer(31) addresses the implementation of the Act; Rosen(47) concerns himself with accountability provisions; Ban, Goldenberg and Marzotto(2) focus on the release of unproductive employees; and Dullea(18) and Flanders and Klauss(19) are optimistic about the potential for executive development.

Chapter 2, Equal Employment Opportunity, addresses affirmative action programs, reverse discrimination, the handicapped worker, sex discrimination and sexual harassment. An integral part of the reform movement in the United States is pressure for a representative bureaucracy. Serious efforts to address discrimination can be traced back to the early 1940s.

However it was not until the passage of the Civil Rights Act in 1964, followed by the 1972 Equal Employment Act, that national attention was focused on this long-standing problem. In combination, these two pieces of legislation prohibited discrimination on the basis of sex, race, color, religion and national origin. In an effort to assure equal opportunity, affirmative action programs were established to bring more women and minorities into the federal service.

Since 1972, the literature is replete with articles and books describing affirmative action programs; refer to Bellone and Darling(76), Berwitz(77), Bocher(80); Clynch and Guadin(86), Farley(93) and Marlin(131). Advice and guidelines for achieving affirmative action goals can be found in Hall and Albrecht(103), Jongeward and Scott(115), Levine(127) and Lovell(128). The issues of reverse discrimination and affirmative action cannot be separated. Both Goldman(98) and Gross(101) raise the issue of justice and corrective preferential treatment. The classic case in this area is *Regents of California v. Allan Bakke* (201) in Chapter 3. Also see Bakaly and Krischer(75), Kelso(117) and Sindler(164).

The literature concerning the Vocational Rehabilitation Act of 1973 (VRA of 1973) and affirmative action programs designed to locate and hire the handicapped worker offers assistance to government contractors and subcontractors in achieving compliance with the provisions of the VRA. Representative works include Asher and Asher(71), Freedman(95), Johnson(114), Pati(142), Pati and Adkins(143) and Paterson(144). Recently, the EEO/AA literature reflects a concern for sex discrimination and sexual harassment in the work place. As the result of large numbers of women entering nontraditional jobs (including management), discrimination, romance in the work place and sexual harassment are fast becoming major management as well as legal concerns. For a discussion of sex discrimination, see Abramson(69), Hoffman and Reed(110), and Korda(119). Concerning romance, see Mead(133), Quinn(146), and Quinn and Judge(147). For more information about sexual harassment, see Backhouse(72), Backhouse et al.(73), Backhouse and Cohen(74), Collins and Blodgett(87), Faucher(94), James(113), MacKennon(129),

Neugarten and Shafritz(140), Rowe(159), Safran(160), and Siniscalo(165).

The next chapter, Constitutional Issues, emphasizes case law. Constitutional case law concerning public personnel management falls into six categories: freedom of expression; political neutrality; freedom of association; liberty; equal protection; and right to hearing. The most significant case currently governing public employee rights to freedom of speech is *Pickering v. Board of Education* (1968)(199). The Supreme Court held that the special duties and obligations of public employees cannot be ignored. The Hatch Acts address political neutrality and were originally promulgated to prevent public employees from being coerced into the performance of partisan services. The growth of unionism, protections against arbitrary adverse actions, and the Supreme Court's rulings in *Elrod v. Burns* (1976)(192) and *Branti v. Finkel* (1980)(185) have made coercion increasingly unlikely.

Freedom of association, the third category, is well established and public employees cannot be compelled to join or support political parties on pain of dismissal. However, in *Abood v. Detroit Board of Education* (1977)(181), the Supreme Court held that a public employee working in an "agency shop" could be required to pay a service fee equal in amount to union dues when he or she did not belong to the union. However, the union could not use the fees for political and ideological purposes unrelated to collective bargaining. During the 1970s, the Supreme Court addressed the next important issue, liberty, several times. *Cleveland Board of Education v. LaFleur* (1974)(187) held that arbitrary mandatory maternity leaves were unconstitutional. In *Kelley v. Johnson* (1976)(193) the Court upheld a municipal regulation limiting the hair length of police. And in *McCarthy v. Philadelphia Civil Service Commission* (1976)(196) the Court upheld the constitutionality of residency requirements for municipal employees.

In *Washington v. Davis* (1976)(207) the Court was concerned with equal protection, the fifth issue, and reasoned that a wide variety of public policies affects blacks differently than whites. Consequently, not result but intent to discriminate was the key constitutionally. In *Massachusetts v. Feeny*

(1979)(194) the Court held that veterans' lifetime preference for state employment was constitutional on the ground that the resulting discriminatory effect on women was not intentional. Finally, although the Supreme Court held in *Bishop v. Wood* (1976)(183) and *Codd v. Velger* (1977)(188) that hearings need not be held, public personnel managers may opt to hold hearings even when they are not constitutionally required to avoid litigation altogether.

In Chapter 4, the central theme is strategic human resources planning. As a strategic planning approach, it involves a systematic process of analyzing external conditions and organizational needs and delineating management response. Biles and Holmberg(209) have assembled a useful book of readings. Denanna, Fombrun and Ticky(218), Foulkes(221) and Geisler(222), Haire(227) and Stybel(248) encourage human resource management to expand its role and get involved at the strategic level of the organization. Practical considerations, such as planning methodologies and supply and demand of appropriately trained labor for manpower planning, can be found in Bowey(211); Bryant, Maggard, and Taylor(212); Burack (213,214); Burack and Mathys(215); Levitan, Mangum and Marshall(233); and Patton(243).

For sophisticated manpower planning models and computer-based technologies available to forecast manpower needs and personnel movement within the organization, see Blakely(210), Dill, Ganer, and Weber(219), Grinold and Marshall(225), Heneman and Sandner(228), Milkovich, Annoni, and Mahoney(235), Nielsen and Young(242), U.S. Civil Service Commission(249), Vroom and MacCrimmon(252) and Weber(254). At the operational level, Feldt and Andersen(220) and Hall(226) address employee turnover costs; Cooper and Davidson(217) and Ivancevich and Matteson(230) examine stress management; and Moore(239) discusses the role of the personnel department in employee relocation. Finally, D. Mills(236) and T. Mills(237) identify human resource management issues of the future.

Chapter 5 can roughly be divided into entries emphasizing position classification and items dealing with pay determination and administration. Position classification uses job descriptions to organize all jobs into classes on the basis of duties and responsibilities to delineate authority, establish chains of command, and provide equitable salary scales in organizations [see, e.g., Baruch(259)]. While position classification is common in personnel programs, it is often criticized. Collett(260) asserts that its technical aspects dominate the process; Klingner(274) finds fault with the traditional job description; Schulkind(288) examines practical classification problems and proposes a legal remedy; and Winchell and Burkett(294) identify role conflicts that contribute to "grade creep," the tendency to reallocate positions upward. A frequent recommendation is the application of behavioral science concepts to position classification [see Atwood(258), Danaker(262), and Shafritz(289)].

The passage of the Job Evaluation Policy Act in 1970 paved the way for the adoption of the factor evaluation system of position classification. Epperson(264) and Ramsay(282) describe its development and implementation at the federal level; Craver(261) reports on its use at the state and county level; and Oliver(280) reports on its development and implementation in Indiana. Since the pay plan ordinarily follows position classification, a great deal of attention is given to compensation determination and administration. Compensation methods can be found in Green(268), Lewin(276), Schmenner(287), Solomon(290), Suskin(291) and U.S. Office of Personnel Management(292). The effects of unionization and market forces on wage determination are addressed by Ashenfelter(257), Freund(267), Karper and Meckstroth(273) and Mode(279). A sound wage and salary program requires maintenance of external and internal equity. Comparability surveys show that some types of public employees earn more than their industrial counterparts while others earn less [Field and Keller(265), Fogel and Lewin(266), and Rosow(285)]. Maintenance of internal equity is much more difficult since position classification forces employees into career lines that are restrictive and because rigid promotional provisions limit employee salary growth. Henderson(270), Lawler(275), Mahoney(277), Patten(281) and Rosen(284) assert that a properly designed compensation system stimulates both performance and motivation.

Chapter 6, Recruitment, Selection and Placement, places

heavy emphasis on obtaining qualified personnel in organizations. After the organization determines its staffing needs (see Chapter 4, Human Resource Planning) and recruits a pool of applicants, selection begins. Selection is the process of reviewing the job candidates and deciding who will be offered the position. Selection, then, automatically affects the placement process, the assignment of the new employee to the position so that work can begin. Examinations are the dominant selection tool: Campbell(298) and Ghiselli(307,308) explore aptitude tests; Guion(309) addresses psychological testing; and Schwartz(333), Schwartz et al.(334) discuss the job sample test. The U.S. Office of Personnel Management(336) has issued a handbook containing testing methods for the small local government. The common objective of the examination is to determine whether an individual has a specific skill or ability. Since the *Griggs v. Duke Power Co.* case, the key dimension test validity (does it measure what it is designed to measure?) has been job-relatedness. For a discussion of validation strategies and job-relatedness of selection procedures, see Cronbach(301), Dreher and Sackett(303), Frank(306), Lawshe(317), Menne, McCarthy and Menne(321), Miner and Miner(323), and Wollack(339).

An elaboration of the examination tool is the assessment center. Proponents of this method assert that it is superior to other selection techniques in matching the appropriate person to the organization, [e.g., Byham(297) and O'Leary(325)]. Hart and Thompson(311) make a case for career development-oriented versus selection-oriented centers. For an account of America's first assessment center, see Office of Strategic Services(324). An integral part of the selection process is the interview. Hariton(310), Huett(313) and O'Leary(326) offer practical step-by-step guides while Kahn and Cannell(315) place emphasis on principles and theory of interviewing.

Chapter 7, Productivity, deals with government efforts to get improved yield out of allocated resources. Adams(341) maintains that, of the three choices — fewer people, fewer hours or greater product—increasing the product seems most feasible; Gilder(363) concurs: either reduce input or expand output; Kenrich(379) proposes using productivity measures to analyze cost and management control; and Chitwood(349) adds social equity to the productivity measurement equation. Because of public sector characteristics, such as budget constraints, and the absence of a discrete product, government faces unique difficulties in the application of productivity improvement concepts. Ammons and King(342) identify lack of familiarity with productivity literature and low priority as limiting factors in local government; Burkhead and Hennigan(346) assert that productivity analysis is difficult in the public sector because of an "absence of discrete units of government output." Notwithstanding these difficulties, Cheek(348), Cummings, Molloy and Glen(354), English and Marchione(358), Harrison(367), Latham, Cummings and Mitchell(383), Newland(401), and Quinn(411) offer strategies and models for productivity improvement.

According to Balk(344), one of the reasons public employees tend to be apathetic about productivity improvement programs is the "lack of involvement they have in productivity improvement planning and implementation." Productivity bargaining holds promise for changing the relationship between unions and management in a positive way [see Capozzola(347), Fremont(361), Goldoff and Tatage(364), Horton(374), McKersie and Hunter(394), Newland(403) and Newland et al.(405)]. Hayward(372), Judson(375), Schaffer(416), Shetty(418), draw attention to managements' role in affecting productivity improvement. For information about motivational techniques designed to address productivity, job satisfaction and quality of work life, see Greiner(365), Katzell and Yankelovich(376), Katzell et al.(377), and National Commission on Productivity and Work Quality(398).

Training and Development, Chapter 8, has traditionally been viewed as a stepchild in the personnel and human resource management family. After all the priority needs of the organization have been attended to, an organization will provide for some form of training and development in an effort to improve the capabilities of its employees. For an introduction to the field of training and development, see Craig(439), DePhillips, Berliner and Cribbin(440), Stockard(476) and Wexley and Latham(479). Since training and development managers routinely have had to justify training expenditures they have developed mechanisms for assessing training needs and evaluating programs. Brown and Wedel(433) write about determining training needs from the perspective of the chief executive; Caldwell(437) ties training to skills needed to achieve organizational objectives; Cooke(438) offers a model to identify situations which can be remedied by training, DiLauro(441) provides an overview of how a government agency assessed its needs; Fraser, Gore and Cotton(444) tell the reader how training requests were handled in the U.S. Department of Agriculture; and Gordon(449) discusses the kind of information necessary to make training program content decisions.

Management development programs target an important group: executives. Levinson(455) argues that educators, not trainers, are needed for executive development; Pomerleau (472) discusses components commonly found in management development programs; Shockley and Staley(474) report on a survey of women in management development programs; and Smith(475) offers guidance to persons responsible for upward mobility programs. Training and development managers do not assume that the number of individuals who have been subjected to a training experience is equal to the number of individuals who have acquired a new skill or expertise. The only way to know what has been gained through training is to evaluate the results. Evaluation seeks to ascertain whether a training effort is worth its cost and whether productive behavior changes have occurred that can be attributed to a specific training program. Byham(435) asserts that the assessment center method of evaluating the effectiveness of training programs shows promise; Caldwell(436) draws a distinction between measurement and evaluation; Goldstein(448) is concerned with internal and external validity in the evaluation process; Kirkpatrick(452) provides guidelines for evaluating training programs; Michalak (458) sees the trainer as a change agent and asserts that all training should be evaluated against desired change; and Mikesell, Willson and Lawther(459) outline a focused training and evaluation program.

Performance Appraisal, Chapter 9, is the process of evaluating employees' level of performance on the job and communicating that information to them. There are a number of potential problems and difficulties encountered in this process. Beaulieu(482) identifies some potential problems; Beer(483) offers ideas for dealing with evaluation, employee development, and feedback; Bernardin and Cardy(485) review obstacles ' stemming from raters' ability and motivation; Brinkerhoff and Kanter(487) caution against uncritical use of formal performance appraisal results; and Whitbeck(563) asserts that the rate of failure of employee evaluation systems remains high because seemingly intractable problems are still with us.

Notwithstanding the failures of the past, performance appraisal systems are used to make judgments about how organizational rewards such as pay, promotion, and training will be distributed among employees. In an effort to pinpoint the high performers, the new thrust in performance appraisal is behaviorally based performance appraisal systems. Kearney (511) asserts that this system gives management the information it needs; Rosinger et al.(545) describe the development of such a system; Levinson(520) advocates job descriptions that are behavior as well as results oriented; Millare, Luthans, and Otteman(530) discuss behaviorally anchored rating scales (BARS) which they developed; Landy et al.(516) describe the development of a BARS used to evaluate performance; Nalbandian(532) and Schwab, Heneman and DeCotiis(552) question the superiority of this technique compared to other evaluation instruments.

Other performance appraisal systems include the critical incident technique, goal setting and principles of reinforcement [see Latham and Wexley(517)]. Obert(536) advises selecting the appraisal system which best fits organizational goals. Cummings and Schwab(494) develop and illustrate three systems for evaluation and development based upon a set of determinants. Taylor and Zawacki(558) report on a field experiment in collaborative goal setting. As previously mentioned, performance appraisal systems are frequently used to decide compensation issues. Adelsberg(480) and DeSanto(596) describe methods of relating performance to compensation; Meyer(528) questions the motivating power of tying pay to performance; Sarin and Winkler(547) suggest performance-based incentive plans for managers; Stimson(556) raises questions about the implementation of performance pay as provided for in the Civil Service Reform Act of 1978; Nigro(534) reports federal employees' doubts about performance appraisal followed by a pay increase.

Chapter 10, Job Design, emphasizes job enrichment, job satisfaction and motivation factors. Job enrichment includes activities intended to alleviate the problems associated with job simplification. Alber(571) studies job enrichment projects in 58 organizations; Ford(588) reports on the American Telephone and Telegraph experience; Hackman(600) analyzes the components of successful and unsuccessful job enrichment projects and he also(601) introduces job characteristics theory and the job diagnostic survey; Herzberg(607,608, 609,610,611) presents and discusses motivation/hygiene theory and job enrichment; McGregor(624) presents Theory X, Theory Y assumptions; Katz(617) concludes that not all employees respond positively to enrichment efforts; Collins and Raubolt(578) identify reasons for employee resistance to a job enrichment program; and Meyers(626) discusses union opposition to job enrichment.

Job satisfaction studies try to determine the variables associated with employee job satisfaction. Rawson and Smith(635) conclude that the determinants of job satisfaction lie in both the job and the work environment; Grupp and Richards(596) report that state executives are more satisfied with their jobs than their federal counterparts; Jauch and Sekaran(615) identify predictors of job satisfaction among professionals in hospitals; Katz(616) relates job satisfaction to Hackman's five task dimensions; Keaveny, Jackson and Fossum(618) and Sauer and York(642) address sex differences and job satisfaction; Weaver(658) explores job satisfaction as a component of happiness among men and women; and Stenson and Johnson(649) examine the relationship among job satisfaction, job tasks and individual differences. Motivation is concerned with the drives and wants within the individual. The central purpose of job design is to create meaningful job tasks within a compatible environment which will stimulate employees to produce their best work. See Aldag(572); Ford(589); Foulkes(590); Gellerman(592); Hackman and Oldham(603); Lawler(622) and Strauss(650).

Envoi

The purpose, then, of this bibliography is to provide students, practitioners, and scholars with a ready reference guide to the public personnel literature. While not exhaustive, this compilation is representative of works central to serious inquiry into the field. Since any bibliography quickly becomes dated, the latest periodical citations can be found in the journals listed on page xxv. Clearly this dynamic area deserves such attention.

We are grateful to Louise Alexander for entering this bibliography into her word processor in the middle of the night with such good humor. Thank you to Kathryn Bowman for searching the card catalog for desired references. We are also grateful to Dennis Becker for such varied assistance that it is impossible to categorize. It might be mentioned that the editor of this series, Jim Bowman, is not related to Sarah or Kathryn Bowman. Finally, we are appreciative to our respective spouses for persevering and coming home anyway.

Sarah Y. Bowman
Jay M. Shafritz

journals searched

Academy of Management
  Journal
Academy of Management
  Review
Administrative Management
Administrative Science
  Quarterly
American Political Science
  Review
American Review of Public
  Administration
Bureaucrat
Business Horizons
California Management Review
Civil Service Journal
Conference Board Record
EEO Today
Employee Relations Law Journal
Harvard Business Review
Health Care Management
  Review
Human Resource Management
Industrial and Labor Relations
  Review
Industrial Engineering
Industrial Management Review
Industrial Relations
Job Safety and Health
Journal of Applied Behavioral
  Science
Journal of Applied Psychology
Journal of Applied Social
  Psychology
Journal of Contemporary
  Business

Management
Management Review
Management Science
Michigan Law Review
Monthly Labor Review
Nation
National Civic Review
Organizational Dynamics
Personnel
Personnel Administration Review
Personnel Administrator
Personnel Journal
Personnel Management Journal
Personnel Psychology
Political Science Quarterly
Public Administration Quarterly
Public Administration Review
Public Interest
Public Personnel Management
Public Personnel Review
Public Power
Public Productivity Review
Review of Economics and
  Statistics
Review of Public Personnel
  Administration
Review of Public Personnel
  Management
Social Science Quarterly
Sloan Management Review
Training
Training and Development
  Journal
Western Political Quarterly

the bibliography

CHAPTER 1

CIVIL SERVICE REFORM

1. Argyle, Nolan J. "Civil Service: The State and Local Response." *Public Personnel Management*, 11 (No. 2, 1982), 157-164.

   Explores the "significant and numerous state and local civil service reforms which have taken place following the federal government's Civil Service Reform Act of 1978. The article also examines the climate for civil service reform and suggests that in many cases the state and local governments provided the direction for the federal government."

2. Ban, Carolyn, Edie N. Goldenberg, and Toni Marzotto. "Firing the Unproductive Employee: Will Civil Service Reform Make a Difference?" *Review of Public Personnel Administration*, 2 (Spring 1982), 87-100.

   Focuses on those provisions of the Civil Service Reform Act of 1978 "intended to facilitate the release of consistently unproductive employees." Gives background and logic of those provisions, "reviews the status of their implementation and offers preliminary evidence on their consequences for personnel management in the federal government."

3. Bellone, Carl J. "Structural vs. Behavioral Change: The Civil Service Reform Act of 1978." *Review of Public Personnel Administration*, 2 (Spring 1982), 59-67.

   "Examines four major assumptions about what was wrong with pre-reform personnel management that led to the Civil Service Reform Act, and the structural changes initiated by the Act to correct these deficiencies. It concludes that without a behaviorally oriented change strategy, these structural reforms are not likely to lead to lasting behavioral change. This failure will result in the law falling short of its goals."

4. Bernstein, Marver H. *The Job of The Federal Executive.*
   Washington, DC: The Brookings Institution, 1958, 219.

   Reports the results of round table discussions sponsored
   by the Brookings Institution in 1957. A group of dis-
   tinguished federal executives considered: "(1) the
   nature of the executive's role and his job, (2) the differences in the functions of political and career executives, (3) the special characteristics of the environment
   in which the federal executive operates, and (4) the
   problem of obtaining and developing effective federal
   executives." Gives the reader the "essence of the discussions."

5. Buchanan, Bruce. "The Senior Executive Service: How We
   Can Tell If It Works." *Public Administration Review*,
   41 (May/June 1981), 349-358.

   Suggests that one of the central problems of S.E.S.
   program implementation will be erosion of "the momentum
   and enthusiasm generated by the legislative stage."
   Four major indicators are offered which will tell "whether
   or not S.E.S. is 'on track' after five years: (1) successful installation and evidence of smooth operation of
   S.E.S. administrative machinery, (2) evidence of positive,
   supportive attitudes among the membership toward S.E.S.,
   (3) evidence of substantial, government-wide preoccupation
   with clarifying the linking individual, agency and program performance objectives, and (4) clear indication
   that the S.E.S. can pass the 'political' test posed by
   periodic changes in presidents and their policies."

6. Campbell, Alan K. "Testimony on Civil Service Reform
   and Reorganization," as reprinted in *Classics of Public
   Personnel Policy*, edited by Frank J. Thompson, Oak Park,
   IL: 1979, 77-102.

   Testimony before the Committee on Post Office and
   Civil Service, U.S. House of Representatives, March 14,
   1978. Supports provisions under Title II which call for
   new systems for appraising employee performance, establish new procedures for removals or demotions and for
   appeals of these actions. "Agencies will be required to
   take action, based on performance appraisals, to:
   (1) recognize employees whose performance significantly
   exceeds requirements; (2) help employees whose performance
   is unacceptable to improve; and (3) remove employees from
   their positions when their performance becomes unacceptable, after warning and an opportunity for improvement."

7. ———. "Revitalizing the Civil Service." *National Civic Review*, 67 (February 1978), 76-79.

Asserts that Civil Service actively seeks out qualified candidates for federal service through programs such as the Presidential Management Intern Program and the Cooperative Education Program for Graduate Students. Well-qualified women and minorities will find these programs an important avenue for entry into management positions in the federal service.

8. ———. "Civil Service Reform: A New Commitment." *Public Administration Review*, 38 (March/April 1978), 99-103.

Advocates passage of the Civil Service Reform Act of 1978 and outlines its major provisions. Argues that the Act will redress many of the disfunctions of the merit system and will "provide greater management flexibility and better rewards for better performance without compromising job security."

9. Carpenter, William Seal. *The Unfinished Business of Civil Service Reform*. Princeton, NJ: Princeton University Press, 1952, 126.

Argues for the "establishment of greater administrative control of public personnel in the hands of the chief executive." Recommends (1) that civil service commissions be replaced by "personnel departments under the direction of single commissioner responsible to the chief executive"; (2) that a law be enacted which creates "adequate machinery to solve the problems of employer-employee relationships"; and (3) that "citizens' organizations interested in the promotion and extension of the merit system be strengthened."

10. Cohn, Barbara, and Darleen Fisher. "The Senior Executive Service: How Do We Get There from Here?" *Management*, 2 (Winter 1981), 2-5.

Outlines the several ways to enter the S.E.S.: "(1) career appointment based on successful manageral experience or special qualities that strongly indicate a likelihood of executive success; (2) career appointment following the successful completion of an approved S.E.S. candidate development program; (3) non-career appointment and limited appointment for those outside the career civil service." Information concerning the several things one can do to prepare for entry into the S.E.S. and a sample developmental assignment are also presented.

11. Colby, Peter W., and Patricia Ingraham. "Individual Moti-
      vation and Institutional Changes Under the Senior Execu-
      tive Service." *Review of Public Personnel Administra-
      tion*, 2 (Spring 1982), 101-118.

      The Senior Executive Service (SES), created by the
      Civil Service Reform Act (CSRA) of 1978, "represents an
      attempt to alter the incentive structure for government
      executives, primarily by introducing new financial incen-
      tives to motivate performance, improve performance ap-
      praisal, and make retention, promotion, and pay truly
      contingent on the results of appraisals." Concludes
      that the impact of "SES to date has been to make matters
      worse. SESers do not perceive improvement in the areas
      that SES was designed to address."

12. Coombs, Vera Vogelsang, and Marvin Cummins. "Reorganiza-
      tions and Reforms: Promises, Promises." *Review of Pub-
      lic Personnel Administration*, 2 (Spring 1982), 21-34.

      "Thesis ... is that executive reorganizations are per-
      vasive rites of presidential politics and that civil
      service reform is a myth based on this rite." Describes
      the "reorganization relationship between the political
      and career governments in terms of a dialogue" and re-
      lates the "dialogue which took place between the presi-
      dent, the bureaucracy, and the Congress in the case of the
      Senior Executive Service." Concludes that the "problem
      of government is largely perceptual; it does not have an
      independent, real-world solution."

13. Couturier, Jean. "The Quiet Revolution in Personnel
      Laws." *Public Personnel Management*, 5 (May/June 1976),
      150-160.

      Traces the historical and political events leading up
      to the passage, by the Chicago City Council, of a person-
      nel ordinance fashioned along the lines of the 1970 Model
      Public Personnel Administration Law of the National Civil
      Service League (NCSL). Also reports the results of the
      NCSL national survey conducted in 1974-1975. The survey
      was designed to test whether the principles of the Model
      Public Personnel Administration Law had taken hold. "The
      results show that 28 percent of the states, 20 percent of
      the metropolitan counties, and 51 percent of the large
      cities have adopted all or all but one of the recommenda-
      tions of the Model Public Personnel Administration Law in
      the first four years after it was promulgated."

14. Crenson, Matthew A. *The Federal Machine: Beginnings Of Bureaucracy In Jacksonian America.* Baltimore: Johns Hopkins University Press, 1975, 174, Bibliography.

Purpose is "to determine when, how, and why bureau-cratic forms of organization were superimposed upon the business of the national government."

15. Crouch, Winston W. *A Guide For Modern Personnel Commissions.* Chicago: IPMA, 1973, 127, Appendices, Glossary, References.

"Outlines and describes the various responsibilities of the commission and discusses the subject of the commission's relationship with its staff, employees and employee groups, and the various publics with which the commission must deal."

16. Dresang, Dennis L. "Diffusion of Civil Service Reform: The Federal and State Governments." *Review of Public Personnel Administration,* 2 (Spring 1982), 35-47.

Public personnel management innovations are not the exclusive property of the federal government. "States and cities have frequently pioneered in personnel management practices. Most of the major features of the 1978 federal Civil Service Reform Act were already practiced by a number of states." Innovations rarely remain the property of a given jurisdiction. "A common pattern" of diffusion of reforms ... "begins with some states, goes to Washington, D.C., and then to another state. Another pattern is one in which change occurs among the states sans Washington involvement."

17. ————. "Public Personnel Reform: A Summary of State Government Activity." *Public Personnel Management,* 7 (September-October 1978), 287-294.

"Surveys major traits of public personnel management in the fifty states and the source and direction of reform efforts during the past five years. There are strong regional differences in the patterns of state personnel systems. Most reform activity is, somewhat ironically, in those states whose practices are already closest to the standards and models suggested by national reform agencies. Among the agencies most involved in reform activity are personnel bureaus although there is a suggestion that their interests may be more defensive than innovative."

18. Dullea, J.F. "Prospects for Executive Development."
     Bureaucrat, 8 (Spring 1979), 40-45.

     Examines certain elements of the Civil Service Reform
     Act of 1978 and concludes that the "time is now ripe for
     executive development in the federal sector. A firm
     legal base and a logical central organizational structure
     have been established. Perhaps most important, there is
     a will to see that a government-wide system will be in-
     stalled. But this determination does not mean that
     there will be a monolithic centrally controlled system
     under which executive development degenerates into a
     'ticket-punching' exercise. It means that agencies will
     not have the option to ignore executive development.
     They will, however, have great flexibility in the design
     and operation of their own programs to realistically meet
     their own requirements."

19. Flanders, Loretta R., and Rudi Klauss. "Developing Future
     Executives: An Assessment of Federal Efforts in an Era
     of Reform." *Review of Public Personnel Administration*,
     2 (Spring 1982), 119-131.

     Preliminary assessment of the Civil Service Reform Act
     of 1978 "indicates that encouraging initial steps have
     been taken in many agencies to establish executive de-
     velopment programs that include a range of work related
     experiences and formal training to prepare individuals for
     the Senior Executive Service. However, the next few years
     will be critical to the long term effort to institution-
     alize executive development programs on a government-
     wide basis."

20. Finkle, Arthur L. "Local Personnel Standards in the
     Federal Grant-In-Aid System." *Personnel Administration
     Review*, 39 (November-December 1979), 572-582.

     A series of court cases in New Jersey are seriously
     challenging the current federal grant-in-aid system as it
     pertains to local personnel standards. "At issue is
     whether local employees paid by federal funds are in the
     employ and under the control of the recipient's merit
     system." Explores this issue, draws conclusions, and
     raises some implications.

21. Fish, Carl Russell. *The Civil Service and The Patronage*.
     New York: Russell and Russell, 1963, 245, Appendices.

     History which views the civil service reform movement
     within an international context and as a "manifestation
     of a stage of national growth."

22. Foster, Gregory D. "The 1978 Civil Service Reform Act:
     Post-Mortem or Rebirth?" *Personnel Administration Re-
     view*, 39 (January–February 1979), 78–86.

     Reviews briefly "three key aspects of the enacted re-
     forms—merit principles, the Senior Executive Service
     (SES) as an entity, and veterans' preference—and a
     related aspect scheduled to be addressed in separate
     legislation—the Hatch Act modifications. Assesses each
     of the above (as appropriate) with respect to its impact
     on equal employment opportunity (EEO) and labor-management
     relations."

23. Hall, Chester G., Jr. "The U.S. Civil Service Commission:
     Arm of the President?" *Public Personnel Review*, 28
     (April 1967), 114–120.

     Reviews presidential styles of Hoover, Roosevelt Truman,
     Eisenhower, Kennedy, and Johnson. Discusses whether the
     Civil Service Commission is, can or should be the manage-
     ment arm of the President "if it is to provide most ef-
     fectively and efficiently for federal personnel administra-
     tion in the public interest."

24. Harvey, Donald R. *The Civil Service Commission*. New York:
     Praeger, 1970, 212, Appendices, Bibliography.

     Motivated by a feeling that the Civil Service Commission
     is not understood well enough, Harvey "endeavored to
     write about the Commission as a human institution re-
     flecting the problems, abilities, successes, and failures
     of the people who have manned it since its establishment
     in 1883.

25. Heclo, Hugh. *A Government of Strangers: Executive Poli-
     tics in Washington*. Washington, DC: Brookings Insti-
     tution, 1977, 264.

     "Describes the relationship between the fleeting (poli-
     tical appointees) and enduring (high-level bureaucrats)
     forces in government and suggests ways in which the in-
     evitable tensions (executive politics) could be handled
     more constructively."

26. Hoogenboom, Ari. *Outlawing the Spoils: A History of the
     Civil Service Reform Movement, 1865-1883*. Urbana:
     University of Illinois Press, 1961, 267.

     Addresses the complex question, "Who were the civil
     service reformers, why did they become reformers, and

what was the impact of reform upon politics and upon the
civil service itself?" Asserts that "the civil service
reform movement fits into an 'out' versus 'in' pattern.

27. Huddleston, Mark W. "Foreign Systems, Familiar Refrains:
     Civil Service Reform in Comparative Perspective."
     Review of Public Personnel Administration, 2 (Spring
     1982), 49-58.

     Suggests that, at least with respect to several central
     issues--non-discrimination, public sector labor relations,
     decentralization, political responsiveness, and private
     sector influences--the United States was "closely paral-
     leled by similar reforms in other Western nations." The
     two sets of explanatory factors are, first, "the dynamics
     of cross-section *learning*," and second, the "underlying
     patterns of *social change*."

28. Josephson, Matthew. *The Politicos: 1865-1896.* New York:
     Harcourt, Brace, 1938, 708, Bibliography, References.

     Provides a "picture of the Politicos as they carried
     out their assignments, as they rose and fell and were
     supplanted, as power passed from the hands of one to the
     other among them." Portrays them "within the frame of
     their social world and real relations."

29. Klingner, Donald E. *Public Personnel Management: Contexts
     and Strategies.* Englewood Cliffs, NJ: Prentice-Hall,
     1980, 459.

     Takes "(1) the importance of law, (2) the perspective
     of the individual employee, and (3) the function of public
     personnel activities in defining public policy" and
     organizes them into a unique approach to public personnel
     management. Combines the "open-and-closed system ap-
     proaches to the topic; evaluates a range of techniques
     for performing each personnel activity; takes a research
     orientation due to the comparative or contextual nature
     of public personnel managment and the variety of possible
     solutions to personnel problems; and discusses laws, ob-
     jectives, and techniques relative to the level, functions,
     type, size and resources of public agencies."

30. Knudsen, Steven, Larry Jakus, and Maida Metz. "The Civil
     Service Reform Act of 1978." *Public Personnel Manage-
     ment*, 8 (May-June 1979), 170-181.

     Explains "the pressures which led to the decision to
     undertake civil service reform and reasons for the suc-

cessful passage of the Act." Also describes the study
recommendations, and law-making processes as well as
updates the progress of implementation. The internal
evaluation plan is discussed and the authors' prognosis
for successful implementation of the legislation is also
included.

Alan K. Campbell, in a Letter to the Editor appearing
in *Public Personnel Management,* 8 (September-October
1979), 337-339, asserts that the Knudsen, Jakus, Metz
article "has many technical errors and distortions of
fact and theory." To illustrate his contentions, he re-
sponds to specific passages in the aforementioned article.

31. Kramer, Kenneth W. "Seeds of Success and Failure: Policy
    Development and Implementation of the 1978 Civil Ser-
    vice Reform Act." *Review of Public Personnel Adminis-
    tration,* 2 (Spring 1982), 5-20.

    Asserts that "any current focus on the implementation of
    the Reform Act of 1978 should be based on a firm founda-
    tion of understanding about the formulation and eventual
    adoption of the legislation." Author poses three ques-
    tions which explore the "nature and potential success
    of the Act: (1) What environmental and other factors led
    to the enactment of this legislation? (2) How did these
    factors affect the nature of the legislation passed?
    and (3) What effect will these factors and the nature of
    the legislation itself have upon the implementation of the
    civil service reforms?"

32. Ling, Cyril C. *The Management of Personnel Relations.*
    Homewood, IL: Richard D. Irwin, 1965.

    Presents a "comprehensive factual record of the his-
    torical development of the field usually labelled person-
    nel." Ling looks at where personnel relations in American
    business firms has been and how it became what it was up
    to 1965. Although this volume "is designed principally
    as a college text, personnel specialists and managers of
    other business specialties may find it useful."

33. Long, Norton E. "S.E.S. and the Public Interest." *Per-
    sonnel Administration Review,* 41 (May-June 1981), 305-
    312.

    Provides an indepth analysis of the potentialities and
    problems of the Senior Executive Service (SES). Discusses
    the relationship among senior officers, political ap-
    pointees and commerce; the extent of political control

of the bureaucracy; "the problems of a bureaucracy out of
hand"; and the "implications of the bureaucracy constitu-
ting a power center of its own."

34. Lynn, Naomi B., and Richard E. Vaden. "Bureaucratic Re-
       sponse to Civil Service Reform." *Personnel Administra-*
       tion, 39 (July-August 1979), 333-343.

Report on the attitudes of top-level federal executives
toward the Civil Service Reform Act of 1978. 1,007 career federal executives at the GS 15-18 levels responded
to a questionnaire. On the negative side, "there was not
a great mandate of support for the Carter proposal";
however, "on the positive side the lack of support is not
high enough to preordain the Act to failure."

35. Mainzer, Lewis C. *Political Bureaucracy*. Glenview, IL:
       Scott, Foresman, 1973, 151, Footnotes, Bibliographical
       Essay.

Asserts that the "continued existence of widespread
public doubt regarding the effectiveness and the credi-
bility of government" cannot be permitted. All Americans
"should know as fully as possible how government operates."
Promotes understanding of government operations by ad-
dressing issues such as: how government employees relate
to their superiors or to their clients; to what extent
their actions are controlled by decisions of the President and Congress; and psychologically how they feel about
the tasks they perform.

36. McBain, Howard Lee. *De Witt Clinton and the Origin of the*
       Spoils System in New York. New York: Columbia Univer-
       sity Press, 1907, 158, Bibliography.

Examines carefully the "development of the civil service
both in the national government and in New York from
the time of the establishment of the federal constitution
down to the year 1801, which marked the first change of
political parties in the nation." Shows De Witt Clinton's
departure from precedents and systematically develops the
"history of patronage in New York and its relation to the
larger question of politics."

37. McCarthy, T.G. "Managers--The Ball is in Our Court."
       Civil Service Journal, 19 (January-March 1979), 10-12.

Civil Service Reform Act of 1978 "calls for performance
standards for each job and performance evaluation systems
tailored to the needs of each agency. It also "makes
fundamental distinctions between managers and other em-

ployees. This difference can be the foundation for managerial team building--a managerial *esprit de corps*.
Managers are to be treated differently because they have
a special purpose and a special responsibility to fulfill
their agencies' missions."

38. Meriam, Lewis. *Personnel Administration in the Federal
    Government*. Washington, DC: Brookings Institution,:
    1937, 62.

    Critical examination of proposals to abolish the Civil
    Service Commission and to transfer "its functions to a
    central personnel agency under a single head." Recom-
    mendations include retention of the Civil Service Com-
    mission with decentralization of its functions.

39. ————. *Public Personnel Problems from the Standpoint of
    the Operating Officer*. Washington, DC: Brookings In-
    stitution, 1938, 387.

    Departs from the usual historical approach and presents
    a view of public personnel administration primarily from
    the standpoint of the operating officer. Draws upon his
    personal experience, expecially in the presentation of
    actual cases.

40. Mosher, Frederick C. *Democracy and the Public Service*.
    New York: Oxford University Press, 1968, 219.

    "Emphasis is on trends and issues in the American public
    service ... [its] philosophical and ideological background,
    the various systems of public employment and the relations
    among them, the public service and the educational system,
    and the expanding roles of the professions and of collec-
    tive organizations in the public service--always with an
    eye to their significance for the traditions, the institu-
    tions, and the practice of democracy in America."

41. Murphy, Lionel V. "The First Federal Civil Service Com-
    mission: 1871-1875." *Public Personnel Review*, Part I,
    3 (January 1942), 29-39; Part II, 3 (July 1942)   218-
    231; Part III, 3 (October 1943), 299-323.

    Detailed account of the creation, short life, and demise
    of the first Civil Service Commission under President
    Grant.

42. Newland, Chester A. "Public Personnel Administration:
    Legalistic Reforms vs. Effectiveness, Efficiency, and

Economy." *Public Administration Review*, 36 (September-
October 1976), 529-537.

Explores the "enormous growth of governments since the
1940's; the rapid growth of unions and of collective
bargaining since the 1950's; and the widespread growth of
litigious, public service-rights populism since the
1960's." Concludes that "collective bargaining, workforce
planning and management and overwhelming bureaucracy and
legal complexity are in urgent need of creative attention."

43. Quaintance, M.K. "The Impact of the Uniform Selection
     Guidelines on Public Merit Systems." *Public Personnel
     Management*, 9 (September 1980), 125-233.

     Describes the broad applicability and legal basis of the
     Uniform Guidelines on Employee Selection Procedures.
     "Key concepts are defined, including: selection procedures,
     employment decisions, applicant, adverse impact, and the
     bottom line. Conflicting mandates inherent in the *Uni-
     form Guidelines* are discussed, and public employees
     operating under merit system laws are advised to select
     a plan of action which is legally defensible under the
     U.S. Constitution."

44. Rainey, Hal G. "Perceptions of Incentives in Business
     and Government: Implications for Civil Service Reform."
     Public Administration Review, 39 (September-October
     1979), 440-448.

     Reports a comparison of questionnaire responses by
     government and business managers which indicates that
     government managers: "(1) perceive a weaker relationship
     between their performance and such incentives as pay,
     promotion, and job security, (2) feel that the formal
     personnel procedures governing their organizations pro-
     vide much less flexibility in administration of such
     incentives (for example, they are much more likely to
     feel that it is difficult to fire a manager who is a poor
     performer), (3) score lower on scales of satisfaction with
     promotion and satisfaction with co-workers. Implications
     for civil service reform, for further research, and for
     theory are discussed."

45. Rich, Wilber D. *The Politics of Urban Personnel Policy:
     Reformers, Politicians and Bureaucrats*. Port Washington,
     NY: Kennikat Press, 1982, 167.

     A book about "politics, values, and visions." The
     politics are those of the government of New York City;

"the values are those of the nineteenth and twentieth-
century civil service reformers striving to impose a
management view on municipal workers; and the vision is
that of an efficient city managed by dedicated men and
women."

46. Rosen, Bernard. "Merit and the President's Plan for
    Changing the Civil Service System." *Public Administra-
    tion Review*, 38 (July-August 1978), 301-304.

    Outlines and discusses four major weaknesses in Carter's
    proposals for changing the federal personnel system: (1)
    "sweeping authority for presidential appointees to re-
    assign and demote almost all top career executives and
    replace them with political or other career appointees
    more to their individual liking," (2) "turning over to
    each agency the authority to examine applicants for jobs
    in that agency," (3) and (4) "splitting the CSC into two
    agencies--a bi-partisan Merit Systems Protection Board
    and the Office of Personnel Management headed by a direc-
    tor who would serve at the pleasure of the president."
    Also offers suggestions for legislation and reorganization
    which would address the aforementioned weaknesses.

47. ————. *The Merit System in the United States Civil Ser-
    vice*. Monograph for the Committee on Post Office and
    Civil Service of the House of Representatives. Wash-
    ington, DC: U.S. Government Printing Office, 94th
    Cong., 1st sess., December 23, 1975, 90.

    Defines the merit system, examines its present condi-
    tion, draws conclusions as to the adequacy of the organi-
    zation for Federal personnel administration, and assesses
    the role of the Civil Service Commission. Twelve recom-
    mendations for legislation are directed toward the solu-
    tion of important, widespread, and persistent problems
    described in the body of the document.

48. ————. "A New Mandate for Accountability in the Nation-
    al Government." *Bureaucrat*, 8 (Spring 1979), 2-8.

    Accountability is the centerpiece of the Civil Service
    Reform Act of 1978. Although the civil service reformers
    gave "federal managers increased discretion and flexibility
    in personnel matters, they also made them more account-
    able for achieving results." Further, "institutional
    mechanisms and statutory means for holding managers ac-
    countable for personnel decisions based on merit princi-
    ples" are also included. "This makes for better government

because it helps attract and keep first-rate people, rewarding excellence and penalizing poor performance."

49. ———. "Uncertainty in the Senior Executive Service."
     Public Administration Review, 41 (March/April 1981),
     203-207.

     Objective of the Senior Executive Service is improved
     government operations. Much has been said about the "new
     flexibility given presidential appointees to move career
     executives from one job to another, but there has been
     very little discussion about the potentially heavy costs,
     expecially during changes in administration."

50. Rosenthal, Harvey A. "In Defense of Central Control of
     Public Personnel Policy." *Public Personnel Review*,
     28 (October 1967), 237-241.

     Reminds the reader that centralized control of personnel
     is the result of abuses and inequities that existed be-
     fore the emergence of strong central personnel agencies.
     These factors have not disappeared. "Could a strong merit
     system really be maintained if a central personnel agency
     were not in control?"

51. Sayre, Wallace. "The Triumph of Techniques over Purpose."
     Public Administration Review, 8 (Spring 1948), 134-137.

     Book review of *Personnel Administration: A Point of
     View and a Method* by Paul Pigors and Charles A. Myers.
     Defines the triumph of techniques over purpose as the
     confluence of (1) elimination of party patronage; (2) guar-
     antee of equal treatment to all; (3) principles of scien-
     tific management; and (4) effort to provide the conditions
     of work which will attract and hold a public service of
     optimum talents, resulting in a formidable system of quan-
     titative techniques and formal rules. Praises the Pigors
     and Myers book for its human relations point of view.

52. Seidman, Harold. *Politics, Position, and Power: The Dy-
     namics of Federal Organization*. New York: Oxford
     University Press, 1970, 286, Bibliography.

     Observed the federal scene for 25 years from his position
     within the Bureau of the Budget (Office of Management and
     Budget). Provides a comprehensive and insightful analysis
     "of the various phenomena which determine and influence
     Federal organization structure and administrative arrange-
     ments." Identifies and describes "the strategic and

tactical uses of organizational type and structure; the interrelationships among the executive branch, the Congress and state and local governments in the administrative process; the linkages between executive branch and congressional organization; institutional culture and personality as a determinant of organizational behavior; and the political and administrative significance of various coordinating devices and the rich variety of institutional types."

53. Shafritz, Jay M. "The Cancer Eroding Public Personnel Professionalism." *Public Personnel Management*, 3 (November-December 1974), 486-492.

Characterizes the fudging process operating in the nether world of public personnel administration as an insidious cancer that quietly and relentlessly erodes the budding professionalism and spirit of the personnel establishment. It serves to subvert the democratic processes of government by institutionalizing a system of governance that is neither known by the public nor formally sanctioned by their elected representatives.

54. ————. *Public Personnel Management: The Heritage of Civil Service Reform*. New York: Praeger, 1975, 178.

Offers a critical analysis of the personnel functions within government and argues for public personnel management which concerns itself with the larger problems of the viability of an organization's human resources. Distinguishes between public personnel administration and public personnel management.

55. Siegel, Efstathia A. "Eight Agencies Link Pay to Performance: Will Merit Pay Work?" *Management*, 2 (Spring 1981), 15-17.

The merit pay system was designed to directly link pay to performance. Eight federal agencies put Office of Personnel Management approved merit pay plans in place in October 1980. Author describes the experience of the eight agencies and suggests procedures to be followed by agencies designing their merit pay plans.

56. Sorauf, Frank J. "The Silent Revolution in Patronage." *Public Administration Review*, 20 (Winter 1960), 28-34.

Argues that the "trend of declining patronage will affect not only local politics but the national party system and the entire political process."

57. Stewart, Frank M. *The National Civil Service Reform
     League: History, Activities, and Problems*. Austin:
     University of Texas, 1929, 227.

     Traces the history of the League beginning with May 1877
     and the formation of the New York Civil Service Reform
     Association. The activities of the League centered
     around "spreading propaganda for the merit system, ex-
     tending it to new jurisdictions, and defending the com-
     petitive principle from all attackers." Elimination of
     the "spoils evil" is the League's paramount goal.

58. Thomas, William V., and Robert Kaper. "Nearsighted Over-
     sight: Patronage Holes in Civil Service." *Nation*, 223
     (December 4, 1976), 591-594.

     Civil Service Commission has not been entirely success-
     ful in its "watchdog" activities. Presidents Eisenhower,
     Kennedy, and Johnson avoided the Commission. Although
     the Sharon Report exposed illegal activities, it failed
     to reform the Commission.

59. Thompson, Duane. "Performance Appraisal and the Civil
     Service Reform Act." *Public Personnel Management*, 10
     (Fall 1981), 281-288.

     "A review of current literature and case law is used to
     support the use of a management-by-objectives (MBO) sys-
     tem" to meet the performance appraisal requirements under
     the CSRA (1980).

60. Tolchin, Martin, and Susan Tolchin. *To The Victor: Poli-
     tical Patronage from The Clubhouse to the White House*.
     New York: Random House, 1971, 312.

     Readable accounts of the use of patronage by political
     leaders to enhance their power and influence with their
     party and the general public. "The major hazard of pa-
     tronage, however, is not that it builds political empires
     or private fortunes, but that it encourages public offi-
     cials to compromise the public interest for private gain
     and to sacrifice the national interest for the needs of
     their regional constituencies."

61. U.S. Civil Service Commission. *Biography of an Ideal*.
     Washington, DC: U.S. Government Printing Office, 1974,
     192.

     A brief history of civil service in the United States.
     It was "first published in 1958, coincident with the 75th

anniversary of the Civil Service of 1883" and updated
coincident with the 90th anniversary. The most significant events in the development of the civil service are
captured and presented in an interesting and readable way.

62. U.S. Office of Personnel Management. *Legislative and
     Regulatory Reforms in State and Local Personnel Systems*.
     U.S. Office of Personnel Management, June 1981, 26,
     Source Index.

     "Report intended to assist public jurisdictions which
     plan to reform their civil service policies and procedures
     through legislative and regulatory processes. Offers
     examples of reform provisions adopted by state and local
     governments."

63. U.S. Office of Personnel Management. *Recapturing Confi-
     dence in Government - Public Personnel Management Reform*.
     Washington, DC: U.S. Office of Personnel Management,
     May 1979, 167.

     Collection of papers delivered at 1979 conference which
     was convened to "examine public personnel management re-
     form efforts and their relationship to public confidence
     in government, to exchange information on new directions
     in reform in personnel management and government produc-
     tivity at the state and local level, and to give advice
     on the directions being taken in federal reform."

64. Van Riper, Paul P. *History of the United States Civil
     Service*. Evanston, IL: Row, Peterson, 1958, 566.

     Presents the "story of one administrative system as it
     developed over time, as it responded to various political
     and social pressures, and as it functioned from day to
     day over more than a century and a half."

65. Vaughn, Robert G. *The Spoiled System: A Call for Civil
     Service Reform*. New York: Charterhouse, 1975, 166,
     Appendices, Notes.

     The Civil Service report (*The Spoiled System*) and the
     Equal Employment Opportunity report (*Behind the Promises*)
     have been edited for publication in this volume. "In
     examining the federal civil service system and the Civil
     Service Commission, the report asks several central ques-
     tions. What are the ways in which the civil service,
     to which Congress delegated the task of administering
     the laws that help determine the quality of justice,
     safety and power in our society, can be held accountable

for the actions of agencies and individual public officials? What are the reasons for and the ways by which
government employees are disciplined? What are their
rights of appeal, and who makes the decisions and by what
standards? What are the informal methods of retaliation
against those who do not choose to get along by going
along? How well does the U.S. Civil Service Commission
carry out its responsibility to prevent the spread of a
new spoils system and to advance and protect procedures
for equal access to federal employment?"

66. Walter, J. Jackson. "The Ethics in Government Act, Con-
     flict of Interest Laws and Presidential Recruiting."
     Public Administration Review, 41 (November-December
     1981), 659-665.

     The Ethics in Government Act of 1978 "requires senior
     federal executives publicly to disclose the details of
     their personal financial interests. The conflict of
     interest criminal statutes establish the standards for
     review of the disclosure reports. The advance review and
     clearance process for presidential nominees, which the
     Office of Government Ethics administers, and upon which
     the confirmation committees of the Senate rely, is in-
     tended to protect the president and his nominees by
     prospectively enforcing prohibitions against abuses of
     public office for private financial gain."

67. White, Leonard D. *The Republican Era*. New York: Macmil-
     lan, 1958. *The Jacksonians*. New York: Macmillan, 1954.
     The Jeffersonians. New York: Macmillan, 1951. *The
     Federalists*. New York: Macmillan, 1948.

     Complete and comprehensive administrative history of
     the federal government.

68. Wilson, Woodrow. "The Study of Administration." *Politi-
     cal Science Quarterly*, 56 (December 1941), 481-506.

     Classic article which states that the "object of admin-
     istrative study [is] to discover, first, what government
     can properly and successfully do, and secondly, how it
     can do these proper things with the utmost possible effi-
     ciency and at the least possible cost either of money or
     of energy."

CHAPTER 2

EQUAL EMPLOYMENT OPPORTUNITY

69. Abramson, Joan. *Old Boys New Women: The Politics of Sex
     Discrimination.* New York: Praeger, 1979, 236.

     Discrimination exists because "a system that requires
     victims will continue to require victims." Understanding
     this broad perspective is the author's purpose. She
     interviewed about 150 people concerning their experiences
     with sex discrimination while collecting materials for this
     book.

70. Anthony, William P., and Marshall Bowen. "Affirmative
     Action: Problems and Promises." *Personnel Journal,*
     56 (December 1977), 616-621.

     Affirmative Action (AA) programs focus on covert discrim-
     ination "which is often subtle enough to prevent detec-
     tion by the employer himself." Outlines problems associ-
     ated with AA programs such as high cost, test valida-
     tions, multiple regulation, effective enforcement, legal
     problems, seniority layoff. As each problem is presented
     and discussed, solutions are offered where they exist.

71. Asher, Janet, and Jules Asher. "How to Accommodate Workers
     in Wheelchairs." *Job Safety and Health,* 4 (October
     1976), 30-35.

     Presents "ideas on machine and building modifications to
     help employers comply with the law and keep handicapped
     workers safe."

72. Backhouse, Constance. *Sexual Harassment On The Job: How
     To Avoid the Working Women's Nightmare.* Englewood
     Cliffs, NJ: Prentice-Hall, 1981, 188.

     Presents carefully selected cases in order to "demon-
     strate that sexual harassment affects all working women."
     Asserts that sexual harassment is a "demonstration of

power politics, an assertion of power that happens to be
expressed in a physical manner. It is the ultimate re-
minder to women that their fundamental status in society
is that of sex object." Provides an historical account of
sexual harassment and perceptions of sexual harassment
from government and private industry managers. Reviews
the law (the courts, Human Rights Commission, and the
EEOC), the women's movement, and asks the question,
"can women sexually harass men?" Also presents "the
other side of the coin: women who exploit their sexuality
for gain." Suggests some prevention do's and don't's
tactics and strategies once harassment begins and action
plans for management and unions. Concludes that "sexual
harassment is rooted in two systematically exploitative
features of North American society and culture: sex discrimination in a hierarchical, undemocratic workplace.
In order to combat sexual harassment either or both of
these syndromes must be addressed."

73.   Backhouse, Constance, and Leah Cohen. *The Secret Oppres-*
      sion: Sexual Harassment of Working Women. Toronto:
      Macmillan, 1978, 206.

      Thorough discussion of sexual harassment, including its
      roots as an expression of power; personnel, management,
      and union perspectives; the law; the women's movement;
      role reversal; women who exploit their sexuality for
      gain; personal solutions; action plans for management
      and unions; and societal solutions.

74.   Backhouse, Constance, et al. *Fighting Sexual Harassment:*
      An Advocacy Handbook. Cambridge, MA: Alliance Against
      Sexual Coercion, 1979, 42, Appendices.

      Purpose of brochure is "to train people in all kinds of
      social service work to recognize when women seeking their
      assistance are experiencing sexual harassment and to pro-
      vide some guidelines on how to deal with this situation."

75.   Bakaly, C.G., and G.E. Krischer. "Bakke: Its Impact on
      Public Employment Discrimination." *Employee Relations
      Law Journal*, 4 (Spring 1979), 471-484.

      Analyzes the Supreme Court's *Bakke* "opinions and ex-
      plores the questions answered and the issues ignored in
      the historic ruling." Concludes that "the decision will
      diminish the use of inflexible goals and quotas based on
      finding of past discrimination."

76. Bellone, Carl J., and Douglas H. Darling. "Implementing
    Affirmative Action Programs: Problems and Strategies."
    Public Personnel Management, 9 (No. 3, 1980), 184-191.

    Report of employee affirmative action survey conducted
    in Alameda County, California, which resulted in a "set
    of issues to address when conducting training, selling
    affirmative action to line managers, and evaluating their
    affirmative action efforts."

77. Berwitz, Clement J. *The Job Analysis Approach to Affirma-
    tive Action*. New York: John Wiley & Sons, 1975, 222,
    Appendices.

    Asserts that "Affirmative Action means good personnel
    management...." Describes how Affirmative Action Plan
    was developed at Wagner College, Staten Island, New York,
    with technical assistance from the United States Manpower
    Administration, a unit of the Department of Labor. Con-
    tinues with a review of the relevant literature; describes
    the Wagner College Affirmative Action Plan; presents struc-
    ture and uses of the Dictionary of Occupational Titles;
    discusses the assumptions, interprets the findings, and
    draws some policy implications.

78. Bishop, Joan Fiss. "The Women's Movement in ASPA."
    Public Administration Review, 36 (July-August 1976),
    349-354.

    Presents the history of the activities of the ASPA
    Task Force on Women in Public Administration and its
    successor, the Standing Committee on Women in Public
    Administration, within the context of the Women's Move-
    ment. Calls for the Decade of Women (1975-1985) to be
    the time for "achievement of the ultimate goals of
    equality."

79. Bittker, Boris. *The Case of Black Reparations*. New York:
    Random House, 1973, 137.

    A discussion of the concept of black reparations with
    the aim of stimulating the debate "that was so strikingly
    missing" in the months after James Forman interrupted the
    Sunday morning service at Riverside Church in New York
    City, May 1969, and delivered a Black Manifesto.

80. Bocher, Rita B. "Does Tradition Affect Affirmative Action
    Results? How Pennsylvania Achieved Changes at the Mid-
    dle Management Level." *Public Administration Review*,
    42 (September-October 1982), 475-478.

Concludes that "qualified women for management jobs do
exist. The problem appears to be that when a higher
level vacancy opens, the decision maker appoints a male--
again."

81. Bolton, Elizabeth B., and Luther Wade Humphreys. "A
     Training Model for Women--An Androgynous Approach."
     Personnel Journal, 56 (May 1977), 230-234.

     Reviews the history of discrimination on the basis of
     sex in the workplace; identifies the differences and
     similarities in ability among male and female managers;
     examines current training practices; and suggests that
     the "existing training model which has worked so well for
     developing males into managers and leaders be expanded to
     include women--an androgynous approach to training."

82. Brown, Marsha D. "Getting and Keeping Women in Nontradi-
     tional Careers." *Public Personnel Management*, 10
     (Winter 1981), 408-411.

     Identifies "strategies to facilitate integration of
     women into nontraditional jobs such as: (1) traditional
     recruitment methods for men need to be changed for women;
     (2) women already working for an agency should be offered
     transfer opportunities; (3) pre-employment and more formal
     on-the-job training should be available."

83. Bureau of National Affairs. *The Comparable Worth Issue:
     A BNA Special Report*. Washington, DC: The Bureau of
     National Affairs, 1981, 60, Appendices, Bibliography,
     Table of Cases.

     "Examines legal issues involved in the comparable worth
     doctrine and analyzes the *Gunther* decision and the major
     federal court decisions prior and subsequent to that
     important Supreme Court ruling"; discusses recent develop-
     ments; summarizes important surveys, studies and reports
     on comparable worth; looks ahead and asks interested groups
     to predict the social, economic and legal trends in this
     area; and includes extensive appendices.

84. Campbell, Alan K. "Approaches to Defining, Measuring,
     and Achieving Equity in the Public Sector." *Public
     Administration Review*, 36 (September/October 1976),
     556-562.

     Equity and its meaning are not new issues. What is new
     is "the current effort to give it operational meaning in
     concrete policy." Selects public school financing, the

provision of municipal services and local government reorganizations to demonstrate the problems of operation-alization.

85. Cayer, N. Joseph, and Lee Sigelman. "Minorities and Wo-men in State and Local Government: 1973-1975." *Public Administration Review*, 40 (September/October 1980), 443-450.

Analyzes the "employment of minorities and women in state and local governments across the country." The two questions which guide the analysis are: (1) "in the most recent year for which data are currently available, where did minorities and women stand with respect to state and local government employment?" and (2) "to what extent did the employment status of these groups change after the EEO act went into effect?"

86. Clynch, Edward J., and Carol A. Guadin. "Sex in the Ship-yards: An Assessment of Affirmative Action Policy." *Public Administration Review*, 42 (March-April 1982), 114-121.

Compares the "impact of affirmative action enforcement in the private and federal sectors. Examines the respec-tive effects of Maritime Administration and Civil Service Commission compliance procedures on female/male employ-ment patterns in private and Naval blue collar shipyard jobs. The findings indicate Maritime enforcement was more successful than Civil Service oversight. Study suggests that achieving equal employment opportunity, especially for women, will continue to be more difficult in the federal than the private sector."

87. Collins, Eliza G.C., and Timothy B. Blodgett. "Sexual Harassment ... Some See It ... Some Won't." *Harvard Business Review*, 59 (March-April 1981), 77-94.

In cooperation with *Redbook*, *Harvard Business Review* conducted a survey on the issue of sexual harassment in the workplace. The questions addressed include: "Is sexual harassment a manufactured issue? Is it widespread? Should it concern top management?" The major findings reported include: "(1) Sexual harassment is seen as an issue of power; (2) Men and women generally agree in theory on what sexual harassment is but disagree on how often it occurs, (3) Top management appears isolated from occurrences of sexual harassment, and middle-level mana-gers are somewhat less aware of misconduct than lower-level managers; (4) Most respondents favor company policies against sexual harassment; (5) In general, most see EEOC

guidelines as reasonable; and (6) Most respondents think
sexual harassment can be a very serious matter."

88.   Cuddy, R.W. "Age Discrimination Amendments and Their Im-
      pact on Personnel." *Employee Law Journal*, 4 (Winter
      1978), 345-399.

      Examines the amendments and "their specific provisions
      and their probable effects. Discusses personnel's role
      in carrying out the congressional decision to protect
      the jobs of employees aged 65 to 70."

89.   Denhardt, Robert B., and Jan Perkins. "The Coming Death
      of Administrative Man." *Public Administration Review*,
      36 (July/August 1976), 379-384.

      The concept of administrative *man*, which has been the
      "model for the culturally dominant version of how people
      in organizations should act" is giving way to new concepts
      of behavior in organizations arising out of the women's
      movement. Considers the implications of the new patterns
      of thinking and acting in organizations.

90.   Diazde-Krofcheck, Maria Dolores, and Carlos Jackson.
      "The Chicano Experience with Nativism in Public Admin-
      istration." *Public Administration Review*, 34 (November/
      December 1974), 534-539.

      Identifies certain "underlying mechanisms existing in
      public institutions which selectively exclude Chicanos
      from participating in policy making and rendering ser-
      vices to the public." Also discusses "the consequence
      of this exclusion" and "explores underlying philosophic
      values and assumptions which are held by the majority
      culture and which are at the heart of perpetuating the
      exclusionary mechanism directed at Chicanos."

91.   Dobbins, Cheryl, and Dollie R. Walker. "The Role of
      Black Colleges in Public Affairs Education." *Public
      Administration Review*, 34 (November/December 1974),
      540-552.

      Discusses "(1) the organizational structure--the expli-
      cit role of black colleges in public affairs education
      present and future; (2) how the role can be implemented;
      (3) the obstacles to fulfilling this role and responsi-
      bilities; and (4) recommendations" for the future. Con-
      cludes that "black colleges and universities, in seeing
      themselves as resources, are intent on becoming forums
      which bring together community people, who are both

fearful and distrustful of local government with public administrators and planners who tend to be the source of such feelings."

92. Dye, Thomas R. *The Politics of Equality*. Indianapolis: Bobbs-Merrill, 1971, 235.

Presents an "overview and analysis of the role of Negroes in the political life of the nation, and raises provocative questions concerning the capacity of the political system to accommodate black demands for legal and social equity. Deals comprehensively with (1) the history of the development of a racially stratified society, (2) the pattern of political and social forces that maintained that society, and (3) the political role of blacks (and whites) in meeting persistent demands for changes in the relative statuses of the two races." Draws from the literature of sociology, economics and political science.

93. Farley, Jennie. *Affirmative Action and the Woman Worker: Guidelines For Personnel Management*. New York: AMACOM, 1979, 210.

Reviews the "situation that promoted enactment of affirmative action legislation and shows why legislators have seen fit to intervene in areas that were traditionally management's domain." Discusses recruitment, selection, and training to "show exactly what is meant by affirmative action in each." Illustrations of plans that are successful, those that appear to work and those which, while sound, have produced few results in industry, business, and the public sector, are presented. Also discusses such related subjects as the minority woman worker, the day-to-day concerns of women workers, and the problem of sexual harassment.

94. Faucher, Mary D., and Kenneth J. McCullock. "Sexual Harassment in the Workplace--What Should the Employer Do?" *EEO Today*, 5 (Spring 1978), 38-46.

Title VII makes it an unlawful employment practice for an employer to discriminate against any individual with respect to conditions or privileges of employment on the basis of sex. "The courts that have addressed the problem of sexual harassment have faced only the issue of a superior's sexual advances, acceptance of which was made the condition of a promotion or job retention. This discussion examines those court decisions, analyzes other forms of sexual harrassment and offers employers faced

with the problem of sexual harassment suggestions including preventing, investigating and avoiding corporate liability for it."

95. Freedman, Sara M., and Robert T. Keller. "The Handicapped
     in the Workforce." *Academy of Management Review*, 6
     (July 1981), 449-458.

     Reviews the literature on "training, placement, and
     employment outcomes for the handicapped, and raises ques-
     tions concerning the methodological soundness of previous
     research and the effects of governmental and industry
     programs designed to aid the handicapped."

96. Gibson, Frank K., and Samuel Yeager. "Trends in the Fed-
     eral Employment of Blacks." *Public Personnel Management*,
     4 (May-June 1975), 189-195.

     Analyzes trends in the federal employment of Blacks and
     concludes that there was a slow increase in black repre-
     sentation in all Civil Service regions from 1962 through
     1970. In most regions, Blacks were over-represented
     when compared to black percentage of population. However,
     when compared to nonblacks, Blacks were underrepresented
     in the upper grade levels (GS 12-18) and over-represented
     in the lower grade levels.

97. Glazer, Nathan. *Affirmative Discrimination: Ethnic In-
     equity and Public Policy.* New York: Basic Books, 1978,
     221.

     Examines public policies in three areas: "employment,
     school desegregation, and residential location. Analyzes
     the position of those who support present policies and
     argues that the consensus of the middle 1960s has been
     broken, and that it was and remains the right policy for
     the United States--right for the groups that had suffered,
     and in some measure still suffer, from prejudice and dis-
     crimination, and right for the nation as a whole." He
     argues that the consensus of the middle 1960s was shaped
     by three decisions: "first, the entire world would be
     allowed to enter the United States. Second, no separate
     ethnic group was to be allowed to establish an indepen-
     dent polity in the United States. Third, no group, how-
     ever, would be required to give up its group character and
     distinctiveness as the price of full entry into the Ameri-
     cna society and polity. The consensus was marked by
     three major pieces of legislation: the Civil Rights Act
     of 1964, the Voting Rights Act of 1965, and the Immigra-
     tion Act of 1965."

98. Goldman, Alan H. *Justice and Reverse Discrimination*.
    Princeton, NJ: Princeton University Press, 1979, 233,
    Notes, Bibliography.

    Presents a "sustained argument for a single coherent
    view on the question of preferential treatment for mem-
    bers of minority groups and women. The question to be
    answered is: When can corrective preferential treatment
    be justified and for whom? Argues that those most compe-
    tent for the positions for which they apply have *prima
    facie* rights to those positions; that reverse discrimina-
    tion is nevertheless justified in order to compensate
    specific past violations of these rights or denials of
    equal opportunity; that a policy of preference is justi-
    fied as well in order to create equal opportunity in the
    future for the chronically deprived; that preference
    cannot be justified when directed indiscriminately at
    groups defined only by race or sex, in order merely to
    increase their percentage representation in various so-
    cial positions; and that affirmative action programs
    are unjust to the extent that they encourage or directly
    mandate such group-oriented preferential policies."

99. Goldstein, Leslie Friedman. *The Constitutional Rights
    of Women*. New York: Longman, 1979, 407.

    Collection of women's rights cases which provide a
    mechanism for "examining the way the Supreme Court of
    the United States both initiates and responds to social
    change." Reader can explore the "role that argument
    plays in this process, the role of changing societal
    mores and assumptions, and the role of political pres-
    sures. Cases provide a stage on which abstract legal
    terms will take on concrete meaning." Reader can "trace
    the roots of [legal] doctrines back into their lego-
    historical origins."

100. Grabosky, Peter, and David H. Rosenbloom. "Racial and
     Ethnic Integration in the Federal Service." *Social
     Science Quarterly*, 56 (June 1975), 71-84.

     Analyzes "integration in the general schedule posi-
     tions of 19 major federal agencies over the period from
     1967 to 1973. Finds that integration has increased at
     all grade levels and in all but one agency during that
     time. This indicates that despite criticisms and program
     weaknesses, the general objective of federal equal em-
     ployment opportunity is being served. Integration varies
     inversely with grade level, however, and grades GS 12-

18 are not well integrated. To a large extent this means
that insofar as it is internal, bureaucratic policy-
making is taking place in an environment which is racially and ethnically different from that of the nation as a
whole. Agency integration is generally highest where
missions involve equality or service to disadvantaged
groups and where work processes involve factory-type
organization or involve tasks not frequently performed
by minority group members. Integration is generally
lowest in agencies having a disproportionately large
share of their positions in the upper-grade levels and
in those that were highly discriminatory in the past
and have little concern with minorities. Agency integration was found to be inversely associated with size,
and no meaningful relationship was found between growth
and integration. Finally, it was found that 'tipping'
has occurred in two agencies."

101. Gross, Barry R. *Discrimination in Reverse: Is Turnabout
      Fair Play?* New York: New York University Press, 1978,
      142.

      Approaches his discussion of reverse discrimination
      from a philosophic point of view and argues his position
      on moral rather than legal grounds. The central issue
      is: "how can we remedy the effects of insidious discrim-
      inatory practices of the past and present without be-
      traying the very principles on the basis of which we
      have condemned such practices as unjust?"

102. Grossman, Harry. "The Equal Employment Opportunity
      Act of 1972, Its Implications for the State and Local
      Government Manager." *Public Personnel Management*,
      2 (September-October 1973), 370-379.

      Examines the more "significant provisions of the 1972
      law and their implications for the managers of units
      of state and local governments."

103. Hall, Francine S., and Maryann H. Albrecht. *The Manage-
      ment of Affirmative Action.* Santa Monica, CA: .:
      Goodyear, 1979, 165, Appendices, Glossary.

      Concerned with the "administration and organization of
      an entire AA/EEO program," the authors "put together
      theoretical perspectives, regulations, guidelines and
      techniques" designed to enable managers to attain their
      AA/EEO goals more effectively."

104. Hall, Grace, and Alan Saltzstein. "Equal Employment in
      Urban Governments; The Potential Problem of Inter-
      minority Competition." *Public Personnel Management*,
      4 (November-December 1975), 386-393.

      The analysis of the black and Mexican-American compo-
      sition of city employment in 26 Texas cities larger than
      50,000 reveals "several sources of difficulty for per-
      sonnel policy makers who attempt to promote and accom-
      plish equal employment. Also presents methodology for
      determining potential problems with EEO implementation
      in cities."

105. Harmon, Michael M. "Social Equity and Organizational
      Man: Motivation and Organizational Democracy."
      Public Administration Review, 34 (January-February
      1974), 11-18.

      Concludes that the "concept of social equity simply
      does not square with the dominant utilitarian premises on
      which the study and practice of public administration
      have for so many years been based. Thus, if social
      equity is to be elevated to a central position among the
      values of the discipline, a serious rethinking is re-
      quired about the manner in which 'responsible' choices
      of administrators are defined and about the appropriate
      structure of and distribution of power within public
      organizations."

106. Harris, Patricia A., and Karen Olivia White. *Assessing
      the Distribution of Minorities and Women in Relevant
      Labor Markets.* U.S. Office of Personnel Management,
      July 1981, 52, References, Appendices.

      "Discusses procedures and general considerations in
      conducting relevant labor market comparative analyses
      for state/local government and non-government occupations.
      The procedures are presented in five steps; I. A descrip-
      tion of the occupation to be analyzed; II. A description
      of recruitment and selection procedures; III. A descrip-
      tion of the jurisdiction's work force; IV. Considerations
      in the selection of appropriate comparison data; and V.
      A discussion of procedures for computing adverse impact
      and evaluating underutilization. Problem areas of the
      labor market approach to EEO program assessment are
      discussed."

107. Hart, David K. "Social Equity, Justice and the Equitable
      Administrator." *Public Administration Review,* 34
      (January-February 1974), 3-11.

Proposes that "social equity is an idea, 'whose time
has come.'" Observes that (1) "social equity needs a
fuller substantive ethical content; (2) its advocates
have based their justifications and their prescriptions
upon the extant American ethical paradigm; the extant
paradigm (a) denies legitimacy to social equity but (b)
is itself suffering from declining public confidence;
(3) a most promising alternative ethical paradigm has
been developed by John Rawls in *A Theory of Justice*;
and (4) his theory of justice can provide a powerful
ethical foundation for (a) a substantive theory of social
equity and (b) for a professional code for 'equitable
public administrations.'"

108. Hellriegel, Don, and Larry Shrot. "Equal Employment Op-
     portunity in the Federal Government; A Comparative
     Analysis." *Public Administration Review*, 32 (Novem-
     ber-December 1972), 851-858.

     Three distinct stages in the development of equal em-
     ployment opportunity in the federal government are identi-
     fied and discussed. "The stages are labelled the period
     of inaction, period of reaction, and period of proaction.
     The policies and procedures with respect to equal oppor-
     tunity of employment are briefly explained for each
     stage. A comparative analysis of the stages is under-
     taken with respect to the levels of employment and ad-
     vancement of racial minorities in the federal govern-
     ment." Concludes that the "policies and procedures of
     the federal affirmative action program may be a worthy
     model for other organizations to emulate, with modi-
     fications to fit their particular situation.

109. Herbert, Adam W. "The Minority Administrator: Problems,
     Prospects, and Challenges." *Public Administration
     Review*, 34 (November-December 1974), 556-563.

     Identifies "six forces which confront the minority
     administrator, and which influence significantly his/
     her potential effectiveness and perhaps perceptions of
     responsibility to both the governmental agency and
     minority peoples more generally." The six role demands
     on minority administrators are: (1) system demands;
     (2) "traditional" role expectations; (3) colleague pres-
     sures; (4) personal ambition; (5) personal commitment
     to community; and (6) community accountability.

110. Hoffmann, Carl, and John Shelton Reed. "Sex Discrimina-
     tion--The XYZ Affair." *The Public Interest*, 62 (Win-
     ter 1981), 21-39.

Reports results of study of personnel practices in a large corporation to determine if sex discrimination existed in promotion decision. The patterns of promotion within the XYZ corporation reflected differences in the behaviors and attitudes of male and female clerks and not discrimination based on sex.

111. Hunsaker, K.A. "Women and Minorities--Changing Roles in Public Power." *Public Power* (January-February 1981), 112-132.

Describes and examines the public power scene in which "comparatively few women and minorities are employed in the public power systems in professional or managerial positions. The problem is not lack of desire or motivation on the part of management, but rather one of seeking out and attracting qualified women and minority candidates." Also looks at alternatives which may help solve this problem.

112. Hunt, Deryl G. "The Black Perspective on Public Management." *Public Administration Review*, 34 (November-December 1974), 520-525.

Addresses the need for a "modification of the practice of administration to better accommodate the perspective of Black Americans. Premise is that the failure of public administration theory to resolve its own state of crisis, coupled with a fundamental misunderstanding of black demands, has produced a condition of severe conflict."

113. James, Jennifer. "Sexual Harassment." *Public Personnel Management*, 10 (Winter 1982), 402-407.

Clarifies the nature of sexual harassment: it is almost *always repetitive*; it is *one-sided*; offender's behavior is *unwelcome*; sexual harassment relates to *power*; and the victim *cannot stop the abuse*. Recommends prevention and the development of a "sexual harassment policy and grievance procedures."

114. Johnson, Harriet McBryde. "Who Is Handicapped? Defining the Protected Class Under the Employment Provisions of Title V of the Rehabilitation Act of 1973." *Review of Public Personnel Administration*, 2 (Fall 1981), 49-61.

Examines the "problems inherent in using handicap as a basis for classification under a civil rights law."

Traces the evolution of definitional issues and assesses "the extent to which the statutory definition is appropriate to different policy areas." The broader question is, "What may reasonably or meaningfully be required of public managers on behalf of a class as problematic as 'handicapped individuals.'"

115. Jongeward, Dorothy, and Dru Scott. *Affirmative Action for Women: A Practical Guide for Women and Managment.* Reading, MA: Addison-Wesley, 1975, 320, Appendices.

     Collection of comments, programs, and articles. Includes "(1) a clear interpretation of the laws affecting organizations and women, (2) the current place of women in organized religion and in government service, (3) the unique problems of black women in organizations, and insights into selecting a professional counselor for a woman."

116. Karnig, A.K., and S. Welch. "Sex and Ethnic Differences in Municipal Representation." *Social Science Quarterly,* 60 (December 1979), 465-481.

     Descriptive study which aims: "(1) to examine and compare the level of municipal government representation of Anglos, Blacks and Mexican-American males and females; (2) to ascertain whether the correlates of equitable representation, including minority population, government structure and minority resources, are similar for both minority males and females; and (3) to determine whether a substantial degree of inter-minority competition exists; that is, whether the rate of representation obtained by one minority-gender group comes at the expense of other minorities or, conversely, generally acts only to reduce the representation of Anglo males." One of the findings is that "women are less well represented than men, and minority women are the most poorly represented."

117. Kelso, William. "From Bakke to Fullilone: Has the Supreme Court Finally Settled the Affirmative Action Controversy?" *Review of Public Personnel Administration,* 1 (Fall 1980), 57-74.

     Examines the affirmative action controversy over quotas in light of the *Bakke* and *Fullilone* Supreme Court decisions. "The major finding is that the Supreme Court has not broken new ground in recent court decisions. Many important quota issues remain to be resolved."

118. Klein, Gerald D. "Beyond EEO and Affirmative Action: Working on the Integraton of the Work Place." *California Management Review*, XXXII (Summer 1980), 74-81.

Offers working assumptions, helpful managerial behavior, and discusses "factors beyond the immediate supervisor-subordinate relationships (such as the presence or absence of broader organizational support for integration, the nature of the opportunity structure) which affect the retention, motivation, and productivity of minority employees."

119. Korda, Michael. *Male Chauvinism! How It Works*. New York: Random House, 1972, 236.

About the "ways in which women are discriminated against by men in the working world, about the reasons men feel, think and behave the way they do, and about the alternatives to a system that makes all sorts of special demands on women and rewards them, on the whole, with lower pay, fewer opportunities and thinly veiled contempt."

120. Krnaz, Harry. *The Participatory Bureaucracy: Women and Minorities in a More Representative Public Service*. Lexington, MA: Lexington Books, 1976, 233, Appendix.

Examines the "development of the bureaucracy, analyzes some of its problems, and presents possible ways to change its current nature. Asserts that the bureaucracy at all levels is unrepresentative of the general population and that it has operated to exclude ethnic minorities and women. Postulates that as government continues to take on additional responsibilities, the bureaucracy will increase despite calls for reducing the size of government." Proposes actions to ensure that the bureaucracy becomes fully representative.

121. Kreps, Juanita. *Sex at the Marketplace: American Women at Work*. Baltimore: Johns Hopkins Press, 1971, 108.

Reviews the literature on the "subject of women's labor force activity, and to examine when women work, at what jobs, and under what arrangements. Raises questions throughout the review, since the ultimate purpose of any such survey is to identify the gaps in information." Since many "aspects of women's work, both market and nonmarket, remain relatively unexplored," Kreps sees it as "important to reexamine their work roles: to ask what conflicts the changing patterns of women's work may be generating."

122. Krislov, Samuel. *Representative Bureaucracy*. Engle-
      wood Cliffs, NJ: Prentice-Hall, 1974, 137, Bibliography.

      Deals with the problems of equality, merit, and reward
      in "terms of one set of social institutions--the public
      bureaucracy--and in terms of a single claim--to societal
      representativeness--offsetting those of 'presumed merit'
      and 'job-skill-related' criteria."

123. ————. *The Negro in Federal Employment*. Minneapolis:
      University of Minnesota Press, 1967, 150.

      Begins with an historical sketch of the Negro in the
      federal service; presents "two concepts central to
      evaluation of success or failure of the equal employment
      program--representative bureaucracy and merit; and de-
      scribes the equal employment program and its achieve-
      ments." Study based upon interviews conducted between
      1963 and 1965 in every department and agency supervised
      by the President's Committee· on Equal Employment Oppor-
      tunity.

124. Lacy, D.P. "EEO Implications of Job Analysis." *Employee
      Relations Law Journal*, 4 (Spring 1979), 525-534.

      Perhaps the strongest impetus for job analysis to
      become an integral part of personnel policy "has come
      from equal employment opportunity cases in which the
      courts have demanded professional standards in the evalu-
      ation of individual job components." Although overt
      discrimination is on the decline, EEO laws seem to foster
      more subtle forms of discrimination. Class action suits
      have replaced individual discrimination cases. "A per-
      formance evaluation that rates employees on other than
      job-related work is a sure source of trouble. The way
      to avoid this trouble is through job analysis." Con-
      cludes that "a well-done job analysis is an important
      step in both complying with and defending against [legal]
      actions."

125. Ledvinka, James. "Technical Implications of Equal Employ-
      ment Law for Manpower Planning." *Personnel Psychology*,
      28 (Autumn 1975), 299-323.

      If an employment practice results in "a substantially
      different impact on different groups, then it is dis-
      criminatory, no matter how impartially it may have been
      applied. As a practical matter, then, managers have
      had to ask how 'different impact' is defined, and particu-
      larly to ask how much of a differential impact is too

much. 'How much' questions invite numerical answers, and the courts have often given numerical answers. One difficulty is that the courts' numerical answers to 'how much' questions vary with the circumstances of the case. There are no explicit numerical thresholds that apply identically from case to case. Nevertheless, the terms in which the 'how much' question is being answered are now emerging from court opinions. Examines those terms and indicates how they might be incorporated into numerical indices of differential impact. Suggests how a probabilistic forecasting model can be used to generate reasonable goals in planning for increased work force integration."

126. Ledvinka, James, and Lyle F. Schoenfeldt. "Legal Developments in Employment Testing: *Albemarle* and Beyond." *Personnel Psychology*, 31 (Spring 1978), 1-13.

Specific provisions of the 1970 revisions of the EEOC Guidelines were upheld in the Supreme Court's 1975 opinion in *Albemarle Paper Co. v. Moody*. Authors conclude that "nothing much has really changed since *Albemarle*."

127. Levine, Charles H. "Beyond the Sound and Fury of Quotas and Targets." *Public Administration Review*, 34 (May-June 1974), 240-241.

Maintains that efforts to evaluate the impact of affirmative action programs must focus on the work experience of minority groups relative to "patterns of mobility, leverage for investment in personal development, human resource investment, levels of authority and responsibility, organizational experiences, and participation in policy making."

128. Lovell, Catherine. "Three Key Issues in Affirmative Action." *Public Administration Review*, 34 (May-June 1974), 235-237.

When affirmative action policies are implemented, three issues arise: "(1) the distinction between affirmative action and 'non-discrimination'; (2) why preferential hiring and the setting of target quotas are necessary to the affirmative action process; and (3) why traditional standards of 'quality' must be re-examined."

129. MacKinnon, Catherine A. *Sexual Harassment of Working Women*. New Haven: Yale University Press, 1979, 312.

Asserts that "sexual harrassment of working women has
been widely practiced and systematically ignored. Men's
control over women's jobs has often made coerced sexual
relations the price of women's material survival. The
author offers a serious attempt to understand sexual
harassment as a pervasive social problem and to present a legal argument that it is discrimination based on
sex."

130. Markoff, Helen. "The Federal Women's Program." *Public
      Administration Review,* 32 (March-April 1972), 144-155.

      Outlines the history of women in the federal work force
      and offers reasons for the establishment of the Federal
      Women's Program. Supports the Program and sees its goals
      and objectives as compatible with those of EEO/AA, the
      merit principles and competent management.

131. Marlin, John Tepper. "City Affirmative Action Efforts."
      Public Administration Review, 37 (September-October
      1977), 508-511.

      Reports the results of a survey conducted by the Coun-
      cil on Municipal Performance (COMP). Analyzes (1) the
      EEO reporting forms from 32 cities (out of 500 who re-
      sponded with usable forms); (2) the answers to whether
      the city (35 responding) "had filed an Affirmative Ac-
      tion Plan with the federal government; had a personnel
      manual (by which such a plan could be implemented); and
      who monitors compliance with the manual." Finally, the
      COMP survey asked, "Have there been any charges or com-
      plaints related to EEO provisions filed against any city
      department?"

132. McGregor, Eugene B. "Social Equity and the Public."
      Public Administration Review, 34 (January-February
      1974), 18-29.

      Discussion of the "implications of the clash between
      'social equity' and 'merit' for civil service employment
      in the United States. The sole concern of this essay is
      with the politics of the struggle to define social equity
      in the public services of the United States." Concludes
      that on the surface it appears that proponents of social
      equity and advocates of excellence are allies. "Both
      find it essential to discover what public servants
      actually do for work and how people come to be educated,
      recruited, selected, and promoted in the work they do.
      Rarely have two so disparate concerns found such common
      ground."

133. Mead, Margaret. "A Proposal: We Need Taboos on Sex at
     Work." *Redbook*, 150 (April 1978), 31-33, 38.

     Discusses forms and extent of sexual harassment and
     proposes "new taboos that are appropriate to the new
     society." Asserts that we need a taboo which says
     "clearly and unequivocally, 'You don't make passes at or
     sleep with the people you work with.'"

134. Meier, Kenneth John. "Representative Bureaucracy: An
     Empirical Analysis." *The American Political Science
     Review*, LXIX (June 1975), 526-542.

     Critically examines the "ideal of a representative
     bureaucracy and empirically tests the existence of a
     representative bureaucracy in the United States." Re-
     views the literature in the field, outlines the under-
     lying theory of representative bureaucracy, and demon-
     strates how the ideal theory might lead to administra-
     tive responsibility. Critically examines the assumptions
     and premises of the ideal theory in order to demonstrate
     certain weaknesses inherent in the theory. United States
     federal bureaucracy is "empirically investigated to de-
     termine if the bureaucracy is, in fact, representative."
     Concludes that "the evidence clearly contradicts the
     existence of representative bureaucracy in the United
     States."

135. Mendenhall, Janice. "Roots of the Federal Women's Pro-
     gram." *Civil Service Journal*, 18 (July-September 1977),
     21-24.

     Executive Order 11375 prohibiting sex discrimination in
     federal employment was issued in 1967. "In the years
     since the Executive Order, attitudes toward working
     women and sex discrimination have improved remarkably,
     and there has been a significant increase in the number
     of women in professional and technical jobs. However,
     many other aspects of women's Federal employment have
     remained relatively unchanged." Examines "some of the
     events leading up to the Executive Order." The author
     participated in many of the developments she covers and
     writes from the vantage point of her experience as "Fed-
     eral Women's Program Director, as a past president of
     Federally Employed Women, Inc., and as an agency FWP
     Coordinator."

136. Milk, Leslie. "What Is Reasonable Accommodation?" *Civil
     Service Journal*, 19 (October-December 1978), 34-36.

Asserts that "no concept has stymied more reasonable
people than the 'reasonable accommodations' provisions
in the regulations governing employment under the Rehabilitation Act of 1973." The two most frequently
asked questions are: "What is reasonable and who is
qualified?" Author provides her answers to these questions and illustrates her point of view with examples.

137. Morishima, James. "Special Employment Issues for Asian
     Americans." *Public Personnel Management*, 10 (Winter
     1981).

     Asserts that the term Asian American is a "catch-all
     phrase for a very diverse group of persons who have a
     special set of employment problems. Takes a look at some
     of these problems and offers some possible solutions."

138. Nachmias, David, and David H. Rosenbloom. "Measuring
     Bureaucratic Representation and Integration." *Public
     Administration Review*, 33 (November-December 1973),
     590-597.

     The concept of "representative bureaucracy" is the basis
     for the development of a new way to measure integration
     (in the sense of socially, ethnically and/or racially
     mixed) in bureaucracies. The Measure of Variation pre-
     sented is explained and applications are suggested.

139. Nelson, William E., Jr., and Winston Van Horne. "Black
     Elected Administrators: The Trials of Office." *Public
     Administration Review*, 34 (November-December 1974),
     526-533.

     Analyzes "a variety of problems faced by black elected
     administrators as they attempt to fulfill the black
     community's urgent desire for institutional reform and
     a radical shift in governmental priorities." Inventories
     the "number of blacks elected to public office in recent
     years, and the kind of positions they hold"; analyzes
     "the significant problems common to black elected admin-
     istrators"; considers the "strategies adopted by black
     elected administrators to overcome these problems"; and
     finally, comments on the "lessons that can be learned
     from the experiences of black elected officials."

140. Neugarten, Dail Ann, and Jay M. Shafritz. *Sexuality in
     Organizations: Romantic and Coercive Behaviors at Work.*
     Oak Park, IL: Moore Publishing, 1980, 157, Bibliography.

     Book of readings divided into four major sections. In
     the first section, the sexual dynamics inherent in the

work setting and the "interplay of sexual attraction and hierarchical processes" are presented. Section two introduces the reader to the "nature and scope of sexual harassment." The third section focuses on organizational responses to sexual harrassment and the final section covers legal issues. Also included are a bibliography and a list of legal cases involving sexual harassment.

141. Ornati, Oscar A., and Margaret J. Eisen. "Are You Complying With EEOC's New Rules on National Origin Discrimination?" *Personnel*, 58 (march-April 1981), 12-20.

National origin discrimination may well be the major issue in the 1980s. Guidelines are also being developed by the EEOC covering religious discrimination. The authors present what's in the new rules, how companies deal with national origin discrimination, and what can be done to eliminate harassment and national origin discrimination.

142. Pati, Gopal C. "Countdown on Hiring the Handicapped." *Personnel Journal*, 57 (March 1978), 144-153.

The Vocational Rehabilitation Act of 1973, "requires federal contractors and subcontractors to take affirmative action (AAP) to seek out qualified handicapped people and fully utilize them." Research supports "(1) Employers must know what handicapped persons can do, rather than what they cannot do. (2) There is no such thing as 'handicapped' people, only people with varied abilities. (3) Legal pressure is not the only reason why employers hire the handicapped. (4) Handicapped employees have positive impact on their peers, managers and organizational climate. (6) The apprehension that insurance, safety and medical costs will skyrocket as a result of employing the handicapped is not valid. (7) A solid working relationship between the business and rehabilitation agency, as well as between the business executive and the compliance officer, must exist. (8) In unionized operations, labor-management cooperation must also exist."

143. Pati, Gopal C., and John I. Adkins, Jr. "Hire the Handicapped--Compliance Is Good Business." *Harvard Business Review*, 58 (January-February 1980), 14-15, 18, 20, 22.

After a discussion of the legal requirements embodied in the Vocational Rehabilitation Act of 1973 and the new enforcement mechanisms, authors offer the reader informa-

tion and illustrations which are designed to make compliance with the law less difficult.

144. Peterson, Donald J. "Paving the Way for Hiring the Handi-
      capped." *Personnel*, 58 (March-April 1981), 43-52.

      Contractors are called upon by federal affirmative ac-
      tion requirements to be ingenious in complying with
      "rules that provide only general guidelines for compli-
      ance." Article is based on the respondents' answers to
      a questionnaire and is organized around the major re-
      quirements of the Office of Federal Contract Compliance
      Programs (OFCCP) rules under the Rehabilitation Act of
      1973: Outreach, interviewing, job accommodation, accessi-
      bility, and human relations training.

145. Porter, David O., and Teddie Wood Porter. "Social Equity
      and Fiscal Federalism." *Public Administration Review*,
      34 (January-February 1974), 36-42.

      Attributes the growing fiscal imbalance among local,
      state and federal levels of government to "(1) tax com-
      petition, (2) uneven distribution of income and wealth
      among jurisdictions, (3) pervasive spillovers of bene-
      fits and costs among state and local governments, and (4)
      the more productive federal income taxes." Concludes
      that what is needed are national policies to guide state
      and local governments in their move to alleviate their
      fiscal problems.

146. Quinn, Robert E. "Coping With Cupid: The Formation,
      Impact and Management of Romantic Relationships in
      Organizations." *Administrative Science Quarterly*, 22
      (March 1977), 30-45.

      Answers three questions: (1) "What aspects of organiza-
      tions facilitate the formation of romance?; (2) What
      is its organizational impact?; and (3) How do superiors,
      coworkers, and subordinates perceive and cope with the
      phenomenon?"

147. Quinn, Robert E., and Noreen A. Judge. "The Office Ro-
      mance: No Bliss for the Boss." *Management Review*, 67
      (July 1978), 43-49.

      Thoroughly discusses the nature of workplace romances,
      the consequences for the organization, offers a pre-
      vention strategy and outlines when the "organizational
      romance is worthy of management attention."

148. Reeves, Earl J. "Making Equality of Employment Opportunity a Reality in the Federal Service." *Public Administration Review*, 30 (January-February 1970), 43-49.

    Major barriers to implementation of "genuine equality of opportunity in federal employment" are reconciliation of "equal employment with the merit system and communication between the federal agencies and minority groups, especially the black community." The need is for a "more flexible approach to the merit system which will place more emphasis on potential" and effective communication. "In seeking to establish communication with the black community, administrators face four barriers: the suspicion felt by Blacks towards all elements of the white establishment; the failure of managers to understand the current black movement; the failure to utilize the pipeline to the community provided by current employees; and the sporadic nature of most attempts at communication."

149. Remick, Helen. "The Comparable Worth Controversy." *Public Personnel Management*, 10 (Winter 1981), 371-383.

    Reviews what "facts" are known about comparable worth; carefully defines terms; and explores "differences between the theory and actual practices of salary setting."

150. Roberts, Robert R. "'Last Hired, First Fired' and Public Employee Layoffs: The Equal Employment Opportunity Dilemma." *Review of Public Personnel Administration*, 2 (Fall 1981), 29-48.

    Relates the conflict between the "application of the 'last hired, first fired' rule and its impact upon equal employment opportunity programs in the public sector." Concludes that "units of government will increasingly face the prospect of using employee layoffs as a way to make significant cuts in expenditures." Traditionally, government relied on "hiring freezes, attrition, and early retirement incentives to avoid employee layoffs."

151. Robertson, David E. "Update on Testing and Equal Opportunity." *Personnel Journal*, 56 (March 1977), 144-147.

    Recently the "courts have upheld tests by not enjoining their use, even in some instances where the employer's actions were found to be discriminatory. Author finds it reasonable "that an employer's conduct be judged in its totality rather than as isolated specific actions without context or purpose." He also is encouraged by the indication that courts are imposing quota systems less often and even occasionally judging them as discriminatory themselves.

152. Robinson, Rose M. "Conference on Minority Public Admin-
      istrations." *Public Administration Review*, 34 (Novem-
      ber-December 1974), 552-556.

      The Conference on Minority Public Administrators (COMPA)
      has been an affiliate of the American Society for Public
      Administration since 1970. The organizational objectives
      are to improve the "quality of public services affecting
      the lives and well-being of minority citizens" and to
      expand the "opportunities for members of minority groups
      to assume leadership roles in public service." Discusses
      "some of the factors which, in the opinion of the author,
      have slowed COMPA's realization of its potential, how
      these are being overcome, some of its accomplishments
      and, finally, what appear to be its prospects for the
      future."

153. Rose, Wenfield H., and Tiang Ping Chia. "The Impact of
      the Equal Employment Opportunity Act of 1972 on Black
      Employment in the Federal Service: A Preliminary Analy-
      sis." *Public Administration Review*, 38 (May-June
      1978), 245-251.

      Sketches the historical development of equal employ-
      ment opportunity and affirmative action in the United
      States, analyzes what they are, and examines the "statis-
      tical record to assess their effectiveness in enhancing
      the number and status of black employees in the United
      States Civil Service."

154. Rosen, Benson, and Thomas H. Herdee. "Sex Stereotyping
      in the Executive Suite." *Harvard Business Review*, 52
      (March-April 1974), 45-58.

      Concludes that "many women do not receive the organiza-
      tional support that their male counterparts automatically
      experience."

155. Rosen, Bernard. "Affirmative Action Produces Equal Em-
      ployment Opportunity For All." *Public Administration
      Review*, 34 (May-June 1974), 237-239.

      Asserts that "affirmative action is the logical exten-
      sion of a non-discrimination policy in employment. The
      United States Civil Service Commission does not think of
      equal employment opportunity as a separate program out-
      side the mainstream of personnel management, nor does it

administer it that way. Equal employment opportunity and employment based on merit principles are truly synonymous concepts."

156. Rosenbloom, David H. "The Civil Service Commission's Decision to Authorize the Use of Goals and Timetables in the Federal Equal Employment Opportunity Program." *Western Political Quarterly*, 26 (June 1973), 236-251.

A memorandum for the heads of departments and agencies concerning the "use of employment goals and timetables in agency equal employment opportunity programs" was issued by the U.S. Civil Service Commission on May 11, 1971. Author's analysis (1) identifies and explains "the importance of the major factors the CSC took into account in making its decision to adopt the new policy"; (2) indicates "how and why ambiguity can be used consciously as a technique for avoiding genuine changes in policy"; (3) raises some fundamental questions concerning the new policy as it relates to overall public policy; and (4) provides "general background information concerning the EEO program itself." Concludes, in part, that "the CSC's decision indicates a need, when analyzing policy-making in the bureaucracy, to search for more or less covert agency considerations and motives which may be largely divorced from the particular policy area openly involved."

157. ————. *Federal Equal Employment Opportunity: Politics and Public Personnel Administration.* New York: Praeger, 1977, 170.

By concentrating on the "politics of the Federal Equal Employment Opportunity Program," author "sheds light on the nature of bureaucratic politics in the federal government and provides a lesson in how administration may be infused with politics." Also "shows the extent to which organizational and administrative choices may be political choices and how agencies can use their control over the implementation of policies to protect their 'cultures' and values. Analysis suggests that the equal employment opportunity (EEO) policy arena is dominated by a contest between those who seek to maintain the merit system as it has traditionally existed and those who see a far more representative federal service. It is argued not only that 'representationists' have made substantial inroads on federal personnel policy, but that representation will occupy a key position in the public personnel administration of the future. In addition, this book

differs from others in its attempt to explore fully the
nature of the contemporary EEO 'problem' and to evaluate
EEO policies from the perspective of their contributions
to its resolution. Hence, it is also a study in public
policy, but implicit in the central argument is the be-
lief that the organizational politics of EEO policy will
continue to dominate its content."

158.   ————. "*Kaiser vs. Weber*: Perspectives From the Public
        Sector." *Public Personnel Management*, 8 (November-
        December 1979), 392-406.

        "Although *Kaiser vs. Weber* allows private employers
        voluntarily to afford preferential treatment to racial
        minorities, its relevance to public sector affirmative
        action practices is political rather than legal or
        constitutional."

159.   Rowe, Mary P. "Dealing with Sexual Harassment." *Harvard
        Business Review*, 59 (May-June 1981), 42-44, 46.

        Recommends (1) complainants take action themselves in
        a "rational and responsible way," (2) conflicts be re-
        solved through "procedures designed to deal with all kinds
        of complaints, not just sexual harassment," and (3)
        corporations "confront the issue of power differences in
        the troubled relationship." Addresses remarks to "offend-
        ed persons whose companies do not yet have policies and
        structures to support them."

160.   Safran, Claire. "What Men Do to Women on the Job: A Shock-
        ing Look at Sexual Harassment." *Redbook* (November
        1976), 149, 217-218, 220, 222, 224.

        Reports results of a survey of 9,000 women who self-
        selected to respond to the survey. Nine out of ten
        women reported "that they have experienced one or more
        forms of unwanted attention on the job." Lists what to
        do and when to do it to discourage unwanted advances.

161.   Samuels, Catherine. *The Forgotten Five Million: Women
        in Public Employment.* (A Guide to Eliminating Sex Dis-
        crimination.) Brooklyn, NY: Faculty Press, 1975,
        298, Appendix.

        Project of the Women's Action Alliance (a national
        non-profit organization and clearinghouse of resources
        and information to assist women), which "highlights the
        serious problems of women employed in state and local
        governments, develops an awareness of discrimination

among these workers, and provides specific and concrete
information on what women can do to improve their employment status. Book written for women employees and
is meant to be a workbook, a handbook, and a detailed
manual for those who seek change."

162. Schlei, Barbara Lindemann, and Paul Grossman. *Employ-
      ment Discrimination Law.* Washington, DC: Bureau of
      National Affairs, 1976, 1472, Bibliographical Refer-
      ences.

      Authors present "issues in employment discrimination
      law, strategy suggestions, a compilation of major author-
      ities, and an edited text of major and illustrative de-
      cisions in the area."

163. Sherman, Mitchell. "Equal Employment Opportunity: Legal
      Issues and Societal Consequences." *Public Personnel
      Management,* 7 (March-April 1978), 127-134.

      "The legal issues which have led to today's Affirmative
      Action programs are reviewed and interpreted. Thesis
      is that current programs do not accurately reflect the
      Rights Act of 1964. Empirical evidence indicates that
      affirmative action programs have not been effective in
      reaching the most needy groups, particularly the younger
      black group. Several studies are reviewed which illus-
      trate the complexity of the Equal Employment Opportunity
      issue and point out some areas for research that would
      aid organizations in successfully integrating their work
      force."

164. Sindler, Allan P. *Bakke, DeFunis, and Minority Admis-
      sions: The Quest for Equal Opportunity.* New York:
      Longman, 1978, 325.

      Addresses the problem of "how to promote equal oppor-
      tunity for disadvantaged minorities through affirmative
      action without engaging in reverse discrimination."
      The focus is "on the problem of minority admissions to
      law and medical schools, where there are many more appli-
      cants than available places, and on two nationally contro-
      versial Supreme Court cases:" *DeFunis* (1974) and *Bakke*
      (1978).

165. Siniscalo, G.R. "Sexual Harassment and Employer Liability:
      The Flirtation That Could Cost a Fortune." *Employee
      Relations law Journal,* 6 (Fall 1980), 277-293.

      Examines the sexual harassment guidelines issued by
      the Equal Employment Opportunity Commission and the pro-

posed regulations issued by the Office of Federal Contract Compliance Programs. This examination finds that
"prevention is the best tool for the possible elimination
of sexual harassment. Preventive measures include af-
firmatively raising the issue of sexual harassment,
expressing strong disapproval, developing appropriate
sanctions, informing employees of their right to com-
plain of sexual harassment, explaining how to make a
complaint under federal and state law, and developing
methods to sensitize employees.

166. Sloan, A. "An Analysis of Uniform Guidelines on Employee
      Selection Procedures." *Employee Relations Law Journal*,
      4 (Winter 1978), 346-356.

      The Equal Employment Opportunity Commission, the De-
      partments of Labor and Justice, and the United States
      Civil Service Commission have come out with their Uni-
      form Guidelines on Employee Selection Procedures. Those
      employers who expected the guidelines to "end the con-
      fusion surrounding EEO selection procedures will be
      disappointed. For although the guidelines do attempt to
      clarify the rules, this article points out that they also
      impose new burdens on the employer and expose the company
      to grave risks in its hiring policies."

167. Stumpf, Stephen A., Martin M. Griller, and Richard D.
      Freedman. "Equal Employment Opportunity Regulation and
      Change in Compensation Practice." *The Journal of Ap-
      plied Behavioral Science*, 16 (January-February-March
      1980), 29-40.

      Over a three-year period, the effects of EEO regula-
      tions on compensation practices of one company were ex-
      amined. Findings suggest that the "EEO regulations and
      top management policy directives had little impact in
      reducing salary inequities of female and minority em-
      ployees who were employed at the time of the policy
      change; newcomers experienced moderate benefit. The
      response of the organization suggests concerns about the
      effectiveness of regulatory intervention designed to
      alter intra-organizational processes."

168. Taylor, Lewis W., and L.S. Tao. "E.E.O.C.'s Improved
      Case Management System." *Management*, 1 (Fall 1980),
      14-15.

      EEOC attached its "backlog problem through a series of
      management initiatives that have resulted in significant
      productivity improvement."

169. Tombari, Henry A. "Determinants of Equity of Rewards for Supervisors." *Public Personnel Management*, 9 (January-February 1980), 25-30.

    Reports summary of survey of 290 first-line supervisors designed "to uncover the determinants of supervisory perceptions of equity of rewards in federal health care organizations. It appears that job-related factors act as determinants of equity of rewards for the supervisory occupations group in this millieu. Discussion of possible means of averting supervisory reward inequities is presented."

170. United States Commission on Civil Rights. *Toward an Understanding of Bakke*, Clearinghouse Publication 58. Washington, DC: U.S. Government Printing Office, May 1979, 189.

    "Intended to increase public understanding of affirmative action by making easily available the complete test of the *Bakke* decision and the Equal Employment Opportunity Commission's voluntary affirmative action guidelines."

171. United States Commission on Civil Rights. *A Guide to Federal Laws and Regulations Prohibiting Sex Discrimination*, Clearinghouse Publication 46. Washington, DC: U.S. Government Printing Office, July 1976, 168, Appendices.

    "Explains Federal laws that prohibit sex discrimination as well as policies and regulations of Federal agencies prohibiting sex discrimination and describes the major provisions of each law and regulation and the complaint procedures established under each."

172. United States Merit Systems Protection Board. *Sexual Harassment in the Federal Workplace: Is It a Problem?* Washington, DC: Government Printing Office, March 1981, 104, Appendices, Tables.

    Summarizes major recommendations and findings "on the views of federal employees about sexual harassment, the extent of sexual harassment in the federal workplace, a description of characteristics of victims and perpetrators of sexual harassment, a discussion of the perceptions and responses of victims to their incidents of sexual harassment, the impact of the behavior on the victims and the estimated dollar cost of sexual harassment to the federal government and views of federal employees about potential remedies and their effectiveness."

173. White, Orion, Jr., and Bruce L. Gates. "Statistical
     Theory and Equity in the Delivery of Social Services."
     Public Administration Review, 34 (January-February
     1974), 43-51.

     Argues "that American society is moving toward a post-
     industrial condition and that public organizations must
     change both their concept of social equity as well as
     their structure and processes if inequities are to be
     reduced or prevented from growing worse in the future."
     We are moving away from a society "centered around the
     process of production and consumption" and toward one in
     which "symbols will replace goods as the substance of the
     economic exchange process." They conclude that "openness
     and participation within our administrative agencies"
     is desirable and in order to achieve this state "it will
     be necessary to educate future generations of administra-
     tors to a view of the world which is itself open."

CHAPTER 3

CONSTITUTIONAL ISSUES

174. Dotson, Arch. "The Emerging Doctrine of Privilege in
Public Employment." *Public Administration Review*, 15
(Spring 1955), 77-88.

The central tenet of the doctrine of privilege in public employment is that "office is held at the pleasure of
the government. Government may impose upon the public
employee any requirement it sees fit as conditional to
employment. From the point of view of the state, public
employment is maintained as an indulgence; from the position of the citizen, his job is a grant concerning which
he has no independent rights." Defines the sources of
this dogma; summarizes and analyzes its content; and
evaluates it, "as a matter of public law and as public
policy."

175. Goldman, Deborah. "Due Process and Public Personnel Management." *Review of Public Personnel Management*, 2
(Fall 1981), 19-27.

Contends that the Supreme Court "has not generally attempted to substitute its judgement for that of executive branch officials on the merits of whether an individual civil servant should be dismissed. Rather, for
the most part, the Court has sought to establish guidelines for the constitutional treatment of public employees
in adverse action cases. Most of the Court's attention
has been paid to matters of procedure."

176. Meir, Kenneth J. "Ode to Patronage: A Critical Analysis
of Two Recent Supreme Court Decisions." *Public Administration Review*, 41 (September-October 1981), 558-563.

The U.S. Supreme Court in *Elrod v. Burns* and *Branti v.
Finkel* "restricted patronage dismissals to only those
positions where 'party affiliation is an appropriate requirement for the effective performance of the public

office involved." This essay argues that the U.S. Supreme Court's decisions have five major flaws: (1) the
positions covered are unclear, (2) effective performance
may involve partisan judgements, (3) several vital state
interests that patronage can attain are ignored, (4) the
decisions are inconsistent with other laws and policies,
and (5) the societal benefits of patronage are minimized."

177. Nalbandian, John, and Donald Klingner. "The Politics of
      Public Personnel Administration: Towards Theoretical
      Understanding." *Public Administration Review*, 41 (Sep-
      tember-October 1981), 541-549.

      Conceptualizes the world of public personnel as a "com-
      plex organizational system rather than primarily a tech-
      nical or political system. This view draws upon the
      theoretical propositions of organization theory as well
      as political science. Article reflects Talcott Parsons'
      assertion that complex organizations exhibit three dis-
      tinct levels of responsibility and control. He labels
      these as institutional, managerial, and technical levels.
      Dynamism is added to this structure with James D. Thomp-
      son's assertion that 'the central problem for complex
      organizations is one of coping with uncertainty.' Thus,
      the central problem for human resource management is to
      attenuate the impact of the political debate which occurs
      at the institutional level so that personnel technicians
      can effectively perform their work."

178. Rosenbloom, David H. *Federal Service and the Constitu-
      tion*. Ithaca, NY: Cornell University Press, 1971, 243.

      Traces the "growth of the federal service from 1776,
      through the spoils system, the reform movement and the
      development of the modern civil service." Principal
      concern is in "the constitutional relationship between
      the citizen and the state in public employment."

179. ————. "Public Personnel Administration and the Con-
      stitution: An Emergent Approach." *Public Administra-
      tion Review*, 35 (January-February 1975), 52-59.

      Analyzes "recent judicial decisions concerning the
      procedural and substantive constitutional rights of
      public employees which indicate that the courts have
      adopted an idiographic approach to many of the issues
      involved. This approach is of greatest importance with
      regard to procedural due process, freedom of speech,
      association and thought, and equal protection. It has
      important implications for public personnel administra-

tion and requires modification of some practices associated with political neutrality, the establishment of moral standards for public employees, and the quest for greater efficiency. The idiographic approach also decreased the utility of public personnel administration's policing function in several respects."

180. ————. "The Sources of Continuing Conflict Between the Constitution and Public Personnel Management." *Review of Public Personnel Administration*, 1 (Fall 1981), 3-18.

Contends that the "root of the conflict between Public Personnel Management and contemporary constitutional law is a major clash between administrative values and those embodied in American constitutional democracy." Argues that "judicial activity in the realm of public personnel administration is but one aspect of a more general judicial response to the rise of the American administrative state."

Legal Cases

181. *Abood v. Detroit Board of Education*, 431 U.S. 209 (1977).

U.S. Supreme Court case, which held that public sector agency shops requiring nonunion employees to pay a service fee equivalent to union dues were constitutional. The court declared unconstitutional a union's use of such service fees for political and ideological purposes unrelated to collective bargaining.

182. *Arnett v. Kennedy*, 416 U.S. 134 (1974).

U.S. Supreme Court case, which held that the administrative procedures afforded federal employees discharged "for such cause as will promote the efficiency of the service" neither violated the due process rights of such employees nor were unconstitutionally vague.

183. *Bishop v. Wood*, 426 U.S. 341 (1976).

U.S. Supreme Court case, which held that an employee's discharge did not deprive him of a property interest protected by the Due Process Clause of the U.S. Constitution's 14th Amendment. The court further asserted that, even assuming a false explanation for the employee's discharge, he was still not deprived of an interest in liberty

protected by the clause if the reasons for his discharge
were not made public.

184. *Board of Regents v. Roth*, 408 U.S. 564 (1972).

U.S. Supreme Court Case, which established the principle that a dismissed or nonrenewed public employee had
no general constitutional right to either a statement of
reasons or a hearing. However, both of these might be
constitutionally required, the court ruled, in individual
instances where any of the following four conditions
existed: (1) Where the removal or nonrenewal was in retaliation for the exercise of constitutional rights
such as freedom of speech or association; (2) Where the
adverse action impaired the individual's reputation; (3)
Perhaps not fully distinguishable from the above, where
a dismissal or nonrenewal placed a stigma or other dis-
ability upon the employee which foreclosed his or her
freedom to take advantage of other employment opportunities; (4) Where one had a property right or interest in
the position, as in the case of tenured or contracted
public employees.

185. *Branti v. Finkel*, 445 U.S. 507 (1980).

U.S. Supreme Court case expanding on the Court's
earlier ruling in *Elrod v. Burns* (1976) that the dismissal of nonpolicymaking, nonconfidential public employees
for their partisan affiliation violates the First and/
or Fourteenth Amendments. The burden is on the hiring
authority to demonstrate that partisan affiliation is an
appropriate requirement for effective performance in
office, which would not be done in this instance involving the position of assistant public defender.

186. *Brown v. General Services Administration*, 425 U.S. 820
      (1976).

U.S. Supreme Court case, which held that Congress intended Title VII of the Civil Rights Act of 1964 to provide the sole statutory protection against employment
discrimination for federal employees--even though it is
not the sole protection for workers in the private sector.

187. *Cleveland Board of Education v. LaFleur*, 414 U.S. 632
      (1974).

U.S. Supreme Court case, which held that arbitrary
mandatory maternity leaves were unconstitutional. The
court held that requiring pregnant teachers to take un-

paid maternity leave five months before expected child-
birth was in violation of the Due Process Clause of the
14th Amendment.

188. *Codd v. Velger*, 429 U.S. 624 (1977).

U.S. Supreme Court case, which held that public employees are not constitutionally entitled to a hearing
in dismissals where no issue of fact is at stake.

189. *Cooper v. Delta Airlines*, 274 F. Supp. 781 (1967).

Case in which a U.S. district court invalidated the
practice of firing women stewardesses who were either
married or more than 32 years old.

190. *Corning Glass Works v. Brennan*, 417 U.S. 188 (1974).

U.S. Supreme Court case, which held that it was a violation of the Equal Pay Act of 1963 to continue to pay
some men at a higher rate ("red circle") than women for
the same work even though all new hires for these same
positions would receive the same salary regardless of sex.

191. *Elfbrandt v. Russell*, 384 U.S. 11 (1966).

U.S. Supreme Court case holding an Arizona loyalty oath
unconstitutional in violation of freedom of association
since, coupled with a perjury statute, it proscribed
membership in any organization having for one of its
purposes the overthrow of the government of the State of
Arizona. The Court reasoned that one might join such an
organization without supporting its illegal purposes.

192. *Elrod v. Burns*, 427 U.S. 347 (1976).

U.S. Supreme Court case, which held that the First
Amendment, which safeguards the rights of political
beliefs and association, prevents political firings of
state, county and local workers below the policymaking
level.

193. *Kelley v. Johnson*, 425 U.S. 238 (1976).

U.S. Supreme Court case, which upheld a municipal regulation limiting the hair length of police.

194. *Massachusetts v. Feeney*, 60 L.Ed. 2d 870 (1979).

U.S. Supreme Court case, which held that a state law
operating to the advantage of males by giving veterans
lifetime preference for state employment was not in
violation of the equal protection clause of the 14th

Amendment. The court found that a veterans' preference
law's disproportionate impact on women did not prove
intentional bias.

195.   *McAuliffe v. Mayor of New Bedford*, 155 Mass. 216 (1892).

Massachusetts Supreme Court case concerning the constitutionality of a city rule prohibiting policemen from
joining labor unions. The logic of this decision has
been rejected by the Supreme Court in more recent years.

196.   *McCarthy v. Philadelphia Civil Service Commission*, 424
       U.S. 645 (1976).

U.S. Supreme Court case, which upheld an ordinance
requiring that city employees live within city limits.

197.   *McDonald v. Sante Fe Trail Transportation Co.*, 424 U.S.
       952 (1976).

U.S. Supreme Court case, which held an employer could
not impose racially discriminatory discipline on employees guilty of the same offense.

198.   *McDonnel Douglas Corporation v. Green*, U.S. 792 (1973).

U.S. Supreme Court case, which held that an employee
could establish a prima facie case of discrimination by
initially showing (1) that he or she was a member of a
racial minority; (2) that he or she applied and was
qualified in an opening for which the employer sought
applicants; (3) that despite qualifications he or she was
rejected; (4) that after rejection the position remained
open and the employer continued to seek applicants.

199.   *Pickering v. Board of Education*, 391 U.S. 563 (1968).

U.S. Supreme Court case, which held that when public
employees' rights to freedom of speech are in question,
the special duties and obligations of public employees
cannot be ignored; the proper test is whether the government's interest in limiting public employees' "opportunities to contribute to public debate is ... significantly
greater than its interest in limiting a similar contribution by any member of the general public." The court
identified six elements which would generally enable the
state to legitimately abridge a public employee's freedom of expression: (1) the need for maintaining discipline and harmony in the workforce; (2) the need for
confidentiality; (3) the possibility that an employee's
position is such that his/her statements might be hard to

counter due to his/her presumed greater access to factual information; (4) the situation in which an employee's statements impede the proper performance of work; (5) the instance where the statements are so without foundation the individual's basic capability to perform his/her duties comes into question; (6) the jeopardizing of a close and personal loyalty and confidence. In addition to the above factors, it has been held that the nature of the remarks or expression, degree of disruption, and likelihood that the public will be prone to accepting the statements of an employee because of his/her position must be weighed. In general, however, only expressions on matters of public concern, as opposed to those primarily of interest to co-workers, are subject to constitutional protection.

200. *Pittsburgh Press Co. v. The Pittsburgh Commission on Human Relations*, 413 U.S. 376 (1973).

U.S. Supreme Court case, which held that a municipal order forbidding newspapers to segregate job announcements according to sex when gender is not a required qualification did not violate the constitutional freedom of the press.

201. *Regents of the University of California v. Allan Bakke*, 438 U.S. 265 (1978).

U.S. Supreme Court case, which upheld a white applicant's claim of reverse discrimination because he was denied admission to the University of California Medical School at Davis when 16 out of the School's 100 class spaces were set aside for minority applicants. The court ruled that Bakke must be admitted to the Davis Medical School as soon as possible, but that the University had the right to take race into account in its admissions criteria. The imprecise nature of taking race into account as one factor among many has created considerable speculation about the potential impact this case may have on voluntary affirmative action programs concerning employment. See Allan P. Sindler, *Bakke, DeFunis, and Minority Admissions: The Quest For Equal Opportunity* (New York: Longman, 1978); Joel Dreyfus and Charles Lawrence III, *The Bakke Case: The Politics of Inequality* (New York: Harcourt Brace Jovanovich, 1979); J. Harvie Wilkinson III, *From Brown to Bakke: The Supreme Court and School Integration 1954-1978* (New York: Oxford University Press, 1979).

202. *Shelton v. Tucker*, 364 U.S. 479 (1960).

     U.S. Supreme Court case, which dealt with the questions
     of whether public employees could have membership in
     subversive organizations, organizations with illegal ob-
     jectives, and unions. Their right to join the latter
     was upheld. With regard to the former two, it was held
     that there could be no general answer. Rather, each case
     has to be judged on the basis of whether a public employee
     actually supports an organization's illegal aims, because,
     as the Supreme Court expressed it, "those who join an
     organization but do not share its unlawful purposes and
     who do not participate in its unlawful activities surely
     pose no threat, either as citizens or as public employees."
     Consequently, it is incumbent upon public employers seek-
     ing to dismiss employees for membership in subversive
     organizations or those with illegal purposes to prove that
     the employees actually shared in the subversive organiza-
     tion's objectionable aims and activities.

203. *Sherbert v. Verner*, 374 U.S. 398 (1963).

     U.S. Supreme Court case, which held it was unconstitu-
     tional to disqualify a person for unemployment compensa-
     tion benefits solely because that person refused to ac-
     cept employment that would require working on Saturday
     contrary to his/her religious belief.

204. *Sugarman v. Dougall*, 413 U.S. 634 (1973).

     U.S. Supreme Court case, which held that a ban on the
     employment of resident aliens by a state was unconsti-
     tutional, because it encompassed positions that had lit-
     tle, if any, relation to a legitimate state interest in
     treating aliens differently from citizens. However, the
     court also stated that alienage might be reasonably tak-
     en into account with regard to specific positions.

205. *United States Civil Service Commission v. National Associ-
     ation of Letter Carriers*, 413 U.S. 548 (1973).

     U.S. Supreme Court case, which upheld the Hatch Act's
     limitations on the political activities of federal em-
     ployees. The *Letter Carriers* decision reaffirmed an
     earlier court ruling, *United Public Workers v. Mitchell*,
     330 U.S. 75 (1947), which had held that the ordinary
     citizen rights of federal employees could be abridged by
     Congress in the interest of increasing or maintaining
     the efficiency of the federal service. In the 1972 case,
     National Association of Letter Carriers v. United States

Civil Service Commission, the Court of Appeals for the District of Columbia Circuit declared the Hatch Act to be unconstitutional because its vague and "overboard" language made it impossible to determine what it prohibited. When this case was appealed to the Supreme Court, the court reasoned that, despite some ambiguities, an ordinary person using ordinary common sense could ascertain and comply with the regulations involved. It also argued that its decision did nothing more than to confirm the judgment of history that political neutrality was a desirable, or even essential, feature of public employment in the United States.

206. *Vance v. Bradley*, 59 L. Ed. 2d 171 (1979).

U.S. Supreme Court case, which held that requiring officers of the U.S. Foreign Service to retire at age 60 did not violate the equal protection component of the due process clause of the Fifth Amendment, even though other federal employees do not face mandatory retirement at such an early age.

207. *Washington v. David*, 426 U.S. 229 (1976).

U.S. Supreme Court case, which held that although the Due Process Clause of the Fifth Amendment prohibits the government from invidious discrimination, it does not follow that a law or other official act is unconstitutional *solely* because it has a racially disproportionate impact. The Court ruled that, under the Constitution (as opposed to Title VII of the Civil Rights Act of 1964), there must be discriminatory purpose or intent--adverse impact alone is insufficient. See Carl F. Goodman, "Public Employment and the Supreme Court's 1975-76 Term," *Public Personnel Management* (September-October 1976).

CHAPTER 4

HUMAN RESOURCES PLANNING

208. Allan, Peter, and Stephen Rosenberg. *Public Personnel
     and Administrative Behavior: Cases and Text*. Monterey,
     CA: Duxbury Press, 1981, 150, Appendices.

     Criteria for cases included in this selection are:
     "First, the cases had to be real; second, they had to
     deal with current problems and with matters likely to be
     of concern in the foreseeable future; third, they had to
     be written so that students and practitioners could readi-
     ly visualize the situation and place themselves within it;
     and fourth, they had to be sufficiently short so that they
     could be read and absorbed quickly."

209. Biles, George E., and Steven R. Holmberg, eds. *Strategic
     Human Resource Planning*. Glen Ridge, NJ: Thomas
     Horton & Daughters, 1980, 342.

     Book of readings designed "to synthesize systematically
     and present the relevant human resource management and
     planning literature, and to (1) facilitate awareness,
     knowledge, understanding, and skills concerning the re-
     lationship of human resource strategic planning to a
     particular organization; and (2) assist in more fully
     incorporating human resource planning into the overall
     strategic management planning of an organization. The
     readings articles in this book are organized into three
     parts. Collectively, these articles represent the full
     range and the best of current and classical research in
     human resource strategic planning: conceptual articles;
     articles dealing with specific tools or techniques; and
     articles which report on current practices of organiza-
     tions. Part I traces the evolving management concept of
     human resource strategic planning. Part II develops the
     specific subelements of human resource strategic plan-
     ning by providing for each subelement the requisite con-
     cepts, tools, and practical examples of their application.
     Part III focuses on the future of human resource strate-

gic planning from the perspective of both individual
organizations and the economy as a whole. Book designed
for: (1) professional managers at both top and middle
management levels in business and nonprofit organizations;
(2) corporate personnel and industrial relations specialists; (3) public and nonprofit sector human resource
policy makers and personnel specialists; (4) personnel
management and industrial relations graduate courses as
a supplement to another textbook; (5) human resource
planning courses at the undergraduate and graduate levels,
as the primary book; (6) management and executive development programs."

210.   Blakely, Robert T., III. "Markov Models and Manpower
       Planning." *Industrial Management Review*, II (Winter
       1970), 39-46.

       Concludes that the Markov technique is "particularly
       helpful in looking at personnel movement within the
       organization. More specifically, the model can be used
       to describe systematically manpower movement and to pro-
       vide estimates of turnover, manpower requirements, and
       statistics related to career paths as well as individual
       career planning."

211.   Bowey, Angela. *A Guide to Manpower Planning*. London:
       Macmillan, 1974, 78.

       A how-to-do-it guide which also "sets out the chains
       of reasoning from which follow the practical steps" that
       are recommended.

212.   Bryant, Don R., Michael J. Maggard, and Robert P. Taylor.
       "Manpower Planning Models and Techniques: A Descriptive
       Study." *Business Horizons*, 16 (April 1973), 69-78.

       Reviews factors giving rise to the need for manpower
       planning. Presents the general characteristics of the
       four main types of manpower planning: (1) judgmental
       techniques including The Delphi Technique; (2) matrix
       models; (3) quantitative techniques including statistical
       methods, operations research methods, and network tech-
       niques; and (4) computer simulation including the Weber
       Model in some detail.

213.   Burack, Elmer H. "Human Resource Planning and Labor Mar-
       ket Information--New for Change, Now." *Public Personnel
       Management*, 7 (September-October 1978), 279-286.

       Asserts that "planners in both public and private sector
       organizations suffer for lack of suitable information re-

garding the numbers, disposition, and characteristics of area manpower. This article seeks to crystallize some of the critical gaps and shortcomings in currently available information and points to some needs and possibilities for the future."

214. ———. *Strategies for Manpower Planning and Programming*. Morristown, NJ: General Learning Corporation, 1972, 213, Bibliography.

Addressed to a variety of audiences, the "overall intention is to develop a comprehensive framework for the understanding of the effective use of manpower resources in organization as well as a practical apparatus for the analysis and resolution of specific manpower problems at the operating level."

215. Burack, Elmer H., and Nicholas J. Mathys. *Human Resource Planning: A Pragmatic Approach to Manpower Staffing and Development*. Lake Forest, IL: Brace-Park Press, 1980, 365.

Focus is on staffing or manpower planning and "various chapters contain: (1) key concepts, which are the cornerstone for building effective systems; (2) specific examples of successful programs and commentaries and suggestions on activities and situations to avoid; (3) skill development, exercises, and applications for those interested in training or self-development; and (4) relevant policies, problems, and issues that must be resolved for successful program implementation."

216. Conroy, W.G., Jr. "Human Resource Development--The Private Sector's Role in Public Policy." *Sloan Management Review*, 22 (Fall 1980), 63-70.

Contends that "the development and employment of our most valuable resource--a productive work force--are imperative in sustaining U.S. social progress and economic growth." Resource development programs are examined and suggestions are offered as to how private industry may participate in public policy formation which affects these programs.

217. Cooper, Cary L., and Marilyn J. Davidson. "The High Cost of Stress on Women Managers." *Organizational Dynamics*, 10 (Spring 1982), 44-53.

"Career women face more work-related stressors than men, which has a detrimental effect on their physical

and mental health--and which, in turn, deters them from
performing at their best or aspiring to high managerial
positions."

218.   Denanna, Mary Anne, Charles Fombrun, and Neil Ticky.
       "Human Resource Management: A Strategic Perspective."
       Organizational Dynamics, 9 (Winter 1981), 51-67.

       Argues that "in both the formulation and the implemen-
       tation of strategic plans, corporations could make better
       use of their human resource management function by en-
       couraging its involvement at a level higher than the
       purely operational one of administering benefit plans and
       running technical programs. Authors present a step-by-
       step approach--the Human Resource Management Audit
       (HRMA), which involves an internal assessment of the
       structure, resources, and process of the personnel func-
       tion. Results from a survey demonstrate how an HRMA
       can be used to define the internal organization needed
       for the function to deliver its services effectively.
       The most important change needed involves forging the
       link between the human resources function and the line
       organization's strategic planning process."

219.   Dill, W.R., D.P. Ganer, and W.L. Weber. "Models and
       Modelling for Manpower Planning." *Management Science*,
       13 (December 1966), B142-B167.

       Explores "some issues in manpower planning" and reviews
       "some of the kinds of approaches that have been tried and
       looks in some detail at two approaches which seem espe-
       cially promising. The first of these involves the de-
       velopment of simple stochastic models for aspects of
       the problem and the exploitation of these by direct
       mathematical manipulation. The second approach is to
       simulate on a computer the histories of a manpower
       system under different kinds of input, policy, and envi-
       ronmental conditions."

220.   Feldt, James A., and David F. Andersen. "Attrition Ver-
       sus Layoffs: How to Estimate the Costs of Holding Em-
       ployees on Payroll When Savings Are Needed." *Public
       Administration Review*, 42 (May-June 1982), 278-282.

       "Principal analytic task facing work force planners is
       to estimate the exact magnitude of holding costs so that
       the relative cost-effectiveness of attrition versus lay-
       off strategies can be determined in any specific case.
       The modified Markov-model presented is capable of esti-
       mating holding costs, using data routinely maintained by

personnel records within an agency. The model provided information on the costs incurred by agencies under different reduction in force policies."

221. Foulkes, Fred K. "The Expanding Role of the Personnel Function." *Harvard Business Review*, 53 (March-April 1975), 71-84.

Discusses the "necessity of a changing role for the personnel department and suggests six areas that a personnel department ought to consider developing expertise in if it is dedicated to change, increased flexibility, and a new tolerance for a diversity of lifestyles within the organization and helping line management with its human resource problems."

222. Geisler, Edwin B. *Manpower Planning: An Emerging Staff Function.* New York: American Management Association, 1967, 28, Appendix, Bibliography.

Based on personal experience (acquired in the government contracting division of an international corporation), research, and analysis, the author "demonstrates why a staff group with responsibility for manpower planning and control is required in an organization and then explores and develops a rationale to support the organizational placement of this staff function at a common and strategic position."

223. Gillespie, Jackson F., Wayne E. Leininger, and Harvey Kaholas. "A Human Resource Planning and Valuation Model." *Academy of Management Journal*, 19 (December 1976), 650-656.

After a brief review of the current literature concerning human resource planning and valuation, the authors "develop a model that can be applied in the areas of manpower planning and human resource valuation. The model is applied to a large certified public accounting (CPA) firm where both the manpower planning and human resource valuation implications are demonstrated."

224. Ginzberg, Eli. *Good Jobs, Bad Jobs, No Jobs.* Cambridge, MA: Harvard University Press, 1979, 207.

Addresses the "complexities of the job problem--more job seekers than jobs--and the national efforts to ameliorate it. The aim is to provide background and understanding about the changes that are occurring in the number and types of jobs available in the U.S. economy

and the parallel changes that are underway in the characteristics of job seekers." Part I provides a framework "within which the job problem must be considered
and solved." Extends the framework which (in his view)
"should bound most discussions of employment, unemployment, and income by delineating recent changes in the
structure of the American family and the changing role
of women. The five chapters of Part II are focused on
'trained manpower' and the chapters in Part III present
three discrete dimensions of the manpower planning and
policy process." Finally, "the three chapters of Part
IV are directed to making room for the political element in manpower economics, particularly in employment
policy."

225.   Grinold, Richard C., and Kneale T. Marshall. *Manpower
       Planning Models*. New York: North-Holland, 1977, 254,
       Appendix, References.

       Concerned with the "strategic role of manpower in large
       organizations, this book is designed to help managers
       and decision makers build and understand mathematical
       models that can be used to analyze manpower policy and
       assist in manpower planning. Presents a unified theory
       of manpower flow that is illustrated by a multitude of
       examples, applications, and exercise problems."

226.   Haire, Mason. "A New Look at Human Resources." *Indus-
       trial Management Review*, 11 (Winter 1970), 17-23.

       Argues that "the management of human resources demands
       greater emphasis in the firm; that both the firm and the
       university must contribute to this--the firm by provid-
       ing a place for the human resource function and the
       university by helping to provide the intellectual con-
       tent that will give it leverage and make it attractive
       to high talent young men; and that the micro-models in
       intra-firm manpower management form one of a series of
       steps for doing this job."

227.   Hall, Thomas E. "How to Estimate Employee Turnover
       Costs." *Personnel*, 58 (July-August 1981), 43-52.

       Presents a "model for estimating total employee turn-
       over costs that is easy to use and inexpensive."

228.   Heneman, Herbert G., III, and Marcus G. Sandner. "Markov
       Analysis in Human Resource Administration: Applications

and Limitations." *The Academy of Management Review*, 2 (October 1977), 535-542.

"Markov Analysis (MA) may be used to examine the movement of personnel into, within, and out of the organization." Administrative applications include description of the internal labor market, audit and control device, career planning and development, forecasting, and affirmative action programs. Describes administrative applications, and potential limitations and concludes that "the range of possible uses of MA suggests that it is often a necessary and/or desirable technique in human resource administration. It appears that the effect of current and proposed government regulations regarding equal employment opportunity will be to increase the use of MA, or something akin to it, in organizations. At the same time, it is crucial to recognize the potential limitations on MA applications. In general MA is best suited to situations involving large numbers of individuals, where substantial movement of individuals occurs on a stable basis among specific job states. The limitations regarding conditional probabilities and forecasting accuracy also involve essentially empirical questions."

229. Hyde, Albert C., and Jay M. Shafritz. "HRIS: Introduction to Tomorrow's System of Managing Human Resources." *Personnel Management*, 6 (March-April 1977), 70-77.

Explains the design and capabilities of the State Department's Human Resources Information System (HRIS), and outlines the needs it was designed to address.

230. Ivancevich, John M., and Michael T. Matteson. "Optimizing Human Resources: A Case for Preventive Health and Stress Management." *Organizational Dynamics*, 9 (Fall 1980), 4-25.

Asserts that it is now "possible and perhaps necessary for managers to intervene early with action to avoid excessive stress that eventually results in physical, mental, and performance problems. Specific techniques and programs encouraged and sponsored by top management are part of the action needed to implement preventive health and stress management. A growing list of organizations, practitioners, and researchers have documented their experiences with such techniques as stress inoculation training, health profiling, role analysis and clarification, establishment of exercise facilities,

management by objectives, and alteration of the physical
environment."

231. Jacobson, Beverly. *Young Programs for Older Workers:
      Case Studies in Progressive Personnel Policies.* New
      York: Van Nostrand Reinhold/Work in America Institute
      Series, 1980, 123.

      Reports on data from 170 organizations "representing
      what industry and government are doing for the older
      worker. Explains how work arrangements are being rede-
      signed and updated to fit the times, including a longer
      life span, extension of mandatory retirement age, infla-
      tion, dual career families, the high divorce rate, high
      unemployment, and other current realities and projections
      for the future."

232. Ledvinka, James. *Federal Regulation of Personnel and Hu-
      man Resource Management.* Boston: Kent Publishing, 1982,
      260.

      Approaches regulation in the areas of equal employment,
      job safety, and retirement benefits from the point of
      view "that it is more important to understand *why* the
      regulations are the way they are than to understand
      what the regulations say management can or cannot do."
      The author's purpose is to provide an understanding of the
      process responsible for the enactment of federal regula-
      tion which, in the past twenty years, has "transformed the
      relationship between employers and employees."

233. Levitan, Sar A., Garth L. Mangum, and Ray Marshall.
      *Human Resources and Labor Markets: Labor and Manpower
      in the American Economy.* New York: Harper & Row, 1972,
      570, Manpower Bibliography.

      The scope of manpower development includes five main
      categories of interest: "(1) factors affecting the supply
      of and demand for labor; (2) allocation of workers among
      jobs and jobs among workers; (3) productivity of the work
      force in its various economic applications; (4) efficiency
      of labor market institutions in utilizing available human
      resources; and (5) public policy. Because human resource
      development deals with such a broad range of subjects,
      its study requires an understanding of changes which are
      transforming our society and economy. First, continued
      gains in productivity have led to rising earnings and
      income. A second major development is the accelerated
      pace of technological change. A third significant de-
      velopment is the drastic redistribution of population

and industry. Fourth, the progress of racial minorities toward equal employment opportunity. A final significant development is the rapid growth of government.

234. Miles, Raymond E., and Howard R. Rosenberg. "The Human Resources Approach to Management: Second-Generation Issues." *Organizational Dynamics*, 10 (Winter 1982), 26-41.

Authors describe their meaning of second-generation human resources organization; homes in on what they believe are the "second generation problems facing HRM organizations; reexamines the concepts and prescriptions of the HRM approach; and describes those aspects they believe to be most useful in a second-generation setting. Finally, they speculate on why the HRM approach is enjoying broader managerial support today than in the 1960s and 1970s and what its developmental course will be in the decade ahead."

235. Milkovich, George T., Anthony J. Annoni, and Thomas A. Mahoney. "The Use of the Delphi Procedures in Manpower Forecasting." *Management Science*, 19 (Part I, December 1972), 381-388.

A case study in the "development, implementation and evaluation of the delphi technique, which systematically makes use of expert judgment in generating manpower forecasts. The study was conducted in a large national retail organization on professional manpower. The results of the delphi technique are compared with results generated by conventional regression based models and the actual experience of the organization served as the criterion. The study also analyzes the informational elements used by experts during the delphi procedures and develops a model based on these elements. The usefulness of the delphi in generating manpower forecasting models is also discussed."

236. Mills, D. Quinn. "Human Resources in the 1980's." *Harvard Business Review*, 51 (July-August 1979), 154-162.

Looks at what the business climate of the 1980s will be and sees greater competition, more technological developments especially in communications, corporate diversification, deregulation of product markets, and an uncertain economy. He sees the changing labor force characterized by a slowing rate of labor force growth, more women and minorities in the labor force, pressure for immigration, and black unemployment increasing. The

principle of "equal pay for equal work" may be replaced
with "equal pay for work of comparable worth" and there
may be challenges to managerial prerogatives and arbitrary limitations of workers' civil liberties at the
work place. There may also be pressure to incorporate
human issues into corporate planning. The challenge for
management is to correctly identify the requirements for
change.

237. Mills, Ted. "Human Resources--Why the New Concern?"
      Harvard Business Review, 53 (March-April 1975), 120-
      134.

      The corporate concern for better management of human
      resources at work seems to be mushrooming. Although
      there is no one name for this corporate concern, the
      field deals with "developing and managing our human
      resources at work toward new goals of greater sharing of
      personal, social, and economic values." Author adopts
      "human resource development" (HRD) as his descriptor.
      He goes on to mention HRD projects in state and local
      governments; why it is hard to get information about HRD
      from industry; the distinguishing characteristics of
      companies moving into the HRD field; unions' attitudes
      toward the HRD movement; and the four schools of thought,
      each with its own explanation of why HRD has emerged at
      this time in our history. Offers a pragmatic reason
      for interest in HRD--it provides a high potential rate
      of return on a relatively low-cost, low-risk investment
      of resources.

238. Montana, Patrick J., and Margaret V. Higginson. *Career
      Life Planning for Americans: Agenda for Organizations
      and Individuals*. New York: AMACOM, 1978, 157, Appen-
      dices.

      Explores in depth "questions and issues of key impor-
      tance to individuals and organizations on career life
      planning." These include: "(1) what social and personal
      influences and determinants affect career life planning?;
      (2) what problems relating to career life planning must
      be solved?; (3) what is currently being done by organiza-
      tions and individuals in terms of career life planning?"

239. Moore, John M. "Employee Relocation: Expanded Responsi-
      bilities for the Personnel Department." *Personnel*, 58
      (September-October 1981), 62-69.

      The role of personnel department in the relocation of
      employees includes: (1) "discussing financial concerns

with employees and helping them handle these; (2) developing effective two-way communication; (3) providing personal counseling; (4) interpreting and implementing relocation policy; and (5) helping establish the family in the new home and community." Author elaborates upon each activity.

240. Muller, David G. "A Model of Human Resource Development." *Personnel Journal*, 55 (May 1976), 238-243.

Proposes that "maximum utilization of human resources" is the goal. Primary elements of the model are: assure an organizational climate conducive to development; define jobs; select qualified candidates; identify employee potential levels; provide developmental opportunities; and assure fair tangible and intangible reward systems.

241. Municipal Manpower Commission. *Government Manpower For Tomorrow's Cities*. New York: McGraw-Hill, 1962, 196.

Report about administrative, professional, technical (APT) people--"the chief executives, attorneys, engineers, accountants, doctors, chemists, psychiatrists, biologists, sanitarians, public safety experts, computer programmers, planners, personnel experts and others who staff our modern cities, urban counties, special districts and authorities. It is about the quality of these APT people, their future roles, and what must be done to get an adequate number of qualified APT people into urban local governments. Report is based on the first national study dedicated solely to the problem of revitalizing local governments through better use of vigorous, capable, dedicated APT people."

242. Nielsen, Gordon L., and Allan R. Young. "Manpower Planning: A Markov Chain Application." *Public Personnel Management*, 2 (March-April 1973), 133-144.

Seeks to demonstrate the "connection between manpower planning and Markov chains within the operational framework of management by objectives."

243. Patton, Arch. "The Coming Flood of Young Executives." *Harvard Business Review*, 54 (September-October 1976), 20-22, 26, 30, 34, 38, 178, 180.

Observes that "in the last decade the supply [of executive talent] was inadequate to fill the numbers of middle- and high-level executive jobs." In the

future "youthful executive talent will be more plentiful,
while experienced talent will still be in short supply."
The coming buyer's market for young executive talent
has implications for the organization's "motivation,
compensation and promotion policies, as well as their
decision making processes." Discusses today's trends
and "what corporations might do to meet them."

244. Prock, Dan, and Bob Hanson. "The Educational Needs of
     and the Future Labor Market Demand for Human Resource
     Managers." *Personnel Journal*, 56 (December 1977),
     602-607.

     Reports a national survey on the content of human
     resource management education. Results indicate pref-
     erence for more 'traditional' skills across personnel,
     labor relations and training/OD, while recognizing the
     need for training in business and the behavioral sciences."

245. Saint, Alice M. *Learning at Work: Human Resources and
     Organizational Development*. Chicago: Nelson-Hall
     Company, 1974, 228, Appendices.

     Objective "is to describe what must happen within an
     organization, both to its framework and its operations
     and to its instructional-learning processes, if the
     organization and its employees are going to learn and
     adapt to their work tasks and roles. The major finding
     was that productive results occur primarily when training
     and learning are integrated with action needed to solve
     real organizational problems and accomplish work goals."

246. Schein, Edgar H. "Increasing Organizational Effective-
     ness Through Better Human Resource Planning and Devel-
     opment." *Sloan Management Review*, 19 (Fall 1977),
     1-20.

     Focuses upon two key issues: "the increasing impor-
     tance of human resource planning and development in or-
     ganizational effectiveness, and how the major components
     of a human resource planning and development system
     should be coordinated for maximum effectiveness. Con-
     cludes that these multiple components must be managed
     by both line managers and staff specialists as part of
     a total system to be effective."

247. Siegel, Gilbert B., editor. *Human Resource Management In
     Public Organizations: A Systems Approach*. Los Angeles:
     University Publishers, 1973, 674.

Collection of 69 essays and articles divided into seven categories: (I) Introduction: Human Resource Management as an Organization System Function; (II) States of the Environment; (III) Human Resource Allocation; (IV) Human Resource Procurement; (V) The Sanction Subsystem; (VI) Resource Development; and (VII) Control and Adaptation. Excellent lead essay [(I) Introduction].

248. Stybel, Laurence J. "Linking Strategic Planning and Management Manpower Planning." *California Management Review*, 25 (Fall 1982), 48-56.

Pairs Maccoby's classification of high-technology manager types (Craftsmen, Jungle Fighters, Company Men, and Gamesmen) with a product life cycle concept (development, growth, maturity, and decline) to produce a "model that can match strategic business unit operational requirements and the leader most likely to succeed."

249. U.S. Civil Service Commission. *Planning Your Staffing Needs: A Handbook For Personnel Workers*. Washington, DC: U.S. Government Printing Office, 1977, 360.

This handbook is a product of the U.S. Civil Service Commission's continuing program of manpower planning research and is divided into two main parts, a narrative text and a series of appendices. The text deals with three principal topics: (1) Staffing needs planning and policy matters (Chapter 1); (2) Manual methods of projecting turnover losses (Chapters 2-5); and (3) Computer methods for analyzing turnover, advancement, and hiring needs (Chapters 6-10). The appendices provide detailed documentation on the manual methods and the computer programs, including full computer program listings, operation manuals and technical analyses. Within the text, all statistics are presented in an elementary, step-by-step manner which thoroughly explains and displays all the techniques which are utilized. In addition, the handbook can be used by organizations with any type of data system; from manual recordkeeping to sophisticated computer systems. Earlier stages of this research have been published in the former *Federal Workforce Outlook* and *Current Federal Workforce Data* publication series.

250. U.S. Civil Service Commission. *Decision Analysis Forecasting for Executive Manpower Planning*. Washington, DC: U.S. Government Printing Office, June 1974, 30.

Describes a forecasting technique "designed to help
determine executive manpower needs at the agency level
and below."

251. U.S. Department of State. *Human Resources Information
      Systems*. Department of State Publication 8911, Septem-
      ber 1977, 78, Appendices.

      An outgrowth of joint task force on HRIS project, this
      document describes in considerable detail an HRIS system
      which does not exist. Discusses the potential of such
      a system and attempts to show what could be accomplished
      through such a system's framework.

252. Vroom, Victor H., and Kenneth R. MacCrimmon. "Toward
      a Stochastic Model of Managerial Careers." *Administra-
      tive Science Quarterly*, 13 (June 1968), 26-46.

      Describes how "the career movements of managers and
      professionals within organizations may be described by
      a Markov chain model. This allows a formal description
      of the results of current career policies which can be
      examined for inconsistencies. Further, it allows predic-
      tions to be made of the effects of continuing present
      policies into the future. Thus, it provides a more ra-
      tional basis for career policies of organizations and
      also for individual managers planning their own careers.
      From a sample of career movements of managers and pro-
      fessionals in a large industrial organization, data are
      presented, a simple model constructed, and inferences
      made. In addition to the normative uses of such models,
      it is important to note that they provide a means for
      examining in a dynamic way some basic behavioral science
      issues that have heretofore been approached in a static
      fashion."

253. Waldron, Ronald J., and John R. Altemose. "Determining
      and Defending Personnel Needs in Criminal Justice
      Organizations." *Public Administration Review*, 39
      (July-August 1979), 385-389.

      Defending legitimate personnel needs of their agencies
      requires that public administrators "be familiar with
      empirical methods of personnel forecasting, methods that
      can be objectively defended as logical and sound, and
      methods that can be used with the framework of a zero
      based budgeting system. Among the approaches that
      might meet the above criteria are the population ratios
      method, the standards method, the needs approach, the

economic determinants method, and the program specific method. Although the focus herein is on criminal justice agencies, the methods used have application in almost any activity, and should be of interest not only to budget personnel but to the generalist administrator who has the responsibility for justifying the budget."

254. Weber, Wesley L. "Manpower Planning in Hierarchial Organizations: A Computer Simulation Approach." *Management Science*, 18 (November 1971), 119-144.

Presents complex system model "as a tool for corporate manpower planning. This approach permits representation of the interrelationships between the behavior of individuals as entities, personnel policy decisions, the labor market, and a large number of individual and organizational outcomes. A computer simulation of the model in the context of a managerial and professional hierarchy is described and tested against hypotheses from the managerial and behavioral science literature. The implications of the results of these tests for the usefulness of this approach for manpower planning and other purposes are discussed."

255. Wikstrom, Walter S. *Manpower Planning: Evolving Systems*. New York: Conference Board, 1971, 72.

A study in which 84 companies were questioned regarding their manpower planning activities. "Only 24 companies reported anything that they considered to be a manpower planning system. Most of those firms were larger organizations selected for the study because it was known that they had recognized and responded to a need for more effective manpower planning. And, in most of these cases, their manpower planning systems were only about five years old."

256. Wilburn, Robert C., and Michael A. Worman. "Overcoming the Limits to Personnel Cut-Backs: Lessons Learned in Pennsylvania." *Public Administration Review*, 40 (November-December 1980), 609-612.

Explores what the authors perceive to be "some of the major limits on retrenchment in the public sector and suggest some techniques and procedures which can facilitate this process. By retrenchment, they mean a reduction in the work force for any purpose."

CHAPTER 5

POSITION CLASSIFICATION AND PAY

257. Ashenfelter, Orley. "The Effect of Unionization on Wages in the Public Sector: The Case of Fire Fighters." *Industrial and Labor Relations Review*, 24 (January 1971), 191-202.

Examines the effects of the International Association of Fire Fighters (IAFF) on the wages of its membership. "Incorporated in this article is information on the IAFF, the dominant union organizing firemen in the United States, including evidence on methods used by locals of the IAFF for increasing wages. A discussion of the conceptual framework used for measurement of the effect of the IAFF on the relative wages of fire fighters follows. Data used and the empirical results are presented next, and some analysis of the economic implications of the results concludes this article."

258. Atwood, Jay F. "Position Synthesis: A Behavioral Approach to Position Classification." *Public Personnel Review*, 32 (April 1971), 77-81.

Sets forth "position synthesis" as an initial step toward the integration of "the findings of the behavioral scientists and the inter-disciplinary organizational theorists about how people and systems interact in a dynamic organizational environment" into effective position classification.

259. Baruch, Ismar, chairman. *Position Classification in the Public Service: A Report Submitted to the Civil Service Assembly.* Chicago: Civil Service Assembly of the United States and Canada, 1941, 335, Appendices.

Report is divided into ten chapters as follows: Position Classification and Personnel Administration; History of Position Classification; Fundamental Concepts; Princi-

pal Uses and Advantages; Position Analysis for Classification Purposes; Basic Legal Authority; Development and
Adoption; Installation; Class Specifications; and Continuous Administration of the Plan.

260. Collett, Merrill J. "Re-Thinking Position Classifica-
      tion and Management." *Public Personnel Review*, 32
      (July 1971), 171-176.

      Observes that "in the name of position classification
      more sins have been committed against persons and against
      the effectiveness of administrative operations than any
      other function in personnel management...." Of all the
      intended functions as described in *Position Classifi-
      cation in the Public Service*, "in actual practice the
      key words have been 'uniform terminology,' 'equitable
      and logical pay plan,' 'informative budgets,' 'meaning-
      ful personnel statistics,' and 'systematize and facili-
      tate ... specific personnel or pay transactions.'"

261. Craver, Gary. "Survey of Job Evaluation Practices in
      State and Country Governments." *Public Personnel
      Management*, 6 (March-April 1977), 121-131.

      Reports that "quantitative methods of job evaluation--
      chiefly factor-point methods--are used to some extent
      by 35 percent of the states and 16 percent of the coun-
      ties reporting (46 states and 31 counties are included
      in the results)." Position classification is still the
      most frequently used method although states and counties
      very often "utilize different methods to evaluate differ-
      ent occupational groups."

262. Danaker, Timothy J. "The Position Classifier's Role in
      Career Planning." *Personnel Administration*, 24 (March-
      April 1961), 33-40.

      Concludes that "effective career planning requires that
      the organization and the position be structured to facil-
      itate the development and advancement of best qualified
      employees over a continuing period of time. Position
      classification has the skills to develop the kind of
      structure and controls necessary."

263. Ellig, Bruce R. "Salary Surveys: Design to Application."
      The Personnel Administrator, 22 (October 1977), 41-48.

      Outlines and elaborates upon the steps to be taken in
      the design and implementation of a salary survey. "A
      hypothetical company has been created and is used as the

focal point of discussion." Steps outlined are: (1) defining the community; (2) identifying the companies;
(3) selecting the jobs; (4) obtaining the data; (5) designing the questionnaire; (6) conducting the survey;
(7) analyzing the data; (8) utilizing the data; and
(9) developing the pay structure.

264. Epperson, Lawrence L. "The Dynamics of Factor Compari-
son/Point Evaluation." *Public Personnel Management*,
4 (January-February 1975), 38-48.

Reports on a cooperative effort among "classification
specialists, seasoned managers, and union representatives in Washington, D.C. and throughout the U.S. federal government ... to come up with a new 'factor ranking
method' for classifying approximately 1.3 million white-
collar jobs in the federal general schedule (GS) service."

265. Field, Charles, and R.L. Keller. "How Salaries of Large
Cities Compare with Industry, Federal Pay." *Monthly
Labor Review*, 99 (November 1976), 23-28.

Reports the results of a city pay scale survey in 24
of the nation's largest cities. He found that city clerical workers earn more than their industry and federal
counterparts while skilled maintenance workers earn less
than their industry and federal counterparts.

266. Fogel, Walter, and David Lewin. "Wage Determination in
the Public Sector." *Industrial and Labor Relations
Review*, 27 (April 1974), 410-431.

Provides evidence "that wages in the public sector
tend to be higher than in the private sector for
most blue-collar jobs and lower level white collar jobs,
but salaries are generally lower in the public sector
for managerial and professional occupations. Argues
that these differentials, many of which are accentuated
by differences in fringe benefits and job security, can
be explained in large part by a combination of two factors: the discretion that public employers must exercise
in implementing the prevailing wage rule adopted by most
cities and larger government units, and the nature of
the political forces that affect governmental wage de-
disions."

267. Freund, James L. "Market and Union Influences on Municipal Employee Wages." *Industrial and Labor Relations
Review*, 27 (April 1974), 391-404.

Tests the "effects of market forces and unionism on
the wages of all municipal employees in a large number of
cities. Regression analysis demonstrates that increases
in the average weekly earnings of municipal employees
from 1965 to 1971 were significantly related to inter-
city difference in market factors such as the rate of
unemployment, the pace of increases in non-government
wages, and the demand for municipal workers as measured
by changes in city expenditures. On the other hand, the
author concludes that unionism exerted only a weak influence on city pay scales during the period studied,
when union impact is measured by factors such as the
extent of organization, the incidence of strikes, and
the legal status of political activity by city employees."

268. Green, Robert J. "Which Pay Delivery System Is Best for
      Your Organization?" *Personnel*, 58 (May-June 1981),
      51-58.

      Presents five approaches to setting individual pay
      rates: fixed-rate, automatic step-rate, step-rate with
      performance conditions, combination step-rate and per-
      formance based. He describes each approach giving "its
      characteristics, the conditions that favor its use, and
      its disadvantages."

269. Greenough, William C., and Francis P. King. *Pension
      Plans and Public Policy*. New York: Columbia University
      Press, 1976, 282.

      Examines in depth "the three major components of our
      old age income support structure: social security, pri-
      vate pensions, and public employee pensions."

270. Henderson, Richard. *Compensation Management: Rewarding
      Performance*. Third Edition. Reston, VA: Reston Pub-
      lishing Co., 1979, 510, Action Words, Glossary of Terms.

      Views compensation from the "point of view of the
      employer. Recognizes that a properly designed and skill-
      fully managed compensation system can establish a work-
      place environment that stimulates employee performance."

271. ———. "Compensation Survey" in *Compensation Management*.
      Reston, VA: Reston Publishing Co., 1976, 191-221.

      "Provides an in-depth analysis of the purpose, methods,
      and procedures for conducting a compensation survey."

272. Jensen, Ollie A. "An Analysis of Confusions and Misconceptions Surrounding Job Analysis, Job Evaluation, Position Classification, Employee Selection, and Content Validity." *Public Personnel Management*, 7 (July-August 1978), 258-271.

Within the context of the content validity model, author defines terms; discusses job evaluation, position classification and employee selection; outlines minimum education, training and experience requirement; compares job evaluation and position allocation vs. employee selection; sets out the nature and extent of need for task data; and finally critically analyzes the "knowledge, skills, abilities, personal characteristics (KSAC's)--that underlie task performance and content validation of tests."

273. Karper, Mark D., and Daniel J. Meckstroth. "The Impact of Unionism on Public Wage Rates." *Public Personnel Management*, 4 (September-October 1976), 343-346.

Report that unionism among sanitation workers in cities over 250,000 population is not a major factor in wage-setting. The local labor market and employer's ability to pay are the major determinants.

274. Klingner, Donald E. "When the Traditional Job Description Is Not Enough." *Personnel Journal*, 58 (April 1979), 243-248.

Many public personnel managers may "admit to one another that the traditional job description is not related to the most basic need of the organization and its employees: improving productivity." Author asserts that "a results-oriented job description can improve performance, as well as fill positions."

275. Lawler, Edward E., III. *Pay and Organization Development*. Reading, MA: Addison-Wesley Publishing, 1981, 229, Appendices.

Begins with argument that pay should be included in organizational development efforts, followed by a chapter dedicated to understanding the impact of pay on individual behavior in organizations. "The remainder of the book focuses on pointing out what options are available in the area of pay system practice and process and when these options should be taken. Because total compensation is the basic building block of any pay system," three chapters are devoted to the "many process and

mechanistic options that are available for determining
the type and amount of total compensation that an individual receives. Because the issues involved in performance based pay are so crucial, they are dealt with
in considerable detail" including how the pay system
"interfaces with other systems" that operate in an organization. "Special issues involved in designing pay
system change strategies" are considered and the author
"concludes with a discussion of future trends in pay and
organizational development."

276. Lewin, David. "Aspects of Wage Determination in Local
      Government Employment." *Public Administration Review*,
      34 (March-April 1974), 149-155.

      Discusses the principle of "prevailing wage" and ex-
      amines its implementation in major American cities, using
      Los Angeles, California, as an example to elucidate the
      wage-setting process among local government employees.
      Also considers some implications (1) for management and
      the quality of public services and (2) of the decision-
      making process in government which vests the final
      authority over wage matters in politically constituted
      governing boards.

277. Mahoney, Thomas A. *Compensation and Reward Perspectives*.
      Homewood, IL: Richard D. Irvin, 1979, 381.

      Collection of readings which integrate "relevant theo-
      ries and models of employee motivation and performance as
      they bear upon the compensation issues of attracting a
      labor force, occupational choice, joining and staying
      with an employer, job performance, and job satisfaction.
      The extensive discussions presented in the introduction
      of and commentary upon readings in the book provide a
      guide to integrate, yet sufficient freedom remains for
      differing interpretations and innovative restructuring of
      the theory presented."

278. McMurray, Carl D. "Position Classification and the Poli-
      tical Executive--A Study in Value Conflict." *Personnel
      Administration*, 24 (May-June 1961), 27-33.

      Asserts that the "classification system is not an iso-
      lated administrative control; rather, it is part of a
      political complex composed of legislative, administra-
      tive and judicial activity carried on by people with
      diverse interests; and standardized treatment of public
      employees is not a value held in common by these inter-

ests. A uniform personnel program is a minor consideration to the chief executive who is primarily concerned
with the implementation of a political program."

279. Mode, V.A. "Salary and the Unionization of Professionals."
     Human Resource Management, 19 (Winter 1980), 26-32.

     Since professionals in increasing numbers "are con-
     sidering unionization it indicates that they do not be-
     lieve in management or that they will receive equitable
     pay." It appears to be in the best interest of management
     "to invest funds in a sound manpower planning program in
     which each individual within the organization is reviewed
     and appraised annually and kept fully informed as to his
     or her current status and potential growth within the or-
     ganization. The entire reward system must emphasize the
     total opportunity package. The professionals are not
     candidates for unionization if they feel that they have
     effective routes to address their grievances and to ob-
     tain generally satisfactory compensation for the jobs
     they do."

280. Oliver, Philip M. "Modernizing a State Job Evaluation
     and Pay Plan." *Public Personnel Management*, 5 (May-
     June 1976), 168-173.

     Reports the development and implementation of a classi-
     fication and pay system for the state of Indiana. The
     existing system was replaced with the "factor ranking/
     benchmark/guide chart system."

281. Patten, Thomas H., Jr. "Linking Financial Rewards to
     Employee Performance: The Roles of OD and MBO." *Human
     Resource Management*, 15 (Winter 1976), 2-17.

     Considers the question," ... should the entire issue
     of management-by-objectives--compensation-by-objectives
     (MB)-CBO) be re-examined so that the hoary field of wage
     and salary administration and fringe benefits is viewed
     as an organizational development (OD) intervention fo-
     cused upon building a trusted reward system in which goal
     setting, performance review, monetary and non-monetary
     rewards, the work itself, and participative teamwork are
     properly interrelated?"

282. Ramsay, Arch S. "The New Factor Evaluation System of
     Position Classification." *Civil Service Journal*, 16
     (January-March 1976), 15-19.

Describes implementation of the Factor Evaluation System (FES), a method to develop "position classification standards for nonsupervisory General Schedule (GS) positions," in the early 1970s which was the "first major change in the job evaluation process since the Classification Act of 1949."

283. Reinke, Roger. *Selection Through Assessment Centers: A Tool for Police Departments.* Washington, DC: The Police Foundation, 1977, 42, Appendix.

Monograph which describes "some of the background, most of the problems, and certain findings in support of assessment centers in the selection of police personnel." Also describes the experience of three police assessment centers--Kansas City, MO; Rochester, NY; and Savannah, GA.

284. Rosen, Hjalmar. "Occupational Motivation of Research and Development Personnel." *Personnel Administration*, 26 (March-April 1963), 37-43.

"The relative merits of pay, promotions, fringe benefits and nonfinancial incentives as motivators are discussed." The research results "suggest that the prime occupational motivators of R & D personnel fall within a rather broad range of job conditions rather than being narrowly delimited."

285. Rosow, Jerome M. "Public Sector Pay and Benefits." *Public Administration Review*, 36 (September-October 1976), 538-543.

Government pay determination, in order of historical development has been legislative, executive and collective bargaining. Employee benefit plans and job security are identified as attractive features of public employment. "The extensive coverage of public employees with generous pension schemes has become a cause for concern. Among the pension issues are: integration with social security, pension benefit formulae, escalation with prices, contributory payments, comparison of benefits to take home pay, and costs."

286. ———. "Public Sector Pay and Productivity." *Harvard Business Review*, 55 (January-February 1977), 6-7.

Reports that average pay in the public sector rose 188% in the past two decades while it rose only 141% in the private, nonagricultural economy. Benefit costs accounted for 31% of the federal payroll. Although the President's Panel on Federal Compensation made a number of proposals to resolve the pay issue, no action on the proposals has been taken.

287. Schmenner, Roger W. "The Determination of Municipal Employee Wages." *The Review of Economics and Statistics*, 55 (February 1973), 83-90.

Suggests "two alternative approaches to the modelling of the wage determination of municipal employees. One approach addresses the issue in terms of the standard supply and demand framework and identifies separate influences on the demand for and supply of municipal workers. The other approach sees wage determination as a bargaining process between the city and the employee union. It models the initial city wage offer, and the concessions the city is forced to make, before agreement on the wage is reached. A choice between the two models has not been made since the reduced formulations of the models are identical."

288. Schulkind, Gilbert A. "Monitoring Position Classification--Practical Problems and Possible Solutions." *Public Personnel Management*, 4 (January-February 1975), 32-37.

Seeks to examine the practical problems and pressures on the monitoring authority in a post-audit system of classification control, and it proposes a change in law to provide grade retention rather than salary retention when jobs are found to be overgraded, as a means of defusing these pressures. It also proposes that the CSC be given authority to require suitable management improvements and organizational changes when necessary or desirable."

289. Shafritz, Jay M. *Position Classification: A Behavioral Analysis for the Public Service*. New York: Praeger, 1973, 133.

Maintains that the negative role of the public personnel agency in guarding the merit system has commonly been more influential than the positive role of aiding management in the maintenance of a viable personnel system. In order to reverse this trend, there should be an application of whatever is presently known about organizational and social behavior to the position classification process.

290. Solomon, Robert J. "Determining the Fairness of Salary
      in Public Employment." *Public Personnel Management*,
      9 (No. 3, 1980), 154-159.

      Presents a method which can identify when salary dif-
      ferences between groups or individuals of different
      races or sexes are legitimate. "A statistical salary
      model is developed for a standard setting group. The
      resulting formula is then used to predict the salary
      that a minority group or individual should have earned
      if compensation had been made on the same basis as the
      standard setting group."

291. Suskin, Harold, ed. *Job Evaluation and Pay Administra-
      tion in the Public Sector.* Chicago: IPMA, 1977, 698.

      Sets forth "the basic principles, objectives, and
      techniques pertaining to job evaluation and pay admini-
      stration in the public sector. While theoretical con-
      cepts and background information are provided, the book
      emphasizes 'how to do it.' Methods that have passed the
      test of time, or have been validated through carefully
      structured field tests, are described in detail. The
      book provides full coverage of both the job evaluation
      and the pay setting processes. Emphasis is also pro-
      vided on administering job evaluation and pay plans."

292. U.S. Office of Personnel Management. *Goals and Tech-
      niques for a Merit Pay System.* U.S. Office of Person-
      nel Management, March 1981, 38.

      "Explains the federal approach to merit pay. Describes
      the goals and techniques that provide the background for
      merit pay policies being established by federal agencies
      in designing their individual merit pay systems and in-
      cludes a model merit pay plan for small federal agencies."

293. Williams, Elmer V. "Administrative By-Products of
      Classification Surveys." *Public Personnel Review*,
      32 (October 1971), 235-237.

      Position classification surveys produce a "tremendous
      amount of information about the organization, functions,
      work flow, work methods, staff and equipment utilization."
      Concludes that this source of information is being
      neglected as a resource for administrative analysis.

294. Winchell, Tim E., and Larry D. Burkett. "Cost Control in
      the Federal Position Classification Program." *Person-
      nel Journal*, 57 (June 1978), 314-318, 336.

A review of available literature reveals that "rarely is there a discussion of such problems as the inconsistent application of grading standards, 'grade creep' or employee distrust. The federal situation results in two significant role conflicts that contribute to the problem of grade creep. These are: (1) the conflict between the role of the agency's public personnel office as staff support to line public personnel and its role in providing interpretations of United States Civil Service Commission job-grading standards, and (2) the dichotomy between the duties and responsibilities of a supervisor and those of a manager." In order to better understand these problems, the authors outline "how federal positions are classified and why certain elements contribute to the development of these conflicts.

CHAPTER 6

RECRUITMENT, SELECTION, AND PLACEMENT

295. Arvey, Richard D. *Fairness in Selecting Employees.*
Reading, MA: Addison-Wesley, 1979, 240, Appendices.

Broad perspective taken on the "full range of decision
making devices available in selecting employees--e.g.,
the interview, height and weight requirements, and so
forth. Reviews the fairness of these selection devices
as they affect blacks, females, the elderly, and the
handicapped. Considerable attention is given to the
legal aspects of unfair discrimination in selection."

296. Blumrosen, Alfred W. "Strangers in Paradise: Griggs v.
Duke Power Co. and the Concept of Employment Discrimination." *Michigan Law Review*, 71 (November 1972), 59-110.

Analyzes the significance of the Griggs v. Duke Power
Co. case. Three concepts concerning the nature of discrimination in employment opportunities are identified:
Concept of Discrimination; Interest Protected and Type
of Conduct Proscribed; and Common Law Parallel.

297. Byham, William C. "Assessment Centers for Spotting Future Managers." *Harvard Business Review*, 48 (July-
August 1970), 150-160, Appendix 162-165.

Explains how the assessment center works, "why it is
superior to others, and the steps a company should go
through in developing a center of its own."

298. Campbell, Joel T. "Tests Are Valid for Minority Groups
Too." *Public Personnel Management*, 2 (January-February 1973), 70-73.

Study shows that "carefully chosen aptitude tests pre-
dict as well for minority groups as for others."

299. Cascio, Wayne F. *Applied Psychology in Personnel Management*. 2nd ed. Reston, VA: Reston Publishing, 1982, 368, Appendices.

Each chapter outlines "the topic under consideration, surveys past practices and research findings, describes present issues and procedures, and, where relevant, indicates future trends and new directions for research." Topics included are "legal requirements for fair employment practice; systems analysis and decision theory; job analysis and human resource planning; performance criteria and measurement and validation of individual differences; theoretical and practical aspects of recruitment and initial screening; personnel selection, placement, training and performance appraisal; compensation/ reward systems; and finally, ethical issues currently confronting human resource management."

300. Committee for Economic Development. *Improving Executive Management in the Federal Government*. New York: Committee for Economic Development, July 1964, 76.

Centers policy statement "on those career and political executives holding senior positions in departments, bureaus, divisions, and independent agencies, on whom the effective management of the federal government depends. Focuses on the need for highly skilled, intelligent, and broad-gauged individuals; describes the changing nature of the management job in government; identifies the kinds of tasks performed by people in the upper echelons of federal service; and recommends specific improvements to enhance the capacity of the federal government to attract, develop, retain, and make productive the kinds and numbers of people needed."

301. Cronbach, Lee J. "Selection Theory for a Political World." *Public Personnel Management*, 9 (January-February 1980), 37-50.

Asserts that "it is necessary to reconsider previously accepted views on test use and validation in the light of theoretical developments and legal challenges. Emerging lines of thought include the possible use of group-specific cutting scores to reduce discrimination at little cost in quality of workers, and the recognition that a defense of 'external validity' is required for most use of tests in selection. This kind of persuasive argument is less formal than construct validation but goes beyond textbook ideas of criterion and content validation."

302. Donovan, J.J., editor. *Recruitment and Selection in the Public Service*. Chicago: International Personnel Management Association, 1968, 390, Appendices.

     Outgrowth of a "week-long seminar conducted by the Public Personnel Association in 1965." Twenty writers contributed to this volume; some from the academic world, some public personnel practitioners and other consultants. Key concepts are summarized as follows: 1. That the end-object of a selection program is to obtain the best available employees. 2. That detailed information about the job to be filled is needed as one of the first steps in the selection process. 3. That success in personnel selection depends heavily on fruitful efforts to attract qualified applicants in adequate numbers. 4. That effective recruitment and selection involves more than a series of stereotyped procedural steps. It requires judgment, decision-making, and advance planning at several levels from top management on down; it calls for making intelligent choices from among the numerous available selection tools and techniques in the light of the task to be performed. 5. That a well-rounded selection program includes research--broadly conceived and systematically pursued--to give management and technicians insight into the effectiveness of the selection program and guidelines to its improvement. 6. That the selection program will gain by exposure to critical evaluation--not only through internal research and the application of objective criteria but also by applying the sometimes-subjective criteria through which the clientele served by the program judges its merits.

303. Dreher, George F., and Paul R. Sackett. "Some Problems With Applying Content Validity Evidence to Assessment Center Procedures." *Academy of Management Review*, 6 (October 1981), 551-560.

     After "reviewing EEOC regulations and judicial opinion," the authors "argue that it is appropriate to use content validity evidence in defense of an employment selection procedure only when current performance is of interest. Because assessment center simulations for first-level supervisors are commonly used to select individuals who will need training and additional experience before they perform adequately, evidence of the job relatedness of such simulations will have to be based on other validation strategies." Authors "suggest some alternative validation strategies in keeping with EEOC guidelines."

304. Dunnett, Marvin D. *Personnel Selection and Placement*.
     Belmont, CA: Wadsworth Publishing, 1966, 224, Appendix.

     Describes "the basic contributions made by psychology
     to effective personnel selection and placement and
     spells out the actual steps in selection and placement.
     Covers the logical and methodological steps in develop-
     ing strategies for making personnel decisions, shows
     how specific programs of selection and placement have
     been developed and summarizes the advantages of careful-
     ly developed programs."

305. Foulkes, Fred K., and Henry M. Morgan. "Organizing and
     Staffing the Personnel Function." *Harvard Business
     Review*, 55 (May-June 1977), 142-154.

     Focuses "on the critical issues of organizing and
     staffing the personnel department for greater useful-
     ness." The critical issues are: (1) the formation
     of personnel policy by top management; (2) implementation
     of the policies; (3) audit and control measures to in-
     sure that policies are properly practiced; and (4) in-
     novation which should provide up-to-date information on
     current trends and new methods of problem solving. It
     is important to the personnel function that the staff
     be competent, knowledgeable people capable of functioning
     at top management levels. In addition, the evaluation
     of the effectiveness of the personnel department should
     include operating measures, quantity measures, and quali-
     ty measures.

306. Frank, E.J. "Reviewing the Obvious of Content Valida-
     tion." *Public Personnel Management*, 9 (No. 4, 1980),
     278-281.

     Observes that "many jurisdictions are struggling with
     their efforts to obtain job analysis documentation with
     which to construct and validate their selection pro-
     cedures. Author responds to some of the basic concerns
     that have been voiced by reviewing some of the 'obvious'
     methodological considerations personnel specialists must
     not forget if they hope to develop effective content
     validity studies."

307. Ghiselli, Edwin E. "The Validity of Aptitude Tests in
     Personnel Selection." *Personnel Psychology*, 26 (Winter
     1973), 461-477.

     Tests, as devices for assessing men and women for
     positions in business and industry, have been in use

for over half a century and an "enormous amount of information has been collected." The author summarizes this information in a simple and compact form. His summary permits "an examination of general trends in the validity of tests for personnel selection."

308. ————. *The Validity of Occupational Aptitude Tests.* New York: John Wiley & Sons, 1966, 127, Appendices.

Presents the "results of the many studies which have been conducted on the validity of tests in the selection and placement of workers in various occupations."

309. Guion, Robert M. *Personnel Testing.* New York: McGraw-Hill, 1965, 513, Appendices.

Intended primarily for advanced students in the classroom, "the book is principally concerned with employment problems and with the implications of psychological testing methods for those problems. Seeks to present scientific procedure and fundamental theory on the premise that, in the final analysis, nothing is more practical."

310. Hariton, Theodore. *Interview!: The Executive's Guide to Selecting the Right Personnel.* New York: Hastings House, 1970, 156.

"How to" primer is a practical step-by-step guide for the non-personnel executive and supervisor "from the first scrutiny of the application form to the close of the interview--and beyond. It includes basic principles, techniques and styles of interviewing and how they are applied to the process of selecting employees."

311. Hart, Garl L., and Paul H. Thompson. "Assessment Centers: For Selection or Development?" *Public Administration Review*, 7 (Spring 1979), 63-77.

Makes the case for "development-oriented centers versus selection-oriented centers and provides a detailed blueprint for an effective assessment center for career development.

312. Holmen, Milton G., and Richard F. Docter. *Educational and Psychological Testing.* New York: Russell Sage Foundation, 1972, 172, Bibliography, Appendix.

Report of a study "of the organizations which comprise the testing industry, the structure and organization of

the industry, the personnel involved, and the manner in
which the professional associations tie into the problem
of technical standards and ethical practices."

313. Huett, Dennis L. *Improving the Selection Interview in
      a Civil Service Setting*. Chicago: IPMA, 1976, 49,
      References.

      Outlines steps in developing, implementing, and evalu-
      ating a selection interview. Also encourages considera-
      tion of alternative selection devices.

314. Isaac, Stephen, with William B. Michael. *Handbook in
      Research and Evaluation*. San Diego: EDITS, 1981,
      226, Appendix.

      "Collection of principles, methods, and strategies
      useful in the planning, design and evaluation of studies
      in education and the behavioral sciences. Presents
      only highlights, outlines, and essentials to achieve
      emphasis, clarity, and brevity."

315. Kahn, Robert L., and Charles F. Cannell. *The Dynamics
      of Interviewing: Theory, Technique, and Cases*. New
      York: John Wiley & Sons, 1957, 351, Bibliography.

      Organized in two parts; part one places emphasis on
      the "principles and theory of interviewing as well as
      on technique. The second part is a series of transcripts
      of recorded interviews, with the authors' comments."

316. Kelly, Michael J. *Police Chief Selection: A Handbook
      for Local Government*. Police Foundation and Interna-
      tional City Management Association, 1975, 110, Appen-
      dices.

      Guidebook which explains the "basic principles of con-
      ducting a search for a police chief." Provides a "gen-
      eral discussion of the problems and possibilities of
      police chief selection. Supplies some convenient check-
      lists of issues that should be addressed during the
      process of selecting a chief, illustrates principles
      with specific examples of selection procedures and docu-
      ments used by municipal executives and search groups."

317. Lawshe, C.H. "A Quantitative Approach to Content Validi-
      ty." *Personnel Psychology,* 28 (Winter 1975), 563-
      575.

      Observes that "civil rights legislation, the attendant
      actions of compliance agencies, and a few landmark court

cases have provided the impetus for the extension of
the application of content validity from academic achievement testing to personnel testing in business and industry. Until professionals reach some degree of concur-
rence regarding what constitutes acceptable evidence of
content validity, there is a serious risk that the courts
and the enforcement agencies will play the major determining role." Author contributes to the "improvement of
this state of affairs (1) by helping sharpen the content
validity concept and (2) by presenting one approach to
the quantification of content validity."

318. Levine, Edward L., and Abraham Flory III. "Evaluation
      of Job Applications: A Conceptual Framework." *Public
      Personnel Management*, 4 (November-December 1975),
      378-385.

      "A conceptual framework to foster programmatic research
      in the area of application evaluation is proffered. The
      major variables included are job relatedness of informa-
      tion, depth of interpretation, and general method of
      education. One approach to application evaluation
      characterized by high job relatedness and surface inter-
      pretation of information along with judgmental combina-
      tion of information was chosen for study. It is shown
      that the method has a high degree of reliability across
      a wide variety of jobs and raters. Agreement between
      raters corrected for chance was .91 on median. Also it
      was found that experience of raters is significantly
      related to interrater reliability."

319. Maier, Norman R.F. *The Appraisal Interview: Three Basic
      Approaches*. La Jolla, CA: University Associates, 1976,
      206, References and Readings.

      Interviews are conducted by management supervisors
      with subordinates to "(a) let them know where they stand;
      (b) recognize good work; (c) communicate directions for
      improvement; (d) develop employees on their present
      jobs; (e) develop and train them for higher jobs; (f)
      let them know how they may make progress within the com-
      pany; (g) serve as a record for assessment of the de-
      partment or unit as a whole, showing where each person
      fits into the larger picture; and (h) warn certain em-
      ployees that they must improve. The three appraisal
      interview methods described and demonstrated are Tell
      and Sell, Tell and Listen, and Problem Solving." Each
      method has slightly different goals and objectives.

320. McClung, Glenn G. "'Qualified' vs. 'Most Qualified': A
      Review of Competitive Merit Selection." *Public Per-
      sonnel Management*, 2 (September-October 1973), 366-
      369.

      "The need for improvement and overhaul of our merit
      systems has been well established elsewhere, as has the
      need for improving the job-relatedness of our tests.
      Suggests that our problems are more ones of delivery than
      basic philosophy, and that there is no viable alternative
      to a merit focus. Also suggests that the adoption of
      some of the 'panaceas' which are being pressed upon us
      may well prove to be cures worse than our maladies.
      For public administrators who press for total autonomy
      of selection, author urges conferences with others who
      have had it. For special interest groups who feel their
      aims can be better served through a system of direct
      pressure on administrators, author urges consideration of
      the impact of collision with the many other special
      interest groups included. Our merit systems are usually
      creatures of our political mainstream. As such, they
      tend to be conservative and slow to move, but once mov-
      ing, the inertia is a powerful force, with a lasting
      effect on the whole of society."

321. Menne, John W., William McCarthy, and Joy Menne. "A
      Systems Approach to the Content Validation of Employee
      Selection Procedures." *Public Personnel Management*,
      5 (November-December 1976), 387-396.

      The systems approach to content validity is composed
      of two important elements: "a precise set of proce-
      dures" and an "extensive computer-based clerical sup-
      port" mechanism. "The procedures involved can be de-
      scribed in two ways: the practical method by which a
      small group of personnel analysts quickly obtain content
      validity documentation on all job classes for which
      they are responsible and then go on to focus their
      efforts on those classes in which the initial documenta-
      tion has indicated problems are present" and a
      delineation of "the logical steps in the process. There
      are three distinct types of computer support provided
      the personnel analyst implementing this system: manage-
      ment/information type reports; computer scoring and analy-
      sis of objectively scored examinations; and computer
      assessed test construction."

322. Miller, Kenneth M., editor. *Psychological Testing in
     Personnel Assessment*. New York: John Wiley & Sons,
     1975, 165, Appendices.

     A "non-technical guide to the purpose of psychological
     tests and how they are used in practice. Part One is a
     brief presentation of information necessary for the
     reader to obtain a general background against which to
     appreciate the case studies in Part Two. Part Three is
     a summary of a survey of the use of tests in British
     industry which indicates the wide and increasing use of
     tests throughout the whole of the industrial and com-
     mercial fields."

323. Miner, Mary Green, and John B. Miner. *Employee Selection
     Within the Law*. Washington, DC: Bureau of National
     Affairs, 1978, 369, Exhibits, References.

     Handbook for "personnel administrators that provides
     detailed guidance on the technical aspects of conduct-
     ing workforce analyses to determine adverse impact of
     employment practices on protected groups, and of conduct-
     ing validation studies to determine the job-relatedness
     of selection procedures."

324. Office of Strategic Services. *Assessment of Men*. New
     York: Rinehart & Co., 1948, 493, Appendices.

     An account "of how a number of psychologists and psychi-
     atrists attempted to assess the merits of men and women
     recruited for the Office of Strategic Services (OSS).
     The undertaking is reported because it represents the
     first attempt in America to design and carry out selec-
     tion procedures in conformity with so-called organismic
     (Gestalt) principles."

325. O'Leary, Lawrence R. *Interviewing for the Decisionmaker*.
     Chicago: Nelson-Hall, 1976, 105, Appendices, Bibliog-
     raphy.

     Offers in "down-to-earth, nontechnical terms techniques
     that can take some of the guesswork out of job inter-
     views."

326. ———. "Objectivity and Job Relatedness: Can We Have
     Our Cake and Eat It Too?" *Public Personnel Management*,
     5 (November-December 1976), 423-433.

     Point of discussion is that "... there are a number
     of steps in the assessment center to minimize subjectivi-

ty, including (1) the use of multiple raters, (2) the use of multiple exercises, (3) the emphasis on 'behavior only' and (4) the requirement that ratings be justified among assessors. The focus is on two major ingredients of predictor validity: objectivity and job relatedness." Also describes the "implementation of the assessment center within the Kansas City, Missouri, Police Department."

327. Ritzer, George, and Harrison M. Trice. *An Occupation in Conflict: A Study of the Personnel Manager*. Ithaca, NY: New York State School of Industrial and Labor Relations, Cornell University, 1969, 85, Appendices.

Monograph concerned with "(1) How professional are the personnel occupations? How professional are the individuals who practice personnel administration?; (2) How committed are personnel managers to their occupation and their organization? If they are committed in part to both, what are the reasons for this dual commitment?; (3) How do personnel managers behave in conflict situations?; and (4) What is the occupational image held by personnel managers? Is it an accurate representation of their role? Data are based largely on a sixteen-page closed-ended questionnaire survey of the members of the American Society for Personnel Administration. Throughout the study, there is a dual focus; on personnel management and on occupational sociology."

328. Rosen, B., and M.F. Miricle. "Influence of Strong Versus Weak Fair Employment Policies and Applicant's Sex on Selection Decisions and Salary Recommendations in a Management Simulation." *Journal of Applied Psychology*, 64 (August 1979), 435-439.

Consequences of fair employment policy statements for managerial selection decisions and salary recommendations are examined in the context of a decision simulation. Two independent variables, strength of fair employment policy statement and applicant's sex, were manipulated in alternate versions of a decision exercise." The findings indicate that "strong and weak policies are equally effective in counteracting sex bias in selection decisions; however, lower starting salaries were recommended for females compared to males in the strong fair employment policy condition."

329. Rosenbloom, David H., and Carole Cassler Obuchowski.
     "Public Personnel Examinations and the Constitution:
     Emergent Trends." *Public Administration Review*, 37
     (January-February 1977), 9-18.

     Outlines the incongruence between the principle of
     "representation" in public service and the original
     intent of the reformers to remove politics from the merit
     system through competitive merit examinations. An
     examination of recent judicial decisions concerning the
     constitutionality of public personnel examinations re-
     veals a trend toward a new perspective in which merit
     examinations must produce a high degree of passive
     representation in the public services in order to with-
     stand constitutional scrutiny.

330. Rouleau, Eugene, and Burton F. Krain. "Using Job Analy-
     sis to Design Selection Procedures." *Public Personnel
     Management*, 4 (September-October 1975), 300-304.

     Explores the many facets of job analysis "from the
     perspective of experienced job analysis practitioners.
     The adequacy and sufficiency of job analysis information
     is questioned in light of the possible pitfalls that may
     befall a study. A table is presented to relate
     various job analytic techniques to sample sizes, cost,
     and complexity of occupations. Limitations as to the
     uses to job analysis information are also presented."

331. Schein, Edgar H. *Career Dynamics: Matching Individual
     and Organizational Needs*. Reading, MA: Addison-Wesley,
     1978, 256, Appendices, Bibliography.

     Pulls together four strands of work author has been
     developing for fifteen years: (1) early career training;
     (2) understanding the concept of a total career; (3)
     problem of human resource development for the sake of
     humanistic values as well as organizational survival; and
     (4) view of life as evolutionary and within ecological
     context.

332. Schwab, Donald P., Herbert G. Heneman III, and Thomas
     A. DeCories. "Behaviorally Anchored Rating Scales:
     A Review of the Literature." *Personnel Psychology*,
     28 (Winter 1975), 549-562.

     Reports on "an evaluation procedure which has been
     developed that attempts to capture performance in multi-
     dimensional, behavior-specific terms. The procedure
     results in an appraisal referred to as behaviorally

anchored rating scales (BARS). BARS are hypothesized to
be superior to alternative evaluation methods in several respects." Authors review and evaluate the research
on BARS and suggest new direction for future research.

333. Schwartz, Donald J. "A Job Sampling Approach to Merit
     System Examining." *Personnel Psychology*, 30 (Summer
     1977), 175-185.

     Presents a technique for applying content validity to
     a merit examining process or rating schedule. "The
     technique, called the job sampling approach, is a
     task-based, structured system of eliciting the informa-
     tion necessary to construct the rating schedule from
     sources most able to provide that information and for
     using the information to construct the rating schedule
     and linking it to job performance." The steps are
     included.

334. Schwartz, Frank L., et al. "Job Sample vs. Paper-and-
     Pencil Trades and Technical Tests; Adverse Impact and
     Examinee Attitudes." *Personnel Psychology*, 30 (Sum-
     mer 1977), 187-197.

     The adverse impact of a job sample test was compared
     to that of a content-valid written test. "The adverse
     impact of the former was considerably less."

335. Sproule, Charles F. "A Strategy for Resource Allocation
     in Public Personnel Selection." *Public Personnel Man-
     agement*, 9 (No. 3, 1980), 116-124.

     Presents "short-range and long-range strategies for
     allocating limited resources" to attack the problem of
     meeting professional and legal standards for personnel
     selection with inadequate resources. "The short-range
     strategy recommends identifying, for each occupation
     where a selection program must be developed, one of three
     levels of resource allocation. What is expected to be
     accomplished with each level of resource allocation is
     outlined. Long-range approaches presented emphasize
     various forms of intergovernmental cooperation."

336. United States Office of Personnel Management. *How to
     Develop Job-Related Personnel Selection Procedures: A
     Handbook for Small Local Governments*. Washington, DC:
     Government Printing Office, November 1977, 56, Appendix,
     Bibliography.

     Handbook designed for administrator who has personnel
     administration as well as other responsibilities in the

organization. "Intended to cover the full scope of the selection process." Helpful in understanding the "theoretical basis for developing personnel testing procedures and offers three methods of testing which have been found appropriate for the small local government.

337. Wanous, John P. *Organizational Entry: Recruitment, Selection, and Socialization of Newcomers.* Reading, MA: Addison-Wesley, 1980, 198, Bibliography.

Begins with an introduction to the various issues in organizational entry and argues for the importance of studying organizational entry.

338. Weisband, Edward, and Thomas M. Franck. *Resignation in Protest.* New York: Penguin Books, 1976.

A book about the "individual at the breaking point" who resigns in protest "compelled by unbearable misgivings." It is "about men and women who disagree with what they see going on around them in the labyrinths of power and who resign in order to be free to tell their story. It is also about top officials who disagree profoundly with key government policies, but who keep silent, placing loyalty to the team or careerism ahead of loyalty to principle and to the public. It is about men and women in power who wrestle mightily with their consciences--and win. And, since silent acquiescence, getting along, became so much the order of the day in government, this book examines the costs of a system based above all on the value of 'team play.'"

339. Wollack, Stephen. "Content Validity: Its Legal and Psychometric Basis." *Public Personnel Management,* 5 (November-December 1976), 397-408.

Discussion centers around "the attempt to reconcile the psychometric and legal standards for establishing the job relatedness of employment tests." Author reviews case law and examines requirements for content validation.

340. Wright, Grace H. *Public Sector Employment Selection.* Chicago: IPMA, 1974, 233.

Annual presents "basic selection concepts and procedures. The first two chapters orient selection within the total employment process. Chapter 3 contains a discussion of job analysis concepts and techniques. A chapter on job performance criteria follows, with dis-

cussions on the appropriate development of measures for
determining job success and their relationships to
other selection elements. Three chapters on tests
(5, 6, and 7) have been included to facilitate the
understanding of what a test is, how to develop or select tests, and finally, how to use tests. Chapter 8
introduces validation as a process. Following the chapter on validation concepts is a chapter on validation
techniques. Completing the manual is a chapter on
statistical procedures."

CHAPTER 7

PRODUCTIVITY

341. Adams, Harold W. "Solutions as Problems: The Case of
Productivity." *Public Productivity Review*, 1 (September 1975), 36-43.

Maintains that "any meaningful increase in productivity
in state government will present problems of adaption.
The choices are few and clear: fewer people, fewer hours,
or greater product. Reducing the public workforce faces
severe political and organizational problems. And,
perhaps, more importantly, fewer people runs counter to
the need of the economy at large to maintain consumer
demand. Fewer hours is a more desirable alternative.
But the problems of reducing the workweek or workyear
will involve serious breaks with tradition and be
politically difficult over the short run. Increasing
the product seems, on the balance, the most feasible
approach though it is not without its problems."

342. Ammons, David N., and Joseph C. King. "Productivity
Improvement in Local Government: Its Place Among Com-
peting Priorities." *Public Administration Review*, 43
(March-April 1983), 113-120.

Reports results of a survey of 298 chief administrators in local government. Survey "reveals that productivity improvement must compete with other pressing
issues for administrative attention and does not generally enjoy top priority. Also suggests that few administrators are very familiar with the productivity literature. Such findings cast doubt on the likelihood of
success of the widely espoused strategy of increased
productivity information dissemination as a means of
improving performance."

343. Balk, Walter L. "Toward A Government Productivity Ethic."
      Public Administration Review, 38 (January-February
      1978), 46-50.

      Believes that "narrowing the definition of productivi-
      ty to that of agency performance gives the term opera-
      tional and control stability." He cautions the reader
      against "imposing prescriptive constructs generated by
      outsiders." Concepts about productivity generated and
      implemented to fit the "economic-rational decision-
      making style" conflict with a "political bargaining
      decision-making style." Valuable insight into produc-
      tivity-improvement methods will come when "agency public
      administrators can articulate how *they* associate improve-
      ment means with results (or ends) *within their particu-
      lar organizations.* The central thrust of productivity
      is clarification of long-term goals and specification of
      performance."

344. ————. "Why Don't Public Administrators Take Produc-
      tivity More Seriously?" *Public Personnel Management*,
      3 (July-August 1974), 318-324.

      Reviews "some of the unique aspects of government
      productivity which have to do with motivation." One
      reason employees are not "enraptured by the notion of
      productivity" is the lack of involvement they have in
      productivity improvement planning and implementation.
      In the face of lay-offs, many employees see productivity
      improvement programs as a threat to their jobs. "Em-
      ployee productivity motivation depends upon what govern-
      ment management people do to set up reward systems
      which relate to the task at hand. Until government
      managers, employees, legislators and the public become
      intensely involved in the processes of controls, reward
      systems and political institutions, motivation is liable
      to remain at a low level."

345. Balk, Walter L., and Jay M. Shafritz, editors. *Public
      Utility Productivity: Management and Measurement: A
      Symposium.* Albany, NY: The New York State Department
      of Public Service, 1975, 241, Appendices.

      Proceedings of a two-day symposium on Public Utility
      Productivity and Managerial Assessment sponsored by the
      New York State Department of Public Service with the
      cooperation of the National Science Foundation and the
      School of Business Administration of the State Univer-
      sity of New York at Albany held August 11 and 12, 1975.

The symposium's "major goal was to produce relevant definitions and a conceptual framework which will facilitate the application of performance standards and productivity analysis and measurement. Each chapter is followed by commentaries." Chapter headings are: Introduction; Aggregate Measures of Productivity; Measurement and Data Requirements; Managerial Efficiency; and Application of Productivity Measurement.

346. Burkhead, Jesse, and Patrick J. Hennigan. "Productivity Analysis: A Search for Definition and Order." *Public Administration Review*, 38 (January-February 1978), 34-40.

Discusses public sector characteristics (public goods consumption, reciprocal externalities); systems-analysis approaches to productivity (fiscal management, vectors: from inputs to social states, efficiency and effectiveness); and a taxonomy of productivity research (activity-output measurement, employment incentives, organizational behavior, productivity bargaining and technology transfer). Concludes that the "difficulties that emerge from productivity analysis in the public sector are, at basis, rooted in the absence of discrete units of government output."

347. Capozzola, John M. "Productivity Bargaining: Problems and Prospects." *National Civil Review*, 65 (April 1976), 176-186.

The need for productivity bargaining becomes more acute as many American cities face fiscal crises. Technical, managerial, legal, political and social problems and issues are within the purview of productivity bargaining. What is needed are meaningful standards of work.

348. Cheek, Logan M. "Cost Effectiveness Comes to the Personnel Function." *Harvard Business Review*, 51 (May-June 1973), 96-105.

Describes a "framework which top operating and personnel executives can use to channel the resources of the personnel function to the most worthwhile undertakings." Procedural steps discussed are: "(1) define and describe each personnel program--whether proposed or ongoing--in a discrete package; (2) separate for special treatment those programs that are legally required; (3) evaluate all programs on the basis of these factors: (a) 'state of the art;' (b) ease of implementation, (c) net economic benefits, (d) economic risk of not acting; and (4)

rank all programs, and allocate and deploy staff resources accordingly." Key advantages of this approach
are rigorous assessment of program benefits and evaluation of the likelihood of achievement.

349. Chitwood, Stephen. "Social Equity and Social Service
      Productivity." *Public Administration Review*, 34
      (January-February 1974), 29-35.

      Examines the "current emphasis on increasing the
      productivity of government activities and briefly
      assesses its historical relation to earlier government
      management movements. This assessment illustrates how
      productivity measures have traditionally neglected a
      basic element in providing public services. The impor-
      tant relationships between productivity measures and
      the determination of social equity in supplying govern-
      ment services are identified." Author provides a "cat-
      egorization of distribution patterns and standards
      which may be used in measuring the social equity with
      which public services are provided."

350. Committee for Economic Development. *Improving Manage-
      ment of the Public Work Force*. New York: Committee
      for Economic Development, 1978, 138.

      The Committee takes a "broad view of the issue of
      managing the public work force." Economic, political,
      managerial, and human concerns are considered and the
      committee "attempts to account for those dimensions and
      to determine how they interact with one another. The
      principal purpose of this statement is to underscore the
      importance of dealing with public personnel management
      in a comprehensive fashion that takes into account all
      its component parts and is sensitive to how they affect
      one another."

351. Committee for Economic Development. *Improving Produc-
      tivity in State and Local Government*. New York: Com-
      mittee for Economic Development, 1976, 92.

      Improving government productivity "is a long-term
      task that requires continuing attention to every phase
      of government operations and a recognition of the inter-
      play between political forces and agency operations,
      between broad policy considerations and detailed admin-
      istrative matters, between technology and people, be-
      tween analytic technique and bureaucratic behavior and
      between local prerogatives and national responsibili-

ties. Government productivity has two dimensions: effectiveness and efficiency. It also requires attention to each of three steps in the process of trans-
forming public desires and tax money into accomplish-
ments: identifying goals and objectives, choosing among
alternative approaches to achieve objectives, and implementing programs."

352. Congressional Budget Office. "The Productivity Problem:
Alternatives for Action." Washington, DC: U.S.
Government Printing Office, 1981, 137.

Asserts that during the 1970s, "productivity growth,
which is the increase in goods and services produced
per hour of work," slowed. Although "government policies can affect productivity growth, it is essential to
recognize that the root causes are complex, interdepen-
dent, and ramify into almost every economic activity."

353. Crane, Edgar G., Bernard F. Lentz, and Jay M. Shafritz.
*State Government Productivity: The Environment for
Improvement.* New York: Praeger, 1976, 246.

Reports the results of research into the political and
social environment in which state government productivity programs are imbedded. "The first two chapters
serve to orient the reader and narrate some of the findings. Then an empirical analysis is made of the influence process between agencies and their environment, followed in Chapter 4 by a comparative study of what appears
to account for various levels of productivity efforts."
Chapter 5 outlines the "productivity variables for one
specific state government function. The last chapter
draws some general conclusions which should be of considerable value to policy makers."

354. Cummings, T.G., Demond S. Molloy, and Roy H. Glen.
"Intervention Strategies for Improving Productivity
and the Quality of Work Life." *Organizational Dynamics,* 4 (Summer 1975), 52-68.

Evaluates "the present state of the strategies for
improving productivity and the quality of work life.
Article is based on a comprehensive review of the empirical literature on job satisfaction, industrial
organization, productivity and focuses on the field
experiments. Divided into three main parts that corres-
pond to the three kinds of knowledge needed to formulate
an effective strategy for improving productivity and

satisfaction: (1) knowledge of 'action levers'; (2) knowledge of contingencies; and (3) knowledge of change strategies."

355. Davidson, Jeff. "Favorite Employee Time Wasters." *Management*, 2 (Winter 1981), 12-15.

Asserts that "a number of activities other than those for which they are paid occupy the time of employees during business hours and infringe upon the productivity of an organization." Provides a list of favorite time wasters: coasting until check-out time; organizing and reorganizing; carefully checking junk mail; taking two lunch breaks; waiting for pay checks; tangential discussions; excessive, elaborate travel arrangements; extensive review of timesheets; and toasting the weekend on Friday afternoon.

356. Downey, Edward H., and Walter L. Balk. *Employee Innovation and Government Productivity: A Study of Suggestion Systems in the Public Sector.* Chicago: IPMA, 1976, 53, Appendices.

Inquiry into the "reasons why suggestion programs do or do not meet their full potential and how they might be improved."

357. Englander, F., and N. Sheflin. "Assessing the Productivity of Workfare in New Jersey." *Public Productivity Review*, 4 (December 1980), 340-351.

Workfare is the "imposition of work requirements on welfare recipients." Authors review "the debate on the relative virtues of workfare, and describe the nature of the New Jersey General Assistance Employability Program."

358. English, Jon, and Anthony R. Marchione. "Productivity: A New Perspective." *California Management Review*, 25 (January 1983), 57-66.

Presents the "productivity-determinant" model which "shows that the external environment as well as the causal variables of structure, process, and leadership are the key determinants influencing emerging employee behavioral patterns." The model is designed to focus management's attention on the causal variables of structure, process, and leadership.

359. Farris, George F. "Chicken, Eggs, and Productivity in Organizations." *Organizational Dynamics*, 3 (Spring 1975), 2-15.

    Documents the importance of "performance feedback loops: favorable environments which foster superior performance; superior performance which contributes to a still more favorable environment. A benevolent cycle."

360. Foster, R. Scott. "State and Local Government Productivity and the Private Sector." *Public Administration Review*, 38 (January-February 1978), 22-27.

    Analyzes productivity from "three different perceptions of economic activity in a state or local jurisdiction: that of a market economy; a pluralistic economy; and a holistic economy." Author believes that each perception "describes some aspects of economic behavior in various jurisdictions more usefully--for the purpose of improving public productivity--than a single model that attempts to synthesize all three. Each perception also suggests a somewhat different definition of public productivity."

361. Fremont, E.G., Jr. "Productivity Bargaining That Really Is." *Personnel Journal*, 49 (January-February 1972), 8-18.

    Argues that collective bargaining is not bargaining at all. In true two-way bargaining--(productivity bargaining)--management is prepared to grant something of value but it expects something of value in return. Management wants to alter the relationship between unions and management in specified ways that will lead to increased productivity. Reports from England on gains for management, unions, and the country as a whole through productivity bargaining.

362. Gannon, Martin J., and Frank T. Paine. "Factors Affecting Productivity in the Public Service: A Managerial Viewpoint." *Public Productivity Review*, 1 (September 1975), 44-50.

    Reports the results of interview with 239 managers in five government agencies. "The objective of the interviews was to ascertain the factors that were acting either as incentives or disincentives to productivity in the federal government." Managers interviewed felt that "productivity would be sharply increased if: (1) they were granted more autonomy in assigning priorities and

work; (2) they had more control over who was hired or
initially allowed in the public service; and (3) they
were allowed to deal effectively with ineffective performance through discharge or reassignments."

363. Gilder, George. "Public Sector Productivity." *Public
      Productivity Review*, 1 (September 1975), 4-8.

      Combines the concepts of efficiency and effectiveness
      in his definition of productivity and states that "to
      improve productivity, one must improve the ratio be-
      tween the resources and results, either by reducing
      input or expanding output, or by some combination."
      Government productivity is partly a management problem.
      Our elected officials are not only charged with making
      policy decisions but must also manage governmental agen-
      cies. "As the public sector absorbs an ever increasing
      portion of the nation's available resources, this role
      of running things productively becomes increasingly
      important to the nation's well-being."

364. Goldoff, Anna C., and David C. Tatage. "Joint Produc-
      tivity Committees: Lessons of Recent Initiatives."
      Public Administration Review, 38 (March-April 1978),
      184-186.

      Essential conditions for successful labor-management
      productivity committees are: a well planned organization-
      al structure, union and management support and a cooper-
      ative attitude between labor and management, keeping
      collective bargaining issues out of the productivity
      program, and program evaluation. The potential for
      better industrial relations in general is present when
      productivity committees are successful.

365. Greiner, John M. "Motivating Improved Productivity:
      Three Promising Approaches." *Personnel Management*,
      61 (October 1979), 2-5.

      Focuses on three motivational techniques--monetary
      incentives, performance targeting, and job enrichment--
      which "appear especially promising for improving employee
      motivation and productivity."

366. Hamilton, Edward K. "Productivity: The New York Approach."
      Public Administration Review, 32 (November-December
      1972), 784-795.

      Hamilton, former Deputy Mayor, City of New York, re-
      ports on former Mayor John V. Lindsay's Productivity

Program. It was instituted "in the wake of repeated city
budget crises" and was "designed to maintain and improve
the quality of service provided to New Yorkers despite
the steady shrinkage in the city work force." The
program called for improvements in productivity which
were "measurable in hard, quantitative terms whenever
possible." Provides cases to illustrate the four objectives of the program: (1) unit cost reduction; (2)
improvement in the deployment of resources; (3) improvement in government organization processing and procedures; and (4) development of new technological devices
and approaches.

367. Harrison, Jared F. *Improving Performance and Productivity: Why Won't They Do What I Want Them to Do?* Reading,
MA: Addison-Wesley, 1978, 163.

About how "to get people to perform the way you want
them to perform" and how "to identify all of the reasons
why they may not be doing so at present." Provides
five steps for redirecting people's efforts: find out
what is happening; who is involved; what it is impacting;
how it is cured; and apply the system. The system
provides mechanisms for people-problem identification,
analysis and deficiency correction. Forms for problem
solving and a checklist of the system are included.

368. Harty, Harry P. "Issues in Productivity Measurement for
Local Governments." *Public Administration Review*, 32
(November-December 1972), 776-784.

In order to justify productivity measurement, it must
lead to improved productivity. "Productivity measurement
can help governments to identify priority areas needing
attention and the degree to which specific actions have
helped. Measurement can help to identify new procedures
or approaches that are worth pursuing, and those that are
not. Used in dealings with employees, they can provide
a basis for incentive plans and the sharing of benefits
of increased productivity."

369. ———. "The Status of Productivity Measurement in the
Public Sector." *Public Administration Review*, 38
(January-February 1978), 28-33.

Report "deals first with what productivity measurement
is, then presents a viewpoint on the current status of
productivity measurement in government in the U.S. and--
finally--briefly examines the likely prospects for the

future, including consideration of facilitating and
inhibiting factors."

370. Hatvany, Nina, and Vladimir Pucik. "Japanese Management
Practices and Productivity." *Organizational Dynamics*,
9 (Spring 1981), 5-21.

Japanese managers contend that "in the long run, human
assets are the most important and profitable. The
concept is backed up by a well-integrated system of
(1) providing long-term, secure employment that attracts
employees of the quality desired and induces them to
remain with a firm; (2) espousing and demonstrating
concern for both employee needs and the importance of
teamwork; (3) searching out new hires with values that
fit well with those of the company and maintaining close
ties thereafter between employees and the company.
Specific techniques emphasize continuous development of
employee skills."

371. Hayes, Frederick O'R. "City and County Productivity
Programs." *Public Administration Review*, 38 (January-
February 1978), 15-18.

Past Director of the Budget for the City of New York
presents his "observations on city and county productivity programs [which] are based primarily upon a
study of programs in eight local governments made between July 1975 and March 1976." He found "no widespread demand for productivity programs and no instance
of significant citizen pressure for the introduction of
a productivity program." Although there is great potential for productivity improvement in local government,
the author concludes that "there is little likelihood
that realization will be very rapid."

372. Hayward, Nancy S. "The Productivity Challenge." *Public
Administration Review*, 36 (September-October 1976),
544-550.

Concludes that "within the constraints of current
knowledge, technology, and legislation, the productivity
of public service delivery can be increased." However,
she believes that the greatest potential for productivity
increases "lies in the management of human resources."

373. Hayward, Nancy S., and George Kuper. "The National
Economy and Productivity in Government." *Public Administration Review*, 38 (January-February 1978), 2-5.

Examines the plight of productivity growth; government's role in national productivity improvement; its impact on other sectors of the economy; government productivity in expanding its own resources; managerial concern for productivity in the federal sector and implications of the intergovernmental system.

374. Horton, Raymond D. "Productivity and Productivity Bargaining in Government: A Critical Analysis." *Public Administration Review*, 36 (July-August 1976), 407-414.

Suggests that "productivity bargaining is likely to yield only minimal impacts on government services, some of these negative, until practitioners and academics better understand the nature of productivity and productivity bargaining in government and further, suggests that the relationship between collective bargaining and the production of services is of greater importance to government officials than the relationship between productivity bargaining and productivity of services."

375. Judson, Arnold S. "The Awkward Truth About Productivity." *Harvard Business Review*, 60 (September-October 1982), 93-97.

A survey of "236 top-level executives representing a cross-section of 195 U.S. industrial companies led to the conclusions that: (1) Management ineffectiveness is by far the single greatest cause of declining productivity in the United States; (2) Most companies' efforts to improve productivity are misdirected and uncoordinated; (3) Tax disincentives, the decline of the work ethic, problems with government regulation, obsolete plant and equipment, insufficient R & D, and poor labor relations have little to do with industry's faltering productivity."

376. Katzell, Raymond A., and Daniel Yankelovich. *Work Productivity and Job Satisfaction: An Evaluation of Policy-Related Research*. New York: The Psychological Corporation, 1975, 368, Bibliographies.

Evaluation of "research dealing with features of work which affect both the productivity and job satisfaction of employees. Convergent findings suggest directions for the future: (1) relatively limited programs, such as job enrichment, participation in decision-making, or incentive pay plans, seem unlikely by themselves to create large or enduring improvements in both produc-

tivity and job satisfaction; (2) socio-technical systems
seem promising in their ability to improve both productivity and job satisfaction. Survey indicates (1) that
managers and union officials alike regard improvements
in both productivity and the quality of working life as
desirable social goals; (2) that barriers to adoption of
needed comprehensive programs along the above lines
stem both from knowledge and political considerations;
and (3) that what seems necessary is a coordinated drive
by many agencies of society."

377. Katzell, Raymond A., et al. "Improving Productivity and
      Job Satisfaction." *Organizational Dynamics*, 4 (Summer
      1975), 69-80.

      Those workers "whose performance, whenever it's effec-
      tive, is both recognized and rewarded in whatever terms
      are meaningful to the workers themselves" tend to be both
      satisfied and productive. "Methods for improving produc-
      tivity exist at various levels and in various spheres of
      knowledge." Also, "various strategies for improving em-
      ployee job satisfaction have been developed." Authors
      assert that although productivity and job satisfaction
      may be achieved simultaneously, they are not necessarily
      causally linked. "The difficulty for the policy maker is
      that to effect large-scale improvements in the produc-
      tive and human use of human resources, he must make num-
      erous and far-reaching changes before the desired effects
      become visible."

378. Keevey, Richard F. "State Productivity Improvements:
      Building on Existing Strengths." *Public Administration
      Review*, 40 (September-October 1980), 451-458.

      Discusses the "efforts of the State of New Jersey in
      strengthening and improving productivity. Past achieve-
      ments are highlighted in such areas as state aid admin-
      istration, capital financing, purchasing, and third-party
      contracting. The author suggests that past achievements
      lay a necessary foundation to facilitate and legitimate
      new productivity endeavors."

379. Kenrick, John W. "Exploring Productivity Measurement in
      Government." *Public Administration Review*, 23 (June
      1963), 59-66.

      Explores the development of productivity measures; de-
      fines the concept and meaning of productivity; discusses
      the measuring of output, special problem areas, the

weighing of certain productivity measures and input
measures (1) cost analysis, budgeting and projection,
and (2) management control; and concludes with suggestions for future work.

380. ――――. "Public Capital Expenditures and Budgeting for
    Productivity Advance." *Public Administration Review*,
    32 (November-December 1972), 804-807.

    Deals with "the chief means by which productivity is
    raised: investments in new and improved capital goods,
    chiefly structures and equipment, and by the 'intangible
    investments' associated with tangible outlays." Recom-
    mends: "(1) a systematic procedure for developing cost
    reducing innovations and related investment projects,
    and reviewing the economic rationality of such pro-
    posed projects, should be instituted within all federal
    government organizations; (2) agencies and existing re-
    volving funds should have separate capital budgets for
    both internal investments and investments designed to
    increase the capacity and/or productivity of the out-
    side economy; (3) the interest and depreciation (or
    amortization) charges on agency investments should be
    carried as a current expense of the agency. This would
    bring government cost accounting more closely in line
    with private practice, and permit better estimates of
    total productivity and cost-saving resulting from the
    investments that promote technological advance; and
    (4) post-investment audits should be made by all govern-
    ment organizations and spot-checked by the General
    Accounting Office to determine whether the anticipated
    cost-savings were in fact realized."

381. Kull, Donald C. "Productivity Programs in the Federal
    Government." *Public Administration Review*, 38 (Janu-
    ary-February 1978), 5-9.

    Reports on the cooperative efforts of the General Ac-
    counting Office, the Office of Management and Budget,
    the Civil Service Commission, the Bureau of Labor Statis-
    tics, the General Services Administration, the Joint
    Financial Management Improvement Program and the Na-
    tional Center for Productivity and Quality of Working
    Life to measure productivity in the federal government.
    Although "substantial progress has been made in the
    development of workable productivity measurement systems,"
    the future should see major emphasis placed on the "in-
    corporation of productivity systems into the planning
    and conduct of federal public programs."

382. Lachenmaeyer, C.W., editor. *Assessing Productivity in
     Hard-to-Measure Jobs.* Hofstra University Yearbook of
     Business Series 15, Vol. 7. Hempstead, NY: Hofstra Uni-
     versity, 1980, 233.

     Discusses the assessment of productivity (1) in mana-
     gerial positions in general; (2) in senior-level manager-
     ial positions; (3) of employees; (4) in large and small
     service firms; and (5) in the delivery of government
     services.

383. Latham, Gary P., Larry L. Cummings, and Terence R.
     Mitchell. "Behavioral Strategies to Improve Produc-
     tivity." *Organizational Dynamics,* 9 (Winter 1981),
     5-23.

     The three-stage process through which performance
     evaluation proceeds on its way to improving employee
     productivity are "(1) identifying poor performance,
     (2) deciding what causes poor performance, and (3) cop-
     ing with the causes(s). Strategies for identifying poor
     performance include examining discrepancies between goals
     set and results achieved; making comparisons across
     people, units, or organizations; and comparing the
     performance of individuals with their own past per-
     formance over a period of time. To help managers diag-
     nose and respond to poor performance, the authors pre-
     sent a model based on attribution theory. The model
     explains why managers may attribute poor performance to
     the wrong cause and thus choose an inappropriate response
     aimed at correcting it; further, the model helps the
     manager maximize the probability of choosing an appro-
     priate response. Steps for coping with the causes of
     poor performance include (1) defining performance
     behaviorally, (2) training managers to minimize rating
     errors, (3) setting specific goals, and (4) ensuring that
     the employee will enjoy positive consequences from
     working hard and achieving the goals set."

384. Layden, Dianne R. "Productivity and Productivity Bar-
     gaining: The Environmental Context." *Public Personnel
     Management,* 9 (No. 4, 1980), 244-256.

     Reviews "attempts to describe key aspects of the
     productivity issue in government as they reflect the
     various perspectives of the participants in the public
     policy-making process, i.e., those of the employee,
     union, management, and public."

385. League of Women Voters of Los Angeles. *Does Civil Ser-*
      vice Enhance or Inhibit Productivity? Los Angeles:
      1977, 53.

      Report presents the complex and stubborn obstacles to
      be overcome in Los Angeles if productivity is to increase.
      There are no sanctions for local governments "which fail
      to install new operating methods or to exploit new
      opportunities. There are few rewards for improving,
      and no generally accepted measures of local government
      productivity. Management can consider a number of
      options for attacking productivity problems, including
      establishing performance standards and adopting flexi-
      ble working hours."

386. Levitt, Theodore. "Management and the 'Post-Industrial'
      Society." *Public Interest* (Summer 1976), 69-103.

      An articulate and readable account of productivity
      performances in various industries throughout the world.
      Author asks the question "whether it is possible to make
      the service economy of the 20th century as productive as
      manufacturing became in the 19th century." His answer is
      in the affirmative. "In the end it is the nature and
      quality of management that makes the real difference."

387. Lovell, Catherine. "Training for Productivity Improve-
      ment: Long Beach, California." *Southern Review of Pub-*
      lic Administration, 2 (March 1979), 458-474.

      Asserts that "productivity improvement requires a total
      system commitment instututionalized as a fundamental
      part of ongoing organizational processes. Productivity,
      from the systemic viewpoint, is not a special set of
      activities or techniques 'added on' to the central pur-
      pose of the organization but is part and parcel of all
      organizational activity. It is not the province of
      special productivity technicians but is an integral part
      of the jobs of everyone in the organization. A central
      problem before the organization which wants to begin a
      productivity improvement effort is how to institutional-
      ize an output orientation throughout the organization.
      A systemwide training effort is a fundamental part of
      the process."

388. Lucey, Patrick J. "Productivity: An Essential Strategy
      for Survival." *Public Productivity Review*, 1 (Septem-
      ber 1975), 30-35.

Observes that "a national effort to improve productivity
is nothing less than a strategy of survival." With the
rapid disappearance of our technological superiority, we
need to develop creative managerial techniques and a new
productivity ethic if we are to restore our economy to
health. Lucey continues by outlining the main features
of the productivity improvement program within the Wisconsin State Government.

389.   ————. "Wisconsin's Productivity Policy." *Public
        Administration Review*, 32 (November-December 1972),
        795-799.

Lucey, a former Governor of Wisconsin, discusses the
Wisconsin productivity program which was instituted in
response to the productivity policy he developed. Included in the appendix is a text of Lucey's policy
statement and the accompanying nine specific instruc-
tions.

390.   ————. "Wisconsin's Progress with Productivity Im-
        provement." *Public Administration Review*, 38 (January-
        February 1978), 9-12.

Reports that "two major trends characterize agency
productivity innovations from 1973-1976. One is the
trend toward agency centralization of management support
services such as typing, payroll, and personnel administration. A variation of this trend is the interagency
exchange of these and other services, particularly among
institutions. A second trend is the continued substitu-
tion of sophisticated technology for human operations to
achieve greater speed, accuracy, and capacity to handle
complex tasks, particularly recording, translation, re-
production, transmittal, storage, and retrieval of information, such as data processing, word processing, and
mailing equipment."

391.   Makielski, S.J., Jr. "The Preconditions to Effective
        Public Administration." *Public Administration Review*,
        27 (June 1967), 148-153.

Suggests four preconditions to effective public administration: (1) "the existence of a basic skill pool;
(2) the existence of general organizational experience;
(3) the existence of a general organizational language;
and (4) an established set of administrative norms."
Asserts that "absence of these preconditions has serious

implications for developing areas and for the nations attempting to aid these areas."

392. Mark, Jerome A. "Meanings and Measures of Productivity." *Public Administration Review*, 32 (November-December 1972), 747-753.

Discusses concepts of productivity and their interpretations; available measures of labor and capital productivity; combined factor input productivity; limitations of available measures; and usefulness of productivity data. Concludes that "measures of productivity have improved substantially in sophistication and accuracy in recent years. While they are still inadequate to answer all the questions that might be asked of them, they do provide insights into many of the economic problems of the day."

393. ————. "Measuring Federal Productivity." *Civil Service Journal*, 19 (January-March 1979), 20-23.

Summarizes the labor productivity efforts within public agencies as measured by the Bureau of Labor Statistics (BLS). Also "examines the concepts and some of the problems involved in developing the measures, and the findings."

394. McKersie, R.B., and L.C. Hunter. *Pay Productivity and Collective Bargaining*. London: Macmillan Press Ltd., 1973, 379.

Authors "take a broad perspective on the developments in productivity bargaining and relate these developments to the conceptual apparatus of current industrial relations." Identify "the usefulness of these concepts in evaluating the achievements and processes of productivity bargaining. Additionally, [they] hoped that the innovations resulting from productivity bargaining might create new concepts and relationships which would in turn spur new theoretical approaches to the changed circumstances. The centerpiece of the study is the analysis of productivity bargaining at the micro-level"; therefore, several chapters are devoted "to discussing the key influences which determined the emergence and development of productivity bargaining, and its sudden fall from grace." Also assess the future role of productivity bargaining.

395. Morris, Thomas, William H. Corbett, and Brian L. Usilaner.
      "Productivity Measures in the Federal Government." *Pub-
      lic Administration Review*, 32 (November-December 1972),
      753-763.

      Report of an inventory, undertaken jointly by the
      Comptroller General, Civil Service Commission and the
      Office of Management and Budget, of federal agency
      practices in using productivity measurement systems in
      the management process. The measurement systems are
      examined in terms of work measurement, unit costs,
      productivity and manpower planning. Construction of
      productivity indices, and their uses and misuses, are
      thoroughly discussed.

396. Morris, William T. *Work and Your Future: Living Poorer,
      Working Harder*. Reston, VA: Reston Publishing Co.,
      1975, 298.

      The three objectives addressed are: "(1) To provide a
      clear, non-technical introduction to the problem of
      productivity and its social, political and economic
      implications. To deal with the myths, conventional wis-
      dom, traditions, research findings, and actual experi-
      ences which surround productivity. (2) To provide ways
      of understanding some of the many curious experiments
      and unexpected developments which we have seen in the
      past. To help one make some sense out of what has
      happened and what is being said about productivity and
      how it may be changed. (3) To suggest some new and
      different hypotheses about the sources of productivity
      improvements and their personal and cultural impacts in
      the future."

397. Mushkin, S.J., and F.H. Sandifer. *Personnel Management
      and Productivity in City Government*. Lexington, MA:
      D.C. Heath, 1979, 185.

      A joint Public Services Laboratory/National League of
      Cities/U.S. Conference of Mayors study on personnel
      management was undertaken in response to the growth de-
      mand for research dealing with administrative services
      and productivity. "Eight cities were selected by the
      Conference of Mayors for participation and study. The
      following municipalities were chosen: Dayton, Ohio;
      Lakewood, Colorado; Nashville-Davidson, Tennessee;
      St. Paul, Minnesota; Savannah, Georgia; Scottsdale,
      Arizona; Tacoma, Washington; and Worcester, Massachu-
      setts." The study "emphasizes the interrelations of

(1) processes of personnel management as an integral part of city management and (2) personnel aspects of program effectiveness. Barriers to productivity improvement in the cities are imposed by the routines of personnel administration. The productivity of personnel management itself initially was regarded as of lesser interest."

398. National Commission on Productivity and Work Quality. *Productivity: Employee Incentives to Improve State and Local Government Productivity.* Washington, DC: National Commission on Productivity and Work Quality, 1975, 147, Appendices.

Report provides "a broad overview of incentive programs throughout the United States. The information is drawn primarily from three sources: (1) studies of incentive programs conducted by The Urban Institute; (2) a survey of state and local government employee incentive programs; (3) other sources, including recent publications and interviews with government officials and other knowledgeable individuals. Report discusses types of incentives used by the state and local governments; describes incentive programs currently in use; presents problems and procedures involved in developing incentive programs; summarizes the survey findings; and offers recommendations."

399. Neugarten, Dail Ann. *The Productivity Puzzle.* Monograph, University of Colorado at Denver, July 1981.

Author states that monograph is written for those government officials (and others) who are willing to tackle the issue of productivity measurement and improvement. The format is question and answer and the contents are divided into seven chapters as follows: (I) Conditions Leading to Concerns About Productivity; (II) Productivity, Productivity Measurement and Productivity Improvement: Definitions and Scope; (III) The History of Productivity Efforts in the United States; (IV) Implementing Productivity Improvement Programs; (V) Strategies and Tactics for Productivity Improvement; (VI) Measuring Productivity; and (VII) The State of the Art and the Future.

400. Newland, Chester A. "Motivation, Productivity, and Performance Appraisal" in *Local Government Personnel Administration*, edited by Winston W. Crouch. Washington, DC: ICMA, 1976, 247-280.

Personnel administration's purposes are: (1) to accomplish the objectives of the organization; and (2) to help employees meet their needs and goals. Performance appraisal has taken on new significance with the growing concern over increasing government productivity. Management by objectives and organizational development are two techniques that are being used to focus on achieved results compared with initial objectives. "In order to have a constructive impact, personnel administration processes need to function as integral aspects of general management."

401.   ————. "Personnel Concerns in Government Productivity Improvement." *Public Administration Review*, 32 (November-December 1972), 807-815.

Identifies three dominant topics among "personnel concerns with productivity improvement in governments." Examines productivity bargaining in some detail and briefly discusses formal production incentive systems and manpower planning.

402.   ————. "Policy/Program Objectives and Federal Management: The Search for Government Effectiveness." *Public Administration Review*, 36 (January-February 1976), 20-27.

Purpose is to examine "MBO in the federal government in the context of dominant federal management and budgeting trends since the 1940s, in which MBO is one of the more important developments." Thesis of the author "is that performance budgeting, productivity measurement, PPB, the social indicators movement, MBO, and program evaluation are intimately related management approaches in an increasingly difficult search for government effectiveness."

403.   ————. "Themes and Issues in Public Sector Productivity." *Public Personnel Management*, 9 (No. 4, 1980), 229-235.

Outlines the "need for increased public sector productivity as well as the issues of definition, measurement and implementation." After disposing of several myths about public sector productivity measurement, author recommends three areas of research: (1) "research devoted to developing better indicators of performance-- for people, for programs and for organizations, (2) research devoted to examining the implications of in-

creased productivity on the budgetary process and (3)
research devoted to the application of behavioral science
knowledge to worker productivity."

404. Newland, Chester A., symposium editor. "Productivity in
Government." *Public Administration Review*, 32 (November-December 1972).

Symposium was "designed to inform practitioners and
scholars in public administration about current productivity concerns, problems, practices and controversies
in government in the United States." Articles in the
symposium addressed: "(1) economic concerns and common
definitions and measures of productivity; (2) major
productivity developments in the federal government;
(3) productivity management in one specific governmental
agency; (4) state and local government programs, specifically Wisconsin, California and New York City; (5)
public capital expenditures, and personnel and employment trends."

405. Newland, Chester A., et al. *MBO and Productivity Bargaining in the Public Sector*. Chicago: IPMA, 1974,
66, Appendix, Bibliography.

Collection of six papers dealing with "principal public personnel management aspects of MBO and productivity
improvement." In the first paper, Newland "emphasizes
that, whatever the management approach, administration
is a process for accomplishing desired results, and that,
in a democracy, both the results and the process must be
meshed with the basic values of human dignity and the
rule of law. Behavioral science applications for productivity improvement in government are analyzed by
John Cole and a practical illustration is provided by
Elsa Porter to show how personnel functions can be
realigned and reorganized in an MBO approach. The last
three papers deal with labor-management relations dimensions of productivity improvement efforts."

406. O'Neill, Michael E., and Ernest A. Unwin. "Productivity
Measurement: A Challenge for Implementation." *Public
Productivity Review*, 2 (Fall 1977), 27-37.

Objective is to "develop an understanding of productivity measurement, specifically in a criminal justice
environment." Article attempts "to develop a common
understanding of productivity from an agency standpoint
and to develop a model for possible implementation by

operational agencies. The model is based upon observations, actual training and feedback from seminar atten-
dees."

407.   Paul, Christian F., and Albert C. Gross. "Increasing
       Productivity and Morale in a Municipality: Effects of
       Organizational Development." *Journal of Applied Be-
       havioral Science*, 17 (January-February-March 1981),
       59-78.

       Reports the results of successful OD intervention de-
       signed "to increase the productivity and to improve
       morale" in the Communications and Electrical Division of
       the City of San Diego.

408.   Peterson, Peter G. "Productivity in Government and the
       American Economy." *Public Administration Review*, 32
       (November-December 1972), 740-747.

       Peterson, former Secretary of Commerce and former
       Chairman of the National Commission on Productivity,
       states that "improving productivity in the public sector
       of the U.S. economy is fundamental to the success of the
       current federal effort to create through a variety of
       policy initiatives an environment that will spur a
       higher rate of productivity growth--over the long term--
       in the economy as a whole." He continues by asserting
       that a "comprehensive national crusade to boost U.S.
       productivity is necessary" and "that the more efficiently
       government uses its resources and performs its services
       for the society, the more productive will the society
       be."

409.   President's Commission for a National Agenda for the
       Eighties. *The American Economy: Employment, Produc-
       tivity, and Inflation in the Eighties*. Washington,
       DC: U.S. Government Printing Office, 1980, 82.

       If the 1980s are to be different from the economically
       frustrating and disappointing 1970s, then "the highest
       economic priority for the U.S. must be to restore sub-
       stantial economic growth, especially growth of output
       per person." We must advocate growth "as a requirement
       for achieving fundamental national goals." The authors
       (former President Carter's Panel on the American Econo-
       my) also discuss constraints on growth, policies which
       promote growth, productivity measurement, labor market
       policies, sources and consequences of inflation, and
       proposals for reforms in industrial policies.

410. Proctor, John R. "Productivity and Effectiveness of
      Inspection Services." *Public Productivity Review*, 1
      (September 1975), 22-29).

      Describes the productivity and effectiveness increas-
      ing techniques developed within the building inspection
      agency of Fairfax County, Virginia. Productivity was
      increased by relieving the inspectors of certain cleri-
      cal and scheduling functions and by reducing travel
      time. "Effectiveness, measured by the degree to which an
      agency or individual meets its stated goals, can be
      increased by devoting more effort to the fulfillment of
      the major responsibilities assigned to the agency.
      Agency effectiveness was increased by placing emphasis
      on the accuracy of the inspectors in detecting possible
      code violations."

411. Quinn, Robert E. "Productivity and the Process of Or-
      ganizational Improvement: Why We Cannot Talk to Each
      Other." *Public Administration Review*, 38 (January-
      February 1978), 41-45.

      Concerned with the meaning of productivity, with frus-
      trations experienced by managers as they view the many
      barriers to productivity improvement and measurement in
      government, and their relief that others experience
      the same frustrations, and finally some guidelines for
      success. Presents an action model constructed around
      "six empirical dimensions of organizational performance
      as preceived by operating public administrators and eight
      means or types of change."

412. Rabinowitz, William, et al. "Worker Motivation: Un-
      solved Problem or Untapped Resource?" *California
      Management Review*, 25 (January 1983), 45-56.

      "A new study of almost eleven thousand hourly employ-
      ees in thirty-seven firms finds that workers are especi-
      ally critical of the way they are treated by organiza-
      tions. But despite complaints about inequities, inade-
      quate opportunities, and lack of communication, workers
      overwhelmingly regarded their work as a source of
      personal satisfaction and pride."

413. Rees, Albert. "Improving Productivity Concepts and
      Measurement Techniques." *Monthly Labor Review*, 102
      (September 1979), 23-27.

      Reports the principal recommendations of the panel to
      Review Productivity Statistics funded by the National

Center for Productivity and Quality of Working Life.
Panel concluded: "(1) Bureau of Labor Statistics' output
measures discount quality changes; and (2) Labor input
may be increasingly overstated by the amount of paid
leave and imputed data. Also suggested development of
mulitfactor productivity series."

414. Rosenbloom, Richard S. "The Real Productivity Crisis is
in Government." *Harvard Business Review*, 51 (September-October 1973), 156-158, 160, 162, 164.

During the 1960s, "government was the most rapidly
growing sector of employment with almost all the growth
taking place in state and local government." Since
government is not subject to the same forces as private
industry--rewards for innovation and penalties for
failure--productivity is less evident and harder to measure. Author suggests four elements necessary for governmental productivity progress: "(1) governments must
learn to make better use of modern techniques of management; (2) greater numbers of talented and technically
trained people must be employed in state and local
government; (3) the businesses which supply goods and
services to government must encourage the use of more
productive technology and systems; (4) the system of
rewards for government executives must be altered to
encourage greater productivity." Considers each element
in turn.

415. Rosener, Judy B. "Improving Productivity in the Public
Sector: An Analysis of Two Tools--Marketing and Citi-
zen Involvement." *Public Productivity Review*, 2
(Spring-Summer 1977), 3-11.

Defines productivity in terms of both efficiency and
effectiveness and asserts that appropriate measurement
tools which might be used to improve productivity in the
public sector are marketing and the involvement of citizens in policymaking.

416. Schaffer, Robert H. "Want Better Performance? Insist
on It!" *Administrative Management*, XL (December 1979),
24, 25, 60, 62, 64.

Outlines reasons managers are sometimes reluctant to
push for major productivity gains and commonly used
avoidance mechanisms. He advises that increasing productivity will take time and energy. However, "the key to
the strategy is to make an initially successful attempt

at upgrading expectations and obtaining a response--and then use this achievement as the foundation for a succession of increasingly ambitious steps." The steps to better results are: (1) select the goal; (2) carve out a first-step achievement; (3) communicate your expectations clearly; (4) monitor the project but delegate responsibility; and (5) expand and extend the process.

417. Schroeder, P. "The Politics of Productivity." *Public Personnel Management*, 9 (No. 4, 1980), 236-243.

Provides a list of "past federal productivity efforts and explains why some efforts have worked better than others and outlines the six common excuses federal managers use as to why productivity efforts cannot work. There are all sorts of disincentives to measuring productivity; however, congress could legislate incentives for increased federal productivity."

418. Shetty, Y.K. "Management's Role in Declining Productivity." *California Management Review*, 25 (Fall 1982), 33-47.

Concludes that although government regulation and labor always come up when productivity declines are analyzed, evidence suggests that "responsibility for our recent productivity decline may belong partly to management." Analyzes the "role of management in declining productivity."

419. Sibson, Robert E. *Increasing Employee Productivity.* New York: AMACOM, 1976, 203.

"A guide for companies who wish to organize their own employee productivity improvements. Topics discussed include: unproductive practices, environment staffing, manpower controls, organization structure, delegation, incentives, personnel management productivity and the responsibilities of the unit personnel manager."

420. Soulier, Mary Ziebell, and Don T. DeCoster. "Productivity Versus Cost Control: Considerations for Health Care Managers." *Health Care Management Review*, 7 (Winter 1982), 15-20.

Concludes that improved financial decision making as well as increased financial awareness may lead to both cost control and productivity increases. "The informed use of budgets is an important first step in achieving the goals" of cost control and increased productivity.

421. Srivastvs, Suresh, et al. *Job Satisfaction and Produc-
tivity.* Cleveland, Ohio: Department of Organizational
Behavior, School of Management, Case Western Reserve
University, 1975, 180, Epilogue, Appendix, Bibliography.

Review of research done between 1960 and 1975 on
"organizational factors which may affect job satisfaction and productivity. The goal of the review is policy-
oriented: to assess the research with regard to knowledge
required by organizational decision-makers. While much
literature propounds one or another approach to work
innovation, no comprehensive analysis has been made of
the tremendous volume of research which could be applied
by those developing strategies for improving productivity and the quality of work life."

422. Staudoher, Paul D. "An experiment in Increasing Productivity of Police Employees." *Public Administration Review,* 35 (September-October 1975), 518-522.

Reports on an experiment in the Orange, California,
Police Department "involving an attempt to increase employee motivation through a group incentive plan." The
police performance incentive plan provided for salary
increases if there was a rate reduction in specific
crimes: rape, robbery, all burglaries, and auto theft.
There was a reduction in the reported target crimes.
Factors influencing this result include: the motivating
effect of the monetary incentive plan; the "Hawthorne
Effect"; the fact that a Crime Prevention Bureau and a
Special Enforcement Team were set up in conjunction
with the incentive plan. Acknowledged weaknesses of the
plan include: no data on unreported crimes; conflict of
interests which arose from those participating in the
incentive plan also being responsible for recordkeeping.

423. Stoltz, Robert E. "Assessing Research Productivity."
Personnel Administration, 25 (January-February 1962),
44-49.

Provides "insights into how the research producer is
perceived both by his superior and, to some extent, by
his subordinates." Five groups of items were developed
and through factor analysis each was examined "to determine which groups of items were most related to the
final evaluation of a man's productive research behavior."

424. Takeuchi, Hirotaka. "Productivity: Learning From the
Japanese." *California Management Review,* 23 (Summer
1981), 5-19.

Analyzes the "factors that have led to the success of
Japanese programs and addresses three questions regarding the Japanese productivity system: (1) What is unique
about the Japanese productivity system? (2) Can a management technique developed within the context of Japanese
companies be transferred to U.S. companies? (3) What can
U.S. managers interested in initiating successful productivity programs learn from past experiences? Describes how U.S. companies can establish and manage productivity systems."

425. Thayer, Frederick C. "Productivity: Taylorism Revisited
      (Round Three)." *Public Administration Review*, 32
      (November-December 1972), 833-840.

Examines the underlying premises of management fads
derived from micro-economics "(where 'inefficiency'
supposedly runs rampant)"; and where we got systems
analysis, and the "currently popular concepts of evaluation and productivity." Begins by outlining "one perspective as to why systems analysis never has been
able to deliver on the promises made on its behalf,"
proceeds to analyze public choice, examines the assumptions of market economics and, finally, looks at the
problems of productivity which tend to get ignored. "The
thrust of the argument is that we are being asked to
return all the way to Taylorism as it first was used by
that gentleman himself and that, if we succumb to the
pied pipers of Taylorism, we will realize only a quantum
jump in repression and alienation among all those employed in organizations which glorify 'productivity,'
and at a time when the survival of the planet is likely
to require limits on production instead of constant
increases in it."

426. U.S. Senate Committee on Commerce, Science, and Trans-
      portation. *Environmental and Health/Safety, Produc-
      tivity Growth, and Economic Performance: An Assessment.*
      Washington, DC: U.S. Government Printing Office,
      August 1980, 94.

Evaluation of "the importance of regulation, relative
to other factors, of the nation's serious productivity
slowdown in the past decade. Defines a frame-work of
economic analyses in which previous studies and future
research can be evaluated and examines a few of the
policy options that Congress might consider in dealing
with these issues."

427. Wallace, Robert J. "Productivity Measurement in the
     Fire Service." *Public Productivity Review*, 2 (Spring-
     Summer 1977), 12-36.

     Reviews "previous attempts at productivity measurement
     and the associated problems of input/output definitions,
     and an alternative approach to productivity measurement
     is proposed. The approach used is to define output as
     workload adjusted for quality changes. Three separate
     fire service functions (inspections, dispatching, and
     fire suppression) are examined."

428. Wildavsky, Aaron. "The Political Economy of Efficiency:
     Cost Benefit Analysis, Systems Analysis, and Program
     Budgeting." *Public Administration Review*, 26 (December
     1966), 292-310.

     Asserts that "the encroachment of economics upon poli-
     tics is not difficult to understand. Being political in
     perspective is viewed as bad; having the perspective of
     the economist is acclaimed as good. As a discipline,
     economics has done more with its theory, however inade-
     quate, then has political science. Under some condi-
     tions economists can give you some idea of what effi-
     ciency requires. It is a rare political scientist who
     would even concern himself with political rationality.
     Economists claim to know and work to defend their in-
     terests in efficiency; political scientists do not even
     define their sphere of competence. Thus the market
     place of ideas is rigged at the start."

429. Yamada, Gordon T. "Improving Management Effectiveness
     in the Federal Government." *Public Administration
     Review*, 32 (November-December 1972), 764-770.

     Describes the "actions which have taken place in recent
     years to improve management effectiveness in the federal
     government. Specifically examines the impact of OMB
     Circular No. A-44 in terms of cost reduction, manage-
     ment improvement and management review." Concludes
     that "Circular A-44 is an 'umbrella' circular under
     which overall agency management review and improvement
     actions can be administered and reported." It is a tool
     to be used by government "to provide the citizenry with a
     more responsive and effective government."

CHAPTER 8

TRAINING AND DEVELOPMENT

430. Bartlett, C.J. "Equal Employment Opportunities Issues
in Training." *Public Personnel Management*, 8 (November-December 1979), 398-406.

Reviews the history of Federal employment regulations;
outlines potential sources of discrimination such as
(1) training as a job prerequisite, (2) selection for
training, (3) the training process, (4) retention, progress and graduation, (5) job placement following training, and (6) promotion, advancement, or compensation,
and concludes with a parody on the EEOC's Guidelines.

431. Benford, Robert J., et al. "Training for Results."
Personnel, 56 (May-June 1979), 17-24.

Report of a training strategy within Norwich-Eaton
Pharmaceuticals which was successful in producing measurable improvements in worker performance.

432. Brim-Donohoe, Lue Rachelle. "A Case for Human Resource
Development." *Public Personnel Management*, 10 (Winter
1981), 365-370.

Asserts that it is "imperative that HRD departments
provide comprehensive, coordinated approaches to its
constituents in order to realize maximum organizational
efficiency." Suggests possible strategies for a "cost-
effective reputable training program which is able to
survive economic crisis and internal and external changes
affecting the organization."

433. Brown, F. Gerald, and Kenneth R. Wedel. *Assessing
Training Needs*. Washington, DC: National Training
and Development Service Press, 1974, 93, Appendices,
Bibliography.

"Written from the perspective of a chief executive or
a training officer within a state or local government
organization, the concern is with training as a means of
organizational goal achievement." Provides the reader
with lists of suggested sources and techniques to determine training needs.

434. Byers, Kenneth T., ed. *Employee Training and Develop-*
      ment in the Public Service. Chicago: International
      Personnel Management Association, 1970, 320, Appendix.

      Divided into two parts, Part One "presents a statement
      of the problems and the resources potentially available
      to solve them. The subject is viewed in broad context,
      but narrows to a more specific focus in the last selec-
      tion. Part Two includes some of the ways by which em-
      ployee development might be more effectively achieved
      in terms of what has been learned of this process to
      date. It is designed primarily for those persons who
      have direct responsibility for, and who actively parti-
      cipate in, organization and employee development."

435. Byham, William C. "How Assessment Centers are Used to
      Evaluate Training's Effectiveness." *Training,* 19
      (February 1982), 32, 35, 38.

      Asserts that "the assessment center method shows
      considerable promise in helping to solve the problem of
      evaluating the effectiveness of training programs.
      Basically, the assessment center method of evaluating
      training is a formal procedure in which individuals are
      put through simulations that mirror work situations."
      Cites a number of organizations and their experiences
      with assessment centers.

436. Caldwell, Lynton K. "Measuring and Evaluating Personnel
      Training." *Public Personnel Review,* 25 (April 1964),
      97-102.

      Draws a clear distinction between measurement and evalu-
      ation of training programs. "Measurement implies some
      standard or criterion for estimating the changes that
      training has induced. It does not necessarily prove
      that the changes are desirable or serve the purposes for
      which the training was intended. Evaluation involves a
      comparison between the objectives sought and the results
      of training; then determining if the effort is justified
      by the results. Evaluation means value judgment." Con-
      cludes that "training plans and programs are not complete

if they do not include first, provisions for measuring
results of the training and second, criteria which, in
the minds of designers of the training, would afford
a fair basis for evaluating results."

437. ———. "Determining Training Needs for Organizational
Effectiveness." *Personnel Administration*, 26 (March-
April 1963), 11-19.

Concludes that "training needs of government depend
upon the personal skills and qualities required to carry
on the activities of government. The effectiveness of
training thus depends upon how well the programs and procedures of government have been defined and clarified.
Training needs are ascertained most accurately as a
part of a survey of the personnel resources needed by
government in the achievement of its objectives." Training costs are difficult to estimate and, finally, "any
plan of training requires establishment of priorities."

438. Cooke, Kathleen. "A Model for the Identification of
Training Needs." *Public Personnel Management*, 8
(July-August 1979), 257-261.

"In facing decisions regarding expenditures to obtain
training, administrators, supervisors and others recognize the need for guidance in the identification of
training programs. The model offers an organized, logi-
cal thought path of seven decision points leading to
the identification of situations, some of which can be
remedied by training. Further, when training is suggested, one or more of the three possible domains of
learning is indicated (cognitive, affective, psycho-
motor). Each of these domains is described in its place
in the model. The model is offered as a diagnostic tool
that can be applied to individuals or groups, and can
be used for self-analysis."

439. Craig, Robert L., editor. *Training and Development Handbook*. Second edition. New York: McGraw-Hill, 1976, 647.

Collection of readings which include "the major recent
applications of the behavioral sciences in management
practices and in the development of human resources; an
emphasis on systematic and quantitative methods for
determining training needs and assessing training outcomes; and overall updating in instructional methods
and media; and coverage of newer concepts in human resources development such as organization development,
work design and group behavior."

440. DePhillips, Frank A., William M. Berliner, and James J.
      Cribbin. *Management of Training Programs*. Homewood,
      IL: Richard D. Irwin, 1960, 439, Bibliography.

      Four units organized around seven central themes:
      "(1) the interdependence of management and training;
      (2) the interpersonal and human relations problems in-
      volved in planning, organizing, and conducting training
      programs; (3) the close integration of training methodol-
      ogy and learning theory; (4) the managerial aspects of
      organizing training programs; (5) the discussion focused
      on various types of training programs, organization of
      training departments, various training techniques, me-
      chanical aids to training, and the other 'how-to' devices
      that are essential for the competent trainer; (6) the
      detailed consideration of the need and importance of re-
      search and evaluation in training; and (7) the considera-
      tion of the future of training as a profession."

441. DiLauro, Thomas J. "Training Needs Assessment: Current
      Practices and New Directions." *Public Personnel Man-
      agement*, 8 (November-December 1979), 350-359.

      Provides overview of the "major steps in the training
      needs assessment process and identifies some of the
      future trends in the field. Article is based on research
      eight staff members conducted as part of work as training
      consultants with U.S. Civil Service Commission (now the
      Office of Personnel Management) to determine how federal
      agencies in the Philadelphia Region assessed their train-
      ing needs."

442. Dinnecenzo, Debra A. "Why Dayton Power Trained Its Man-
      agers 'Before the Beginning.'" *Training*, 19 (August
      1982), 36-37, 40.

      Describes Dayton Power and Light Company's "proactive
      approach to training all levels of personnel in prepara-
      tion for a new power plant coming on line."

443. Dyer, William G., editor. *Modern Theory and Method in
      Group Training*. New York: Van Nostrand Reinhold, 1972,
      251.

      A number of experts in the field of "group training in
      individual and organizational behavior have contributed
      to this volume on the role, skills, and professional
      experience and personal behavior of the trainer. Con-
      tents: Pt. 1, Theory and method of trainer style; Pt. 2,
      Theory and method of trainer interventions; Pt. 3, De-

sign developments in group training; Pt. 4, Group methods
and organization development; Pt. 5, Ethical issues in
group training."

444. Fraser, Richard F., John W. Gore, and Chester C. Cotton.
      "A System for Determining Training Needs." *Personnel
      Journal*, 57 (December 1978), 682-685, 697.

      Reminds the reader that "in the Federal system, the
      Government Employees Training Act (GETA) of 1958 requires
      agencies to carefully determine employee training needs
      and to relate such training to improved job performance.
      Guide, developed for the U.S. Department of Agriculture,
      prescreens training requests and thus simplifies the
      approval decision process."

445. Gardner, James E. *Helping Employees Develop Job Skill:
      A Casebook of Training Approaches*. Washington, DC:
      Bureau of National Affairs, 1976, 163, Appendix, Bibli-
      ography.

      Treats the "job-learning process in a realistically
      broad way, discusses it as the developing thing it is and
      makes a balanced statement about training approaches
      as useful not only early in the training but at those
      crucial stages when the employee moves close to job
      competency or is faced with the problem of maintaining
      it."

446. Gellerman, Saul W. "Developing Managers Without Manage-
      ment Development." *Conference Board Record*, 10 (July
      1973), 32-37.

      "Develops in some detail the possibilities for and
      importance of developing managers through the experience
      of managing rather than through formal management
      training programs. Organization structure, job design,
      career planning and control systems are four specific
      aspects of the organization's management that he sees as
      keys to providing a continuing supply of talent."

447. Gilbert, G. Ronald, and John V. Sauter. "The Federal
      Executive Institute's Executive Development Programs."
      Public Personnel Management, 8 (November-December 1979),
      407-415.

      Reviews "some of the practices of executive development
      in the federal government. While not an exhaustive
      study, it identifies some of the discrepancies which cur-
      rently exist between the espoused policy in federal execu-

tive development and that which is actually practiced.
Of particular focus is the practice of executive development at the United States Office of Personnel Management's (OPM) Federal Executive Institute (FEI)."

448. Goldstein, Irwin L. "The Pursuit of Internal and Ex-
      ternal Validity in the Evaluation of Training Pro-
      grams." *Public Personnel Management*, 8 (November-
      December 1979), 416-429.

      Concerned with "where in the pursuit of internal and
      external validity do problems occur that result in com-
      plaints" from trainees, trainers, and organizations.

449. Gordon, Michael E. "Planning Training Activity."
      Training and Development Journal, 27 (January 1973),
      3-6.

      Discusses "an approach to acquiring information on
      which to base decisions about the course of action an
      organization should pursue in developing new training
      products or revising old instructional materials." De-
      scribes "three kinds of survey information the average
      trainer might rely on in making decisions about the
      content and level of training in an organization."
      Also, describes "methods used to analyze this informa-
      tion."

450. Huse, Edgar F. "Putting in a Management Development
      Program That Works." *California Management Review*,
      9 (Winter 1966), 73-80.

      Concludes that in order to be successful "a change
      process needs to be carefully planned and implemented."
      Also describes Work Planning and Review (WP&R) and
      asserts that "it is effective as a management develop-
      ment program at all levels of management in a wide var-
      iety of management positions."

451. Hyde, Albert C., and Jay M. Shafritz. "Training and De-
      velopment and Personnel Management." *Public Personnel
      Management*, 8 (November-December 1979), 344-349.

      Authors' opinion is "that trainers must first be con-
      cerned about human development objectives and then focus
      on upgrading the activities and techniques to be used."
      Lists an agenda for trainers in the 1980's.

452. Kirkpatrick, Donald L. "Evaluating In-House Training
      Programs." *Training and Development Journal*, 32
      (September 1978), 6-9.

When evaluating supervisory training programs four
stages or steps should be considered. They are: Reac-
tion, Learning, Behavior, and Results. Author provides guidelines for evaluating such training programs.

453. Klauss, Rudi. "Formalized Mentor Relationships for
Management and Executive Development Programs in the
Federal Government." *Public Administration Review*,
41 (July-August 1981), 489-496.

Examines "mentor relationships in the public sector,
with special attention to the role of formal mentor-
advisor systems in management and executive development
programs within the federal government. Draws on the
experience of three case studies of formal mentor systems, as well as other recent experience in the public
and private sector. Intent is to extract from this experience some major themes and lessons which can be
used to facilitate the development of more effective
mentor relationships."

454. Klingner, Donald E. "Career-Life Planning and Development Management." *Public Personnel Management*, 8
(November-December 1979), 382-391.

"Examines the theoretical roots, techniques and reasons for success or failure" of career-life planning.

455. Levinson, Harry. "Executive Development: What You Need
to Know." *Training and Development Journal*, 35
(September 1981), 84-95.

Executives are increasingly required to function at a
high level of abstraction, "to conceive of what they
are doing in a historical context, to recognize the effects of what they do on the community, and therefore to
be governed by a concept of sound business policy."
Challenges people in the training function to understand
the needs of the executive and design a "more sophisticated, more comprehensive, more academic kind of effort
which will require not trainers but educators--people
who have a more comprehensive perception of what goes
on in the world, greater capacity to abstract and to
integrate, and certainly the capacity to organize and
teach in high level inhouse educational programs."

456. Mager, Robert F., and Peter Pipe. *Analyzing Performance
Problems or "You Really Oughta Wanna."* Belmont, CA:
Fearon Publishers, 1970, 109.

"About how to find solutions to problems of human
performance. Describes a procedure for analyzing and
identifying the nature and cause of performance problems.
Provides a series of questions for each step of the
analysis, and a quick-reference checklist to help you
determine which solution is most likely to work."

457. Mealica, Laird W., and John F. Duffy. "An Integrated
      Model for Training and Development: How to Build on
      What You Already Have." *Public Personnel Management*,
      9 (No. 4, 1980), 336-343.

      Model offered for economically implementing an effec-
      tive training and development program which integrates
      "(a) job analyses, (b) needs assessment, (c) motivation-
      al theory, (d) performance appraisals, (e) assessment
      center technology, (f) feedback, (g) effective training
      evaluation, and (h) career path/development."

458. Michalak, Donald F., and Edwin G. Yager. *Making the
      Training Process Work*. New York: Harper & Row, 1979,
      148.

      Based on two assumptions: (1) "The trainer is an agent
      of change and the employer who pays wages expects the
      trainer to change people and situations; and (2) All
      training can and should be evaluated, and if it cannot,
      the trainer should review seriously his or her involve-
      ment. Three distinct threads run through the book:
      (1) organizational analysis; (2) need for a correlation
      between training and organizational development; and
      (3) the trainer's role as analyst, writer, presenter,
      helper, counselor and evaluator."

459. Mikesell, John L., John A. Willson, and Wendell Lawther.
      "Training Program and Evaluation Model." *Public Per-
      sonnel Management*, 4 (November-December 1975), 405-411.

      "Training can improve many government activities.
      Several public sector tasks, specific to particular
      duties, are not taught in traditional academic institu-
      tions. Focused training can make major job performance
      improvements in reasonably short periods of time. In
      some areas, including revenue administration, it can
      sometimes be shown directly and immediately that train-
      ing adds more revenue to the state than the out-of-
      pocket training cost. Outlines a training development
      and evaluation program used by the School of Public and
      Environmental Affairs of Indiana University and funded

through the Intergovernmental Personnel Act. Its application to a program for tax auditors in the Indiana Department of Revenue proivdes one example of how problems
of course relevance and evaluation can be overcome.
The inclusion of job performance data emerging from this
workshop experience further emphasizes the inseparability
of program development and program evaluation."

460. Miner, John B. "Management Development and Attitude
      Change." *Personnel Administration*, 24 (May-June 1961),
      21-26.

      Concludes that "(1) a favorable attitude toward super-
      visory work is an important factor in managerial per-
      formance; (2) management development courses can modify
      attitudes; (3) one very effective method of producing
      attitude change is a lecture course which places con-
      siderable emphasis on scientific theory and research
      findings relevant to supervisory practice, and which
      presents clearly the challenges, pleasures and respon-
      sibilities inherent in managerial work; and (4) attitude
      change through management development is equally possible
      during the early stages in a man's career when he is
      preparing himself for a business position and at a
      later date when he has already assumed managerial re-
      sponsibilities."

461. Mitchell, Elizabeth, and Albert C. Hyde. "Training De-
      mand Assessment: Three Case Studies in Planning Train-
      ing Programs." *Public Personnel Management*, 8 (Novem-
      ber-December 1979), 360-373.

      Briefly presents and discusses three training demand
      surveys, one each from the City of Indianapolis; the
      Johnson-Space Center (NASA); and twenty local governments
      in the Houston-Galveston area. Concludes that "training
      demand information can be important to training planning
      as long as trainers realize that training demand may or
      may not be the same as training need."

462. Moses, Joseph L., and William C. Byham. *Applying the
      Assessment Center Method*. New York: Pergamon Press,
      1977, 302, Appendix.

      Summarizes "what is known about applying assessment
      center methods and provides an insight into prospective
      research and implementation strategies. Divided into
      three parts: Part One (Method) describes the process,
      its history, and its current status; Part Two (Impemen-

tation) deals with installing this method; and Part
Three (Evaluation and Beyond) stresses the research
base of assessment."

463. Myers, M. Scott. "Overcoming Union Opposition to Job
     Enrichment." *Harvard Business Review*, 49 (May-June
     1971), 37-49.

     Four models are described for developing cooperation
     between management and union officials in OD programs:
     the confrontation model, the management training model,
     the reorientation model and the negotiated collaboration
     model.

464. Nadler, Leonard. *Developing Human Resources*. Second
     edition. Austin, TX: Learning Concepts, 1979, 315.

     Discusses the definition of human resource development
     (HRD); outlines its history; asserts the HRD is an "um-
     brella" term for training, education, and development;
     and assigns three major roles to the HRD specialist:
     "learning specialist, administrator and consultant."
     The three concluding chapters review the "conceptualiza-
     tion of HRD and explore five implications for organi-
     zations applying this concept: responsibility, mutual
     expectations, learning theory, human resource account-
     ing and evaluation; report the results of a study of
     manager's perceptions and expectations of the role of
     the human resource developer; and view training educa-
     tion and development from the standpoint of economic
     classification evaluation and risk level as a way to per-
     mit organizations to re-examine their HRD goals and
     practices."

465. Nigro, Felix A., and Lloyd G. Nigro. "The Trainer as a
     Strategist." *Public Personnel Management*, 3 (May-
     June 1974), 193-198.

     "Focuses on the dimensions of the trainer's role that
     he uses to select the appropriate strategy for evaluat-
     ing training goals and means. Trainers must attempt
     to create conditions in which it is possible to make
     decisions while keeping the cost at the lowest point
     for the organizations."

466. Odiorne, George S. *Training by Objectives: An Economic
     Approach to Management Training*. New York: Macmillan
     Company, 1970, 348, Cases.

Looks at "economics of training and applied learning
theory" and then integrates them into an approach to
training. Asserts that training should be designed to
achieve a needed objective. "Part I deals with the
economic approach to training, pointing out the
fruitlessness of many past training efforts. Part II
presents the systems approach to training as means of
reorienting training to economic objectives. Part III
outlines the various kinds of learning theories, classified with hard criteria and soft criteria, and shows
what the demands of the future will be for hard criteria
training. It then goes on to illustrate how these will
look in terms of training methods and action training."

467. O'Toole, James. "Integrating Work and Learning."
      Training and Development Journal, 31 (June 1977), 36-
      48.

      Asserts that "if employers are to attract, motivate
      and retain workers in the future, they will probably find
      it necessary to create conditions in which educated work-
      ers can realize their desire to learn on the job." Fo-
      cuses upon the "development of human resources as socie-
      ty's central goal, with education, work and leisure act-
      ing as continuous strands throughout each person's life."

468. ————. *Work Learning and the American Future*. San
      Francisco: Jossey-Bass Publishers, 1977, 222, Bibliog-
      raphy.

      Divided into four parts, Part One "identifies and de-
      fines the major problems of work and education to which
      the entire volume is addressed. Part Two discusses the
      role of government in securing full employment and the
      roles of employers and unions in improving the quality
      of working life. Part Three outlines alternative ways
      in which education might be made more relevant to the fu-
      ture world of work while not becoming a passive hand-
      maiden of industry or the economy. Part Four teases
      out several untried policies that might lead to fuller
      utilization of the nation's human resources."

469. Otto, Calvin P., and Rollen O. Glaser. *The Management
      of Training: A Handbook for Training and Development
      Personnel*. Reading, MA: Addison-Wesley, 1970, 389,
      Appendix.

      Divided into three parts: "Part I presents a detailed
      look at the training director's major responsibilities

in any enterprise; Part II is devoted to an identification of some of the basic conceptual skills needed by
training personnel in their day-to-day work; and Part
III describes some of the basic training media and the
techniques for producing them at the lowest cost."

470. Passett, Barry A. *Leadership Development for Public Service*. Houston, TX: Gulf Publishing, 1971, 112, Appendix, Bibliography.

Asks the question, "How have today's trends influenced
the requirements for new styles of leadership and administration?" Asserts that the "challenge of a more
effective public service is a challenge to the leadership and management capability of people in government."
Critical of the track record of management development
in the public sector, and the lack of dialogue between
HRD personnel in the public and private sectors, the author hopes the "common experience to be gained from reading this book will enable them to communicate more
effectively with each other."

471. Patton, Arch. "The Coming Flood of Young Executives."
Harvard Business Review, 54 (September-October 1976),
20-22, 26, 30, 34, 38, 178, 180.

Predicts that employment opportunities for executives
will be fewer in the future while the supply of young
executives graduating from business schools will increase. "When promotional changes are slim and starting
salaries decrease, and self-interest seems to offer more
to young people than company loyalty, keeping a high
quality staff is not going to be easy." In order for
top managers to meet these challenges, author recommends
that corporations "rethink their motivation, compensation, and promotion policies, as well as their decision-
making processes."

472. Pomerleau, Raymond. "The State of Management Development in the Federal Service." *Public Personnel Management*, 3 (January-February 1974), 23-28.

Defines management development by making clear distinctions between terms, training, education, and development.
Reviews the literature that falls within this management
development definition and discusses components commonly found in management development programs. Cites the
Federal Executive Institute and the Executive Seminar
Centers as examples of the Federal government's commitment to management development in the public service.

473. Schimel, Ruth M., and Torrey S. Whitman. "Training and Development: Institutional and Decentralized Approaches." *Public Personnel Management*, 8 (November-December 1979), 374-381.

"Discusses ways in which trainees can school their thinking and shape their training 'style' to varying organizations." The critical question is, "How much central management control should be exerted over training, and how is that choice influenced by the nature of the overarching organization."

474. Schockley, Pamela S., and Constance M. Staley. "Women in Management Training Programs: What They Think About Key Issues." *Public Personnel Management*, 9 (No. 3, 1980), 214-224.

Reports on questionnaire developed and administered to 30 women "focusing on the attitudes and behaviors of women in management training programs. Responses are reported in ten general categories: knowledge of the organization, individual role in the organization, individual role in the organization as compared with the role of male counterparts, goal development, risk taking, power, communication behavior, supervisory responsibilities, mentors and perception of other women in the organization. In conclusion, survey results and their implications are discussed."

475. Smith, Janice B. *Upward Mobility: Consideration for Program Planning and Development*. U.S. Office of Personnel Management, March 1981, 31, Reference List.

"Outlines upward mobility program issues, strategies, and approaches and serves as a comprehensive information guide to planners in state and local agencies who are developing, refining, or expanding upward mobility programs."

476. Stockard, James G. *Career Development and Job Training: A Manager's Handbook*. New York: AMACOM, 1977, 383, Appendices.

A "practical handbook, in four parts which equate to the four basic steps in a sound approach to employee education, training, and career development: sorting out the needs (Part I), planning and developing solutions (Part II), delivering new knowledge and skill (Part III), and examining results and determining the future course of action (Part IV). Board policy issues, management objectives and options, and operational strategies and techniques are detailed."

477. Tolbert, E.B. *Counseling for Career Development*. Boston: Houghton Mifflin, 298, Bibliography.

Textbook designed for course in "preparation programs for secondary school counselors. Emphasis is upon practical applications supported by relevant theory and research. Illustrative cases are presented and programs are described. The framework of principles and practices provides a foundation upon which the counselor can build as he tries out his ideas, gathers new insights from research reports, and reviews the results of field testing of new programs."

478. Van Maanen, John. *Organizational Careers: Some New Perspectives*. New York: John Wiley & Sons, 179, Bibliography.

Original essays which deal with "careers in organizations, and the relationship of 'work' experience to family and personal needs of the individual. The central concern is with the life-long development of the individual and with constraints which may be imposed upon such personal growth by career requirements in organizations." Contributors include: John Van Maanen, Edgar H. Schein, David A. Kolb, Mark S. Plovnick, Peter G.W. Keen, Lotta Bailyn, Ralph Katz, and Richard Beckhard.

479. Wexley, Kenneth N., and Gary P. Latham. *Developing and Training Human Resources in Organizations*. Dallas, TX: Scott, Foresman, 1981, 235, References.

Begins by presenting "a general understanding of the nature of the training and development function within organizations; covers the functions of both the training director and the training staff within an organization; gives special attention to task analysis, since task analysis should be used to determine the content of training programs; deals with what the training staff needs to know to maximize learning by the trainees; describes approaches to be used for evaluating training program effectiveness; describes specific approaches to employee development; and focuses on current topical issues in the training and development literature.

CHAPTER 9

PERFORMANCE APPRAISAL

480. Adelsberg, Henri van. "Relating Performance Evaluation
    to Compensation of Public Employees." *Public Personnel
    Management*, 7 (March-April 1978), 72-79.

    "Provides a variety of approaches to administering
    individual salaries on the basis of evaluated perform-
    ance, as alternatives to in-range longevity. Describes
    methods of precalculating and controlling salary ex-
    penditures while simultaneously administering salaries
    on a 'relative' rather than 'absolute' performance rating
    system."

481. Allan, Peter, and Stephen Rosenberg. "Getting a Manageri-
    al Performance Appraisal System Under Way: New York
    City's Experience." *Public Administration Review*,
    40 (July-August 1980), 372-379.

    In 1975, voters approved changes in NYC's Charter
    which required the city's central Department of Person-
    nel to establish a Management Services Plan. "The
    revised charter also mandated the installation of a per-
    formance evaluation system for managers to be used as the
    basis for a variety of personnel decisions. The authors
    trace and analyze the city's efforts to install two dif-
    ferent performance evaluation systems."

482. Beaulieu, Rod. "An Easier Look at Performance Apprai-
    sal." *Training and Development Journal*, 34 (October
    1980), 56-58.

    Potential problems concerning performance appraisal
    are examined, such as: (1) personnel managers' famili-
    arity with the organization and employee fit within the
    organization; (2) performance standards preparation; (3)
    identification of employee competence; (4) measurement
    of performance standards; and (5) performance appraisal
    results.

483. Beer, Michael. "Performance Appraisal: Dilemmas and
     Possibilities." *Organizational Dynamics*, 9 (Winter
     1981), 24-36.

     Explores the difficulties involved in appraising
     performance and offers some ideas on dealing with them.
     Addresses: "(1) separating the evaluation aspect from
     employee-development aspect by conducting two appraisals,
     (2) focusing feedback on specific behavior or specific
     performance goals, and (3) conducting the appraisal in
     ways that won't leave the employee feeling powerless."

484. Beer, Michael, and Robert A. Ruh. "Employee Growth
     Through Performance Management." *Harvard Business
     Review*, 54 (July-August 1976), 59-66.

     Corning Glass designed and implemented a "management
     development plan to help managers counsel as well as
     judge their employees." Authors describe how it works.

485. Bernardin, H. John, and Robert L. Cardy. "Appraisal Ac-
     curacy: The Ability and Motivation to Remember the
     Past." *Public Personnel Management*, 11 (Winter 1982),
     352-357.

     Reviews "the obstacles to accurate performance apprai-
     sal that stem from both ability and motivational per-
     spectives. A considerable amount of research on human
     information processing and cognition suggests that even
     when in a desirable climate and motivated to rate ac-
     curately, raters have highly fallible perceptions and
     recall. One of the major conclusions centers on the
     level of trust raters have in the appraisal system and
     how that impacts raters' ability and motivation."

486. Beyer, Janice M., John M. Stevens, and Harrison M. Trice.
     "Predicting How Federal Managers Perceive Criteria
     Used for Their Promotion." *Public Administration
     Review*, 40 (January-February 1980), 55-66.

     Reports results of a study of 634 managers in nine
     executive departments of the U.S. government and their
     "expectations regarding factors that contribute to their
     career advancement. The complex interactions found
     suggest that attempts to improve motivation and perform-
     ance through promotion policies must incorporate suf-
     ficient flexibility to allow them to be tailored to
     fit personal and work situations if they are to succeed."

487. Brinkerhoff, Derick W., and Rosabeth Moss Kanter. "Appraising the Performance of Performance Appraisal." *Sloan Management Review*, 21 (Spring 1980), 3-16.

Article provides a "critical examination of formal performance appraisal systems in organizations. Argues that the role, effectiveness, and validity of appraisal data are limited by a number of organizational factors: the purposes of the appraisal (both avowed and covert), the characteristics of the tasks for which the appraisal is performed, and the location in the structure of the organization of both appraisers and appraisees. Authors conclude that data from formal performance appraisal systems should never be utilized alone and uncritically, without full consideration of the context in which the appraisal is being performed and used."

488. Brown, Robert W. "Performance Appraisal: A Policy Implementation Analysis." *Review of Public Personnel Administration*, 2 (Spring 1982), 69-85.

Outlines and analyzes five conditions for effective public policy implementation: "(1) Program must be based upon a valid 'technical' theory which links target group behavior to the statutory objectives; (2) Statute should contain unambiguous policy directives and structure the implementation process to maximize the probability of target group compliance; (3) Leaders of the implementation agencies should possess substantial political and managerial skills and have a commitment to the statutory objectives; (4) Program should be actively supported by organized constituency groups and by key legislators (or the chief executive) throughout the implementation process, with the courts being neutral or supportive; (5) Relative priority of the statutory objectives are not significantly undermined over time by the emergence of conflicting public policies or by changes in relevant socioeconomic conditions that undermine the reform's 'technical' theory or political support." Concludes, with guarded optimism, that the aforementioned conditions may be created if "certain actions are taken by policy administrators, and favorable rulings emerge from third-party institutions such as the Federal Labor Relations Authority, Merit Systems Protection Board, General Accounting Office, and the courts." Recommendations include "increased use of nonmonetary incentives, development of legislative support and organized constituents, melding of performance appraisal into the regular manage-

ment processes, and a vigorous program of research and
evaluation."

489. Brumback, Gary B. "Toward a New Theory and System of
     Performance Evaluation: A Standardized, MBO-Oriented
     Approach." *Public Personnel Management*, 7 (July-
     August 1978), 205-211.

     Presents a theory and model of individual performance
     planning and evaluation which was derived from the pro-
     gram management model. "The Individual's model can
     become a theoretical argument for the integration of
     performance evaluation and management, a linkage which
     is a practical necessity if performance evaluation is to
     be taken seriously."

490. Byham, William C., and Carl Wettengel. "Assessment
     Centers for Supervisors and Managers." *Public Person-
     nel Management*, 3 (September-October 1974), 352-364.

     Evaluates the Assessment Center method positively and
     attributes its popularity to its "great flexibility in
     adaptation to different jobs and job levels; inherent
     potential for higher degrees of content validity (job
     relatedness); potential for higher criterion-related
     validities than available from test or interviews alone;
     and enthusiastic acceptance by involved participants and
     managers."

491. Caldwell, David S. "Performance Appraisal and Produc-
     tivity in the Civil Service Reform Era." *Public Per-
     sonnel Management*, 11 (Winter 1982), 332-334.

     "Understanding the significance of Civil Service Re-
     form is critical for an evaluation of renewed efforts to
     improve performance appraisal. Reform is premised on
     multiple objectives involving delegation of authority
     to individual agencies, decentralization of much of the
     personnel practice and deinstitutionalization of per-
     sonnel regulation. Expected and actual changes can
     only be assessed in the context of these reform objec-
     tives."

492. Cascio, Wayne F. "Scientific, Legal and Operational
     Imperatives of Workable Performance Appraisal Sys-
     tems." *Public Personnel Management*, 11 (Winter 1982),
     367-375.

     "Develops two themes that are critical for workable,
     effective performance appraisal systems: scientific and

legal imperatives and operational imperatives. These
imperatives dictate that performance appraisal systems
be relevant, sensitive, reliable, acceptable, and practical. Citing a number of examples, the article con-
trasts the need for administrative convenience with the
necessity of motivating and involving raters in a developmental process designed to produce more careful and accurate ratings. It also urges that performance appraisal systems be viewed in a wider context--as a developing decision system. As such, relevance, sensitivity,
and reliability should be evaluated with as much care as
the technical components of any system designed to make
decisions about individuals.

493. Committee for Economic Development. *Improving Productivity In State and Local Government.* New York:
Committee for Economic Development, 1976, 92.

An overview that "identifies and links together the
numerous elements that bear on government productivity
so that more effective and coordinated action can be
taken toward improvement. Its purposes are to define
the dimensions of state and local government productivity, to identify the principal opportunities for improvement, to determine approaches for strengthening the
forces that can motivate government, and to suggest
how the federal system can encourage and assist states
and localities in getting on with the task."

494. Cummings, Larry L., and Donald P. Schwab. *Performance
in Organizations: Determinants and Appraisal.* Glenview, IL: Scott, Foresman, 1973, 130 Bibliography.

Begins by elaborating on a model which asserts that
"performance is determined primarily by ability and
motivation; explores the roles of performance appraisal
as a managerial tool; examines the key concepts in
constructing an effective appraisal system, and the
techniques for appraisal from which the manager may
select; treats key issues relating to who should
appraise, how often appraisals should be conducted, who
should receive feedback, and how feedback should be
given; develops and illustrates three systems for evaluation and development, each aimed at a specific set of
performance and task situations; and finally, offers
an annotated bibliography."

495. Davies, Celia, and Arthur Francis. "The Many Dimensions
of Performance Management." *Organizational Dynamics*,
3 (Winter 1975), 51-65.

Concludes that there is "no one best way to get high
performance, both because there is no 'best performance'
to be had and because what influences the performance
outcomes of an organization is a complex array of variables not all of which can either be easily measured or
put in causal sequence."

496. DeSanto, J.F. "Higher Pay for Good Performance: The
Average Grade Approach." *Public Personnel Management*,
9 (No. 4, 1980), 282-284.

The Average Grade Concept is "a mathematical device
designed to regulate position classification in various
units throughout an organization. Employees are moved
from one salary level to another based on individual
performance and ability. The basic premise is that
managers can and should reward good performance."

497. Field, Hubert S., and William H. Holley. "Performance
Appraisal: An Analysis of State-Wide Practices."
Public Personnel Management, 4 (May-June 1975), 145-
150.

Analyzes the material from 39 state-wide performance
appraisal systems. "The appraisal information was
content-analyzed in four major areas: purposes of appraisal information, administration of appraisal programs, use of appraisal techniques, and use of performance rating procedures." Findings include: the most
frequently listed purposes were "to provide justifica-
tion for decisions concerning promotions, demotions, and
layoffs (26%) and manpower planning and utilization
(22%); the typical state-wide appraisal system was
approximately four years old. Each of the 39 states
required that the rated individual's immediate supervisor, as well as the supervisor's superior, sign the appraisal form. All of the states noted that employees'
performance was evaluated at least once a year; the most
prevalent technique employed on a state-wide basis was
the numerical rating scale (62%); and over 80% of the
states used some form of rating scale (numerical, graphic). The vast majority of the states employed a
person-oriented rating system." Authors recommend that
if the appraisal system is to be used to make decisions
regarding promotions, demotions, layoffs and manpower
planning and utilization, then steps should be taken to
validate the appraisal forms. It is also recommended
that states move toward a results-oriented system and
away from the person-oriented rating system.

498. Field, Hubert S., and William H. Holley. "Traits in Performance Ratings--Their Importance in Public Employment." *Public Personnel Management*, 4 (September-October 1975), 327-330.

     Purpose of research was "to obtain judgments from a large sample of managers in public employment on the importance of various traits in explaining the successful job performance of nonsupervisory personnel. Results should be useful to organizations contemplating the construction of rating forms or revision of those forms currently used in performance appraisal in public settings."

499. Giglioni, Giovanni B., Joyce B. Giglioni, and James A. Bryant. "Performance Appraisal: Here Comes the Judge." *California Management Review*, 24 (Winter 1981), 14-23.

     Presents the essence of Title VII of the Civil Rights Act; identifies and discusses those "characteristics of a performance appraisal system that are likly to result in a judicial scrutiny"; and suggests a "modern philosophy of performance appraisal" and specifies the "modifications that must be adopted in order to avoid the complications and costs of a lengthy lawsuit."

500. Gilbert, Ronald G. "Performance and Organizational Practice: A Post Reform Review." *Public Personnel Management*, 11 (Winter 1982), 318-321.

     "Addresses the questions of 'why have a performance appraisal system?' and 'what concerns need to be raised about formal performance appraisal systems?'"

501. Greene, Charles N., and Philip M. Podsakoff. "Effects of Withdrawal of a Performance-Contingent Reward on Supervisory Influence and Power." *Academy of Management Journal*, 24 (September 1981), 527-542.

     Experiment conducted "to investigate effects of removal of a performance-contingent reward on subordinates' perceptions of their supervisors' sources of influence. A significant increase was found in perceptions of supervisors' use of punishment, but reward, referent, and organizationally-sanctioned power declined significantly. Expert power was unaffected by removal of the incentive system."

502. Griffin, Ricky W., and Gregory Moorhead. "Perceived Task Characteristics and Employee Performance: A

Literature Review." *Academy of Management Journal*,
(October 1981), 655-664.

Reviewed thirteen studies which addressed "empirical
relationships between perceived task scope and employee
performance. Results from these studies are contra-
dictory and inconclusive. Most studies use less than
adequate measures of employee performance. Moreover,
although a causal relationship is assumed, reciprocal
or reverse causality may exist. There is a clear need
for further theoretical explication and improved labora-
tory and field research aimed at enhancing both construct
validity and substantive considerations."

503. Henderson, R. *Performance Appraisal: Theory to Practice*.
      Reston, VA: Reston Publishing, A Prentice-Hall Company,
      1980, 310.

      Presents and analyzes "successful performance apprai-
      sal programs and shows how to construct a system based
      solely on job content and specified employee achieve-
      ments."

504. Heyel, Carl. *Appraising Executive Performance*. New
      York: American Management Association, 1958, 189.

      Assumes that formal performance appraisal is a good
      idea, and emphasizes that "appraisal and the communica-
      tion process that goes with it are both continuing re-
      sponsibilities and that environmental factors need to
      be considered in appraising an executive."

505. Holley, William H., and Hubert S. Field. "Will Your
      Performance Appraisal System Hold Up in Court?" *Per-
      sonnel*, 59 (January-February 1982), 59-64.

      "Human resources managers can measure the vulnerability
      of their performance appraisal systems by comparing them
      with ones involved in discrimination suits."

506. Hopkins, Anne H. "Perceptions of Employment Discrimina-
      tion in the Public Sector." *Public Administration Re-
      view*, 40 (March-April 1980), 131-137.

      Examines the "scope and correlates of employee percep-
      tions of discrimination based on age, sex and race. Al-
      most one in five state employees perceive some form of
      job discrimination. Women, older workers and non-whites
      who feel sex, age and race discrimination share feelings
      of dissatisfaction with their jobs, that promotions are
      not handled fairly, and that supervisors do not take a
      personal interest in them as employees. Possible

remedies for such perceptions of discrimination are
discussed as well as the kind of research needed to more
fully understand the nature of the problems."

507. Huse, Edgar. "Performance Appraisal: A New Look." *Per-
      sonnel Administration*, 30 (March-April 1967), 3-6.

      Explores the problem of linking performance apprai-
      sal and productivity. Describes a program of performance
      appraisal that "considerably increased productivity be-
      cause the objectives of the program were developed before
      specific techniques were established to accomplish these
      objectives."

508. Hyde, Albert C., and Melanie A. Smith. "Performance
      Appraisal and Training: Objectives, A Model for Change,
      and a Note of Rebuttal." *Public Personnel Management*,
      11 (Winter 1982), 358-366.

      "A general conclusion of the performance appraisal
      literature is that training programs for both raters
      and ratees can play a significant role in reducing
      appraisal system bias and error. Current initiatives
      in the public sector have largely recognized this factor
      and special training efforts are already underway in
      many jurisdictions. The training model generally used
      incorporates four phases: orientation to the new system,
      analysis of evaluation methods and errors, opportunity
      to 'practice' performance appraisal, and evaluation of
      training results. Concludes that although training may
      well have a significant impact on reducing subjective
      errors in evaluation, the impact on other systemic pro-
      grams will be minimal."

509. Ingle, Henry T. "Contemporary Issues in Federal Evalua-
      tion Policy: New Linkages Between Personnel and Pro-
      gram Assessment Processes." *Public Personnel Manage-
      ment*, 11 (Winter 1982), 322-331.

      "Highlights the changing and evolving nature of the
      evaluation of Federal government programs and the Fed-
      eral workforce and the potential impact of these changes
      on both the growth of assessment and appraisal prac-
      tices and the conduct of the business of the Federal
      government."

510. Kaufman, Herbert. *Administrative Feedback: Monitoring
      Subordinates' Behavior*. Washington, DC: The Brook-
      ings Institution, 1973, 80.

      Review of "administrative feedback" in nine bureaus of
      the federal government in Washington. Administrative
      feedback is defined "as all the processes by which the
      bureau leaders--the whole headquarters--are apprised of

subordinate behavior down to the lowest organizational
level." Study concludes that "if the leaders of any of
the agencies fail to detect any persistent, pronounced,
or widespread patterns of noncompliance on the part of
their subordinates, it is not because of any breakdown
of administrative feedback or because such patterns are
inherently undetectable at headquarters. The leaders
have the means at hand to keep track of what goes on
below, and these means currently produce enough data in
seven of the nine cases to disclose such behavior if the
leaders want to know about it."

511. Kearney, William J. "The Value of Behaviorally Based
     Performance Appraisals." *Business Horizons*, 19
     (June 1976), 75-83.

     Concludes that behaviorally based performance apprai-
     sal is designed to tell management how results were
     achieved as well as what behaviors are associated with
     getting results. "Behaviorally based performance apprai-
     sal pinpoints the individual's contribution to results
     since it focuses on specific behaviors that are control-
     lable. Inherent in behaviorally based appraisal is the
     generation of specific job-centered prescriptions for
     improving performance."

512. Klingner, Donald E., and John Nalbandian. "Personnel
     Management by Whose Objectives." *Public Administra-
     tion Review*, 38 (July-August 1978), 366-372.

     Outlines a framework for the study of public personnel
     administration. Suggests that "any personnel management
     issue can be classified according to agreement/disagree-
     ment on outcomes desired and means of achieving the out-
     comes and that the agreement/disagreement results from
     interplay of actors at three different levels: environ-
     ment, organization, and employee. Once the issue is
     classified, a context is available, signalling the
     appropriateness of different problem-solving strategies:
     computational, compromise, judgmental, or inspirational."

513. Koontz, Harold. *Appraising Managers as Managers*. New
     York: McGraw-Hill, 1971, 183, Bibliography, Appendices.

     Sets forth an "appraisal program that emphasizes both
     appraisal against objectives and appraisal of managers
     as managers. Conclusions and suggestions are based upon
     participation in an experience with appraisal in both
     business and government operations, as well as research

and experience reported by many practitioners and scholars."

514. Kotter, John P. "Power, Success, and Organizational Effectiveness." *Organizational Dynamics*, 6 (Winter 1978),
27–40.

Argues "that the importance of power-oriented behavior
to managerial career success varies depending upon some
factors that define the managerial jobs involved." He
defines "when and why power-oriented behavior promotes
organizational health and effectiveness and when and why
it does not." Concludes by "demonstrating a simple but
powerful analytical technique that derives from" his discussion.

515. Landy, Frank J. *Performance Appraisal in Police Departments*. Washington, DC: The Police Foundation, 1977,
33, Appendices.

Monograph which considers the "technical aspects of
performance appraisal, the uses of appraisal information
as well as the human problems involved such as the reactions of supervisors and subordinates to the system and
the motivational properties of a performance appraisal system." Describes how the Dade County Public
Safety Department, Dade County, Florida, approached a
change in personnel evaluation systems.

516. Landy, Frank J., et al. "Behaviorally Anchored Scales
for Rating the Performance of Police Officers." *Journal of Applied Psychology*, 61 (December 1976), 750–758.

Goal of study was to "develop supervisory and peer rating scales that could be used to evaluate the effectiveness of municipal police officers. Authors hoped to
demonstrate that the behaviorally anchored scales could
be used effectively, even though the raters were not
directly involved in the construction of the scales."

517. Latham, Gary P., and Kenneth N. Wexley. *Increasing Productivity Through Performance Appraisal*. Reading, MA:
Addison-Wesley, 1981, 205, Appendices, Bibliography.

Describes an "appraisal system that is valid, that
satisfies legal requirements and, most importantly, defines and simulates employee productivity. The system
is based in part on three milestones in organizational
psychology--the critical incident technique, goal setting, and principles of reinforcement."

518. Lazer, Robert I., and Walter S. Wikstrom. *Appraising Managerial Performance: Current Practices and Future Directions*. New York: The Conference Board, 1977, 82, Appendices.

Data obtained from "responses to a survey questionnaire from 293 U.S. corporations, performance appraisal forms and manuals supplied by 125 of these companies, and interviews with personnel executives and consultants. Report is concerned with the state of the management performance appraisal "art," examining current corporate practice in the context of criticisms that are widely expressed and legal challenges that threaten to overthrow some common appraisal practices. Four case studies illustrate attempts made by various firms to tailor their appraisal systems to their own particular needs. Appendix goes into detail on the advantages and disadvantages of different approaches to performance appraisal."

519. Lefton, R.E., et al. *Effective Motivation Through Performance Appraisal*. Cambridge, MA: Ballinger Publishing Company, 1980, 294, Appendices, Bibliography.

Shows how to "conduct performance appraisals that pay off for the organization in terms of higher profits, greater efficiency, better morale, faster growth, lower costs, better public image, etc." Written from the manager's point of view it meets head on the difficult and diverse issues without the use of jargon and technical terms. Using two models, the Dimensional Model of Superior Appraisal Behavior and the Dimensional Model of how and why people behave as they do in performance appraisals."

520. Levinson, Harry. "Appraisal of What Performance?" *Harvard Business Review*, (July-August 1976), 30-32, 34, 36, 40, 44, 46, 160.

Describes the basic functions of performance appraisal and asserts that most performance appraisal mechanisms focus on the outcomes of behavior, not the behavior itself. Advocates "job descriptions that are behavior-as well as results-oriented; a critical incident program in which managers write reports regularly on the behavior of their employees; and support mechanisms to help managers honestly appraise the behavior of their employees as well as their bosses."

521. Levinson, Priscilla, and Mary Sugar. "Performance Evaluation and Rating." *Civil Service Journal*, 18 (July-
September 1977), 28-31.

Asserts that the emphasis in the revised Federal Personnel Manual, Chapter 430, Performance Evaluation and
Rating, issued by the United States Civil Service Commission, is on "advantages, opportunities, and methods
for improved communication between supervisors and employees." The Guide for Improving Personnel Evaluation
has been added as Appendix A to Chapter 430. "The chapter describes what should be done; the Guide explains
how to do it."

522. Locker, Alan H., and Kenneth S. Teel. "Performance Appraisal: A Survey of Current Practices." *Personnel
Journal*, 56 (May 1977), 245-247, 254.

Report on survey of private industries' performance
appraisal systems. Conclusions are "1. Most organizations have formal appraisal programs and use two or
more different appraisal techniques for different groups
of employees. 2. Large corporations (500 employees) are
no more sophisticated than small in their appraisal programs. 3. The graphic rating scale, despite its well-
known limitations, is still by far the most widely
used appraisal technique. 4. MBO, despite its widespread
publicity, is not widely used. 5. Most appraisals are
annual. They are made by the immediate supervisor of
the employee being appraised, without any direct employee
input. 6. Very few organizations provide adequate
training for appraisers. Recommendations can be summa-
rized as follows: 1. Identify in detail the objectives
of your appraisal program. 2. Audit your current program to see if it is achieving those objectives. 3.
Modify it whenever your objectives change, or data indicate that it is no longer satisfying your objectives.
4. Provide formal training for appraisers, to insure that
they understand both the objectives and mechanics of
the program."

523. Lockwood, Jay H. "A Local Government Perspective on 'Performance Appraisal in the Post-Reform Era.'" *Public
Personnel Management*, 11 (Winter 1982), 338-339.

Believes that there "is a pervasive resistance on the
part of local government employees, supervisors and
managers to sincerely participate in a process which
differentiates, on some alleged quantitative basis, the

'worth' of other humans sharing the same work environment."

524.   Lopez, Felix M. *Evaluating Employee Performance.* Chica-
       go: Public Personnel Association, 1968, 283, Epilogue,
       Appendices.

       Develops a model of a viable performance evaluation
       program, a "vocabulary to explain it more precisely,
       and an operational plan to implement it." Explores
       "those elements of the organization system that affect
       performance evaluation most--values, principles, and
       purposes; examines the nature of formal performance
       evaluation; discusses ways of transforming basic princi-
       ples into a practical program; lists the strategies and
       the tactics that have been employed by many companies and
       government agencies to implement their programs; presents
       a model of performance evaluation that is multi-purpose
       and multi-method; discusses the difficulties and the
       hazards encountered in day-to-day [activities]; and finally
       addresses the question of program continuity and renewal
       and the problem of adaption."

525.   Lovrich, Nicholas P., Jr., et al. "Do Public Servants
       Welcome or Fear Merit Evaluation of Their Performance?"
       Public Administration Review, 40 (May-June 1980), 314-
       222.

       Reports on the results of "a survey among Washington
       State employees, which indicates that there may be a
       far more supportive environment for merit evaluation of
       performance in the public sector than would be suggested
       by the conventional wisdom of personnel management liter-
       ature. Furthermore, there is evidence to suggest that
       public employees will respond quite favorably to the
       emphasis placed upon 'employee participation' in the
       performance appraisal processes established in the Civil
       Service Reform Act of 1978."

526.   McCrensky, Edward. "Increasing the Effectiveness of
       Staff Performance Appraisal Systems." *Public Personnel
       Management,* 7 (July-August 1978), 212-220.

       Focuses upon "constructive results that should be
       obtained from national performance appraisal systems,
       particularly among developing countries." Asserts that
       "a personnel appraisal system has to be judged on its
       capacity for satisfying the special requirements and
       goals of individual national personnel management sys-

tems." Proposes an "operationally oriented plan for a performance appraisal system that might serve the requirements of developing countries although the basic concepts have universal applicability."

527. McGregor, Douglas. "An Uneasy Look at Performance Appraisal." *Harvard Business Review*, 53 (May-June 1975), 35, 89-94.

First appeared in the May-June 1957 issue of *Harvard Business Review*. Critical of conventional performance appraisal approach because it forces the manager to make a judgment about the personal worth of a fellow employee. Proposes employees be analyzed on basis of performance.

528. Meyer, Herbert H. "The Pay-for-Performance Dilemma." *Organizational Dynamics*, 3 (Winter 1975) 39-50.

Argues that merit pay demotivates rather than motivates "because most people exaggerate their own performance and feel cheated whenever they get a raise. To the extent pay is attached directly to the performance of the task, intrinsic interest in the task itself decreases. When pay becomes the important goal, the individual's interest tends to focus on that goal rather than on the performance of the task itself. Recommends each person be employed on the basis of implicit contract and a starting salary negotiated. Pay increases would be withheld from those who do not perform up to their implicit contract."

529. Meyer, Herbert H., Emmanuel Kay, and John R.P. French, Jr. "Split Roles in Performance Appraisal." *Harvard Business Review*, 43 (January-February 1965), 123-239.

Report of intensive year long study of work planning and review at General Electric. Appraisal of performance and salary action interviews were held separately from performance improvements planning. Authors conclude that comprehensive annual performance appraisals are of questionable value; that coaching should be a day-to-day, not a once-a-year activity; that goal setting, not criticism, should be used to improve performance; and separate appraisals should be held for different purposes.

530. Millard, Cheedle W., Fred Luthans, and Robert L. Ottemann. "A New Breakthrough for Performance Appraisal." *Business Horizons*, 19 (August 1976), 66-73.

"Gives a brief background of the Behaviorally Anchored Rating Scales (BARS) technique which was developed by these authors, goes through the steps of how the scales are developed and implemented, and presents the data, analysis and conclusions on the effectiveness of BARS."

531. Morrison, Ann M., and Mary Ellen Kranz. "The Shape of Performance Appraisal in the Coming Decade." *Personnel*, 58 (July-August 1981), 12-22.

Projects the effect economic conditions, federal legislation, technological advances and cultural trends will have on performance appraisal and provides some "insight into how organizations' performance appraisal programs could be structured so they will have meaning in the larger environment and contribute to an organization's prosperity."

532. Nalbandian, John. "Performance Appraisal: If Only People Were Not Involved." *Public Administration Review*, 41 (May-June 1981), 392-396.

Critiques the trend toward "the replacement of subjectivity in the evaluation process with objectivity anchored in job-related behavior and explicit goal statements."

533. Newland, Chester A. "Performance Appraisal of Public Administrators: According to Which Criteria?" *Public Personnel Management*, 8 (September-October 1979), 294-304.

Examines "three double sets of criteria for performance appraisal of public administrators: (1) agency and subordinate expectations, focusing principally on new United States Government performance appraisal criteria for executives, using the National Aeronautics and Space Administration approach for illustration; (2) requirements of the law and responsibility to the public and (3) professional standards and self-expectations. Executive functions are identified on which evaluation of organizational, not individual, performance may be required.

534. Nigro, Lloyd G. "CSRA Performance Appraisals and Merit Pay: Growing Uncertainty in the Federal Work Force." *Public Administration Review*, 42 (July-August 1982), 371-375.

Reports survey results which suggest that federal employees are becoming increasingly uncertain about the likelihood of experiencing a performance appraisal followed by a salary adjustment in their favor.

535. ————. "Attitudes of Federal Employees Toward Performance Appraisal and Merit Pay: Implications for CSRA Implementation." *Public Administration Review*, 41 (January-February 1981), 84-86.

Reviews "findings of two major surveys and draws some tentative conclusions about the following questions: (1) How do federal employees feel about the existing (pre-CRSA) performance appraisal system? and (2) Do they trust their organizations to develop and implement performance appraisal methods that are fair and equitable?"

536. Oberg, Winston. "Make Performance Appraisal Relevant." *Harvard Business Review*, 50 (January-February 1972), 61-67.

Fitting "practice to purpose when setting goals and selecting appraisal to achieve them" can make performance appraisal programs considerably more effective. Author "presents a catalog of the strengths and weaknesses of nine of these techniques; then he shows how they can be used singly and in combination with different performance appraisal objectives."

537. O'Reilly, Charles A., III, and Barton A. Weitz. "Managing Marginal Employees: The Use of Warnings and Dismissals." *Administrative Science Quarterly*, 25 (September 1980), 467-484.

Examines how marginal employees are identified and managed by first-level supervisors. Findings suggest that "appropriate use of sanctions may be perceived by employees as legitimate and may be conducive to the development of productive group norms."

538. Patz, Alan L. "Performance Appraisal: Useful But Still Resisted." *Harvard Business Review*, 53 (May-June 1975), 74-80.

Survey of 19 companies revealed (1) "traditional forms of performance appraisal are still in use, even though many companies have adopted MBO or other development systems, and (2) managers are unwilling to abandon performance appraisal, although they still experience difficulty in carrying out the process." Author concludes

that managers think performance appraisal is helpful and
he offers a "four-point strategy emphasizing manageabili-
ty and directness."

539. Perry, Lee T., and Jay B. Barney. "Performance Lies Are
      Hazardous to Organizational Health." *Organizational
      Dynamics*, 9 (Winter 1981), 68-80.

      Focuses on situational causes of "lies designed to
      deceive others in an organization about individual or
      group performance. In explaining the structural incen-
      tives that foster lies by people below top management,
      the authors introduce the 'coalition to effect and pre-
      serve the organizational performance lie.' By cooperat-
      ing in the lie, loyal members of the coalition are able
      to control the information top management receives about
      performance and prevent an interruption of the flow of
      organizational rewards."

540. Ralph, Pierson M. "Performance Evaluation: One More
      Try." *Public Personnel Management*, 9 (No. 3, 1980),
      145-153.

      Asserts that "performance evaluations can serve both
      administrative and behavioral purposes. Performance
      evaluation systems often fail because this distinction
      is not made and the objectives of the system are not
      defined before the system is designed. Failure to take
      behavioral considerations into account can also create
      distortion in the system. By defining objectives, de-
      signing elements of the system to address objectives
      independently, and taking explicit steps to minimize
      distortion, an effective system can be constructed."

541. Rifkind, Bernard D., Raymond A. Conner, and Seymore W.
      Chad. "Applying Work Measurement to Personnel Admin-
      istration." *Public Administration Review*, 17 (Winter
      1957), 14-19.

      Major factors affecting manpower requirements are:
      mission of the agency, scope of field activities, and
      stability of agency programs. Author reports on re-
      search, undertaken for the USAF, designed to apply work
      measurement to personnel administration. Summary of
      program results discusses the "potential contribution to
      program effectiveness and economy and efficiency of
      operation" of the work measurement project.

542. Rona, W.W., Charles L. Anderson, and Terry L. Talbert. "A Psychometric Approach to Job Performance: Fire Fighters." *Public Personnel Management*, 5 (November-December 1976), 409-422.

Identifies the "dimensions of the job of fire fighter" and develops "psychometric devices to measure as many of the dimensions as possible." The data indicate that (1) "it appears to be possible to construct objective tests that measure at least some of the relevant dimensions of fire fighter job performance," (2) "some performance dimensions seem impossible to test--in particular, the areas of interpersonal relationships, motivation, etc.," and (3) "subjective evaluations showed minimal relationships with the objective performance measures, and the peer and supervisory evaluations did not agree to any great extent."

543. Ronel, Simcha, and Sophia B. Primps. "The Impact of Flextime on Performance and Attitudes in 25 Public Agencies." *Public Personnel Management*, 9 (November 3, 1980), 201-217.

Reports the results from "25 U.S. public sector organizations which have implemented flextime." Findings are subdivided into four general categories: "organizational effectiveness, employee attitudes, membership behavior, and personal time management. In general, it was found that the organization can improve its effectiveness through flextime implementation: data on productivity, performance, interpersonal relations, tardiness and absenteeism support this conclusion. Employee attitudes towards the job, the work environment and home/work fit are consistently improved, although supervisors and managers tend to be somewhat less positive."

544. Rosenbloom, David H. "Public Sector Performance Appraisal in the Contemporary Legal Environment." *Public Personnel Management*, 11 (Winter 1982), 314-317.

Asserts that "the judiciary has increased its scrutiny of public bureaucrats and chosen to exercise greater authority. This development has entailed creating new rights for individuals who interact with public organizations, curtailing the immunity of public officials, and directly involving the judiciary in overseeing public facility administration. The thrust of judicial activity involving public personnel, including performance appraisal, is to reduce the authority of administrative hierarchies over their employees."

545. Rosinger, George, et al. "Development of a Behaviorally
      Based Performance Appraisal System." *Personnel Psy-
      chology*, 35 (Spring 1982), 75-88.

      Describes the "development of a behaviorally based
      performance appraisal system. Items in the present
      scale were developed to described proficiency levels of
      specific job tasks. This characteristic is expected to
      enhance the objectivity of the evaluation system for
      both appraisal and job counseling purposes. The apprai-
      sal instrument was subjected to a series of reliability
      and validity tests that demonstrated its high reliability
      and validity. Although the content of the appraisal sys-
      tem described here included highway patrol tasks, a simi-
      lar system could be developed using the procedures de-
      scribed for a wide variety and level of jobs."

546. Rowland, Virgil K. *Evaluating and Improving Managerial
      Performance*. New York: McGraw-Hill, 1970, 323.

      Attempts to "pull together the management practices of
      successful managers and to classify, explain, evaluate
      and illustrate these practices." Divided into six sec-
      tions, "Parts One and Six discuss management philoso-
      phies, problems, and the future. Parts Two through Five
      are devoted to specific management tools or techniques."

547. Sarin, Rakesh K., and Robert L. Winkler. "Performance-
      Based Incentive Plans." *Management Science*, 26
      (November 1980), 1131-1144.

      Describes how incentive plans can be devised employ-
      ing multi-attribute preference theory in the design.
      "The basic idea is to state empirically verifiable con-
      ditions on the decision maker's preferences that imply
      some particular forms of the incentive function." First,
      the authors show how an "incentive plan can be devised
      when incentive compensation to managers is based on their
      actual performance on some predetermined criteria."
      Next, they "consider goal-based plans that encourage
      managers to set accurate goals and motivate them to
      strive for a better performance subsequent to goal
      setting." Finally, they "extend the goal-based plans to
      include situations in which the goals are reported
      probabilistically. Several suggestions for further re-
      search are also provided."

548. Sauer, William I., Jr. "Evaluating Employee Perform-
      ance: Needs, Problems and Possible Solutions." *Pub-*

lic Personnel Management, 9 (January-February 1980), 11-18.

Some benefits of a "well constructed evaluation system" are considered; "the merits and drawbacks of two sources of performance information" are examined; and "four possible solutions for problems in the performance rating process" are discussed.

549. Schimel, Ruth Mara. "Making Performance Evaluation Work Better: A Supervisor's Viewpoint." *Public Personnel Management*, 11 (Winter 1982), 335-337.

Objective of performance appraisal "is to improve managerial effectiveness. This requires both environmental analysis to include social and cultural delineations and individual analysis focusing on personal values, degree of identity and sense of purpose. The performance appraisal process, to be effective, must involve supervisors and managers in a mediating interactional role."

550. Schinagl, Mary S. *History of Efficiency Ratings in the Federal Government*. New York: Bookman Associates, 1966, 100, Notes, Bibliography.

Develops a "chronological history of efficiency ratings in the Federal government and shows that, although they were first introduced to eradicate politics, favoritism, and inefficiency, all three still exist in civil service. Despite its failure, however, employee evaluation is considered important enough by the legislative and executive branches of government to warrant continual experimentation."

551. Schneir, Craig Eric. "Multiple Rater Groups and Performance Appraisal." *Public Personnel Management*, 6 (January-February 1977), 13-20.

Reviews the "advantages and disadvantages of using multiple groups as raters. A set of techniques is explained whereby organizations can assess the perspectives of the potential rater groups, diagnose their degree of difference and similarity, and utilize the results of such a diagnosis to strengthen their performance appraisal system."

552. Schwab, Donald P., Herbert G. Heneman III, and Thomas A. DeCotiis. "Behaviorally Anchored Rating Scales:

A Review of the Literature." *Personnel Psychology*,
28 (Winter 1975), 549-562.

Concludes that "despite the intuitive appeal of BARS,
findings from research have not been very encouraging.
On the three issues that have been investigated most
thoroughly to date (leniency, dimension independence
and reliability) there is little reason to believe that
BARS are superior to alternative evaluation instruments."

553. Slusher, E. Allen. "A Systems Look at Performance Appraisal." *Personnel Journal*, 54 (February 1975), 114-
117.

Analyzes performance appraisal from a systems perspective. "The existence of a system boundary implies that
those elements not within the system lie in a larger
suprasystem or environment. The suprasystem affects
the system by providing inputs to the system and accepting outputs from the system. In the human resource system presented here, there are three inputs: organizational goals, human talent and other suprasystem factors.
The outputs from the human resource system are organizational performance and human need satisfaction. By
meeting performance standards, the organization strives
to insure its own survival. The human resource system's
ability as an open system, to progress toward organizational goals, depends chiefly on the supply of comprehensive feedback from the appraisal subsystem. The appraisal subsystem's feedback contribution can be fully under-
stood by analyzing resource subsystems. Few organizations utilize all the potential feedback interfaces that
sound appraisal offers."

554. Speroff, B.J. "Experimental Procedures and Techniques
for Evaluating Supervisory Performance." *Personnel
Administration*, 24 (May-June 1961), 4-10.

Briefly discusses trait evaluation, detailed job description evaluation, evaluation training, forced choice
evaluation, paired comparisons evaluation, critical incident evaluation, progress review evaluation, supervisory goals evaluation, actual results analyses evalua-
tion, area evaluation, leadership type and evaluation
and follow-up and evaluation.

555. Starling, Grover. "Performance Appraisal in the Z Organization." *Public Personnel Management*, 11 (Winter
1982), 343-351.

Presents an overview of "what can be learned from
Theory Z organizations regarding working and management
style variables and formal evaluation systems. In Theory
Z organizations, formal performance evaluation is slow
and insulated while informal performance feedback is
emphasized and made smooth and continuous. A tentative
conclusion is that current performance appraisal systems
must reflect more of the appraisal embodied in prevailing trends toward Theory Z organizational and management
styles."

556. Stimson, Richard A. "Performance Pay: Will It Work?"
     The Bureaucrat, 9 (Summer 1980), 39-47.

     The Civil Service Reform Act of 1978 "provides that
middle level managers and above be paid according to
their performance" and that the establishment of performance goals: (1) be an annual event, (2) be a collaborative effort between superior and subordinate,
and (3) include both the organizational and personal
objectives. Questions addressed are "What is the extent
of theoretical support for the new federal program,
what are the limiting factors, and what might work?"

557. Sushkin, Marshall. "Appraising Appraisal: Ten Lessons
     From Research for Practice." *Organizational Dynamics*,
     9 (Winter 1981), 37-50.

     Presents ten guidelines designed to help evaluate
performance appraisal systems. The guidelines are "il-
lustrated with case examples and include specific recommendations for helping an organization upgrade its
own system. In addition, the discussion shows how the
presence or absence of specific characteristics or
practices promotes the general aims of appraisal--that
is, personnel development, performance feedback, and
the generation of information on which to base administrative action decisions. Some examples: whether and
how managers are rewarded for subordinate development,
whether skill training is provided in rating and counseling subordinates, whether and how subordinates are
involved in the appraisal process, and whether the communication of judgmental feedback is separated from
coaching and counseling activities."

558. Taylor, Robert L., and Robert A. Zawacki. "Collabora-
     tive Goal Setting in Performance Appraisal: A Field
     Experiment." *Public Personnel Management*, 7 (May-
     June) 1978), 162-170.

"An organization's performance appraisal and development system (PADS) was changed to measure the effects
of collaborative goal setting. Subjects were divided
into experimental and control groups. Pretest and post-
test measures revealed significant differences in perceived involvement, feedback, and attitudes between
groups with the experimental group feeling more involved,
more satisfied with the PADS, and receiving more positive feedback."

559. Taylor, Robert L., and William D. Wilsted. "Capturing
      Judgment Policies in Performance Rating." *Industrial
      Relations*, 15 (May 1976), 216-224.

      Introduces "'policy capturing,' a process by which
      actual decisions are analyzed. The process provides a
      mathematical description of the way the decision maker
      uses information to make decisions. The mathematical
      description can be used to predict and understand the
      information used by the decision maker and builds a
      model which, through certain statistical techniques,
      weights each piece of information according to its
      actual influence on a decision. The research reported
      here sought to explore the usefulness of the policy
      capturing technique in understanding and improving the
      semi-annual rating received by U.S. Air Force Academy
      Cadets."

560. Teel, Kenneth S. "Performance Appraisal: Current Trends,
      Persistent Progress." *Personnel Journal*, 59 (April
      1980), 296-301, 316.

      Most large organizations are placing increasing empha-
      sis on the importance of performance appraisal systems
      such as narrative evaluations, tying pay to performance
      and frequent changes in the appraisal system.

561. Thayer, Fred C. "Civil Service Reform and Performance
      Appraisal: A Policy Disaster." *Personnel Management
      Journal*, 10 (No. 1, 1981), 20-28.

      Contends that "performance appraisal systems do not
      and cannot possibly work." Purpose is to "stimulate
      readers to consider the possibility that the defects of
      appraisal systems in general, and the emerging problems
      of the new reform, are not traceable to supervisory care-
      lessness, nor to the inevitable 'shakedown period' which
      follows any major change, but are inherently a part of
      any appraisal system."

562. Thompson, Frank J. "Performance Appraisal of Public Mana-
      gers: Inspiration, Consensual Tests and the Margins."
      Public Personnel Management, 11 (Winter 1982), 306-
      313.

      "Argues that the effective functioning of an apprai-
      sal system depends in large part on the presence of mana-
      gers gifted in decision making via inspiration rather
      than just calculation and those involved in appraisal
      initiatives need to be adroit in forging consensus about
      the merits of appraisal systems."

563. Whitbeck, Philip H. "A Critique on the Theme of Change
      in Performance Appraisal." *Public Personnel Manage-
      ment*, 11 (Winter 1982), 340-342.

      Asserts that the problems associated with employee
      evaluation are as "intractable" today as they were fifty
      years ago. "While past failures have not prevented the
      development of many new approaches to old problems, the
      rate of failure remains high."

564. White, B. Frank, and Louis B. Barnes. "Power Networks
      in the Appraisal Process." *Harvard Business Review*,
      49 (May-June 1971), 101-109.

      "Describes a concrete effort to develop managerial
      skills and talents of subordinates in a large organiza-
      tion."

565. Williams, Michael R. *Performance Appraisal in Manage-
      ment*. London: Cox and Wyman, 1972, 142, Appendices.

      Explores "problems involved in appraising managerial
      effectiveness--particularly in those areas where it is
      impracticable to quantify performance and where qualita-
      tive yardsticks must be the principal means of evaluat-
      ing a manager's contribution. Presents the process of
      appraising performance as a natural and inevitable func-
      tion of management."

566. Williams, Richard, James Walker, and Clive Fletcher.
      "International Review of Staff Appraisal Practices:
      Current Trends and Issues." *Public Personnel Manage-
      ment*, 6 (January-February 1977), 5-12.

      Reports a survey of public administrations which re-
      vealed a number of trends, among them a move toward
      greater involvement of employees in the appraisal pro-
      cess. The authors interpret the trends as an indication
      that there is a general shift toward greater fulfill-

ment of the employee's needs. However, when appraisal
schemes are used for organizational purposes, the likelihood of conflict between employee and organizational
goals is enhanced.

567. Wise, Charles R., and Eugene B. McGregor, Jr. "Government Productivity and Program Evaluation Issues."
Public Productivity Review, 1 (March 1976), 5-19.

Summary and discussion of questions addressed at
conference: "(1) What is the importance of government
productivity improvement in the US' economic system?
(2) What are the different forms of government output
measurement and to what purposes are they best suited?
(3) How do productivity and effectiveness measurements
relate to other management improvement efforts? (4)
How long does it take to implement productivity measurement efforts? (5) How can productivity be integrated
into the management process? (6) What impact do employee relations and managerial acceptability have on productivity improvement? What can be done to avoid dis-
functional behavioral reactions to productivity improvement programs? (7) What are the implications for personnel management and training?"

568. Zawacki, Robert A., and Robert L. Taylor. "A View of
Performance Appraisal From Organizations Using It."
Personnel Journal, 55 (June 1976), 290-292, 299.

Study reports on the "results of a national survey of
key industrial firms whose top personnel administrators
were queried as to the current state of performance
appraisal in their organizations. From the respondent
organizations, an almost even split between the traditional and collaborative approaches to supervisory ratings" is observed.

569. Zedlewski, Edwin W. "Performance Measurement in Public
Agencies: The Law Enforcement Evolution." *Public Administration Review*, 39 (September-October 1979),
488-493.

During the past ten years, the LEAA supported attempts:
"(1) to develop performance measurement systems for the
police, prosecution and public defense, courts, and
corrections functions; (2) to promote performance and
professional standards; and (3) to launch an extensive
program of evaluation research." Author "traces the
contributions of these experiences to the current effort;

discusses some of the conceptual advances anticipated
from the program and how these concepts might proceed
from research to action; and offers some concluding
observations to other mission-oriented funding agencies."

CHAPTER 10

JOB DESIGN

570. Abdel-Halim, Ahmed. "Employee Effective Response to
      Organizational Stress: Moderating Effects of Job
      Characteristics." *Personnel Psychology*, 31 (Autumn
      1978), 561-579.

      Examines role conflict, ambiguity and overload and the
      role these factors play in job stress and dissatisfac-
      tion among managerial level employees. For employees
      holding low-enriched jobs, overload and role ambiguity
      are more adverse. Role ambiguity has the strongest re-
      lationship with job dissatisfaction and stress.

571. Alber, A. "Job Enrichment for Profit." *Human Resource
      Management*, 18 (Spring 1979), 15-25.

      Report of job enrichment projects in 58 organizations.
      Reasons for undertaking job enrichment programs are dis-
      cussed under the following headings: (1) economic strate-
      gy; (2) non-economic strategy; (3) economic-humanistic
      strategy; and (4) economic benefits. Benefits realized
      as a result of job enrichment programs are in the areas
      of: (1) quality; (2) resource utilization; (3) operating
      benefits; (4) absenteeism (reduced); (5) turnover (re-
      duced); and (6) work force reduction. The reader is
      reminded that there is risk involved when job enrich-
      ment programs are instituted. They are not always
      successful in producing the desired results.

572. Aldag, Ramon J., and Arthur P. Brief. *Task Design and
      Employee Motivation*. Glenview, IL: Scott, Foresman,
      1979, 146.

      Presents theories of human behavior, summarizes re-
      search findings pertinent to the theoretical models,
      and takes a pragmatic viewpoint. "Explores the behavior-
      al backgrounds to the issue of job redesign, focusing
      upon employee need structures, motivation, and perform-

ance, examines the historical backgrounds of the job design issue; offers a synthesized theory of job redesign
based upon a set of five specific task attributes; recog-
nizes that not all employees respond in like manner to
job redesign interventions; presents evidence that job
redesign efforts should not be attempted without an
assessment of the organizational context of the target
jobs," and concludes with a futuristic look at the
changing role of the worker.

573. Beehr, Terry A., and John E. Newman. "Job Stress, Em-
      ployee Health, and Organizational Effectiveness: A
      Facet Analysis, Model and Literature Review." *Per-
      sonnel Psychology*, 31 (Winter 1978), 665-699.

      Presents a literature review of research into job
stress. The material is organized as follows: (1) environmental facet; (2) personal facet; (3) process facet;
(4) human consequences facet; (5) organizational consequences facet; (6) adaptive responses facet; and (7) time
facet. (Facet--a conceptual dimension underlying a set
of variables.) Two models are used to demonstrate stress
responses over time.

574. Berg, Ivar, Marcia Freedman, and Michael Freeman. *Mana-
      gers and Work Reform*. New York: The Free Press, 1978,
      316, Bibliography.

      Central theme is that potential managers have to in-
tervene in the work setting and alter the level of satisfaction of the worker, reduce labor costs, labor strife,
and increase productivity and profits. Authors conclude
that the "linkage between satisfaction and productivity
is hard to measure, harder to establish and almost impossible to affect through direct interventions."

575. Birchall, David, Ray Wild, and Colin Carnall. "Redesign-
      ing a Way to Worker Participation." *Personnel Manage-
      ment*, 8 (August 1976), 26-28.

      The Henley Work Research Group of England approached
job design from the view that one critical element is
decision making participation at the shop floor level.

576. Blumberg, Paul. *Industrial Democracy: The Sociology of
      Participation*. New York: Schocken Books, 1968, 234.

      Presents the view that "workers' management" may be
an important issue in the 1970s, 80s, and 90s. Major

forces "pushing in the direction of a renewal of the issue of workers' management" are examined. Issues such
as: (1) mitigation of alienation through direct workers'
participation, (2) growth and significance of public
ownership, (3) internal logic of Socialist ideology,
(4) liberal ideology acting to "extend participation
beyond political boundaries, (5) and Yugoslav experiment
with workers' management.

577. Champagne, Paul J., and Curt Tausky. "When Job Enrichment Doesn't Pay." *Personnel*, 55 (January–February
1978), 30-40.

Report of a job satisfaction project judged to be a
failure because management did not increase compensation
as responsibility increased.

578. Collins, Donald C., and Robert R. Raubolt. "A Study of
Employee Resistance to Job Enrichment." *Personnel
Journal*, 54 (April 1975), 232-235 and 248.

Resistance to job enrichment in a large manufacturing
firm among engineers, engineering associates and drafts-
men was relative to: (1) economic factors; (2) job security; (3) social influences; (4) job convenience; (5)
self-actualization; and (6) employee-management cooperation.

579. Cooper, M.R., B.S. Morgan, P.M. Foley, and L.B. Kaplan.
"Changing Employee Values: Deepening Discontent?"
Harvard Business Review, 57 (January–February 1979),
117-125.

Presents trends in employee attitudes toward the company and the job, security and pay, management and supervision, and esteem-related factors over a 25-year
period. Major findings include: "(1) managers are usually more satisfied than are clerical and hourly employees; (2) most employees agree that their company is not
as good a place to work in as it once was; (3) discontent
among hourly and clerical employees seems to be growing;
(4) most employees rate their pay favorably; (5) currently there is a downward trend in employees' rating of
the equity with which they are treated; and (6) employees increasingly expect their companies to do something
about their problems and complaints." The reader is
reminded that changing employee values are real and
must be addressed in innovative ways.

580. Cummings, Thomas G., and Edmund S. Molloy. *Improving Productivity and the Quality of Work Life*. New York: Praeger, 1977, 291, Bibliography.

The basis for much that is presented in this book is the research supported by the National Science Foundation dealing with policy-related research on productivity, industrial organization, and job satisfaction. Fifty-eight experiments were assessed. The material is organized into seven parts: (1) autonomous work groups; (2) job restructuring; (3) participative management; (4) organization-wide change; (5) organizational behavior modification; (6) flexible working hours; and (7) Scanlon plans.

581. Cummings, Thomas G., and Suresh Srivastva. *Management of Work: A Socio-technical Systems Approach*. Kent, OH: Comparative Administration Research Institute, 1977, 247, Bibliography.

Presents a historical perspective of management and a definition of work at the individual level, group organization level and societal level. Socio-technical systems are thoroughly discussed and strategies for applying the concepts of socio-technical systems design in organizations are presented.

582. Davis, Louis E. "Job Design and Productivity: A New Approach." *Personnel*, 33 (March 1975), 418-430.

Presents job design as a concept and outlines some approaches. The traditional view of job design is challenged. This article is a report of a study designed to test how productivity could be improved by altering job content. He reports reduced cost and a gain in productivity.

583. Davis, Louis E., and James C. Taylor, editors. *Design of Jobs*. Second edition. Santa Monica, CA: Goodyear Publishing, 1979, 459, Bibliography.

The first edition was one of the first books of readings on job design. This second edition shows "that the concepts and requirements for the design of jobs have changed in recent years." Works have been carefully selected to bring the reader up to date on what is happening in organizations today. A volume well worth reading and owning.

584. Davis, Louis E., and Albert B. Cherns, editors. *The Quality of Working Life, Volume I: Problems, Prospects and the State of the Art, Volume II: Cases and Commentary.* New York: The Free Press, 1975.

Addresses the problems of being a working person in an organization in this post industrial era. The seven parts of the first volume are: (1) Enhancing the Quality of Working Life; (2) Defining and Measuring the Quality of Working Life; (3) Changing the Quality of Working Life; (4) Technology and the Quality of Working Life; (5) Quality of Working Life--The Context of Change; (6) Quality of Working Life--The Context of Bargaining; and (7) Quality of Working Life--A Central Issue in Industrial Relations. Volume II presents cases and commentary.

585. Dawis, R.V. "Personnel Assessment From the Perspective of the Theory of Work Adjustment." *Public Personnel Management*, 9 (No. 4, 1980), 268-273.

The Theory of Work Adjustment is based on the "interaction between an individual and his work environment and focuses on two aspects of the individual--needs and skills--and on two parallel aspects of the work environment--task requirements and reinforcers. The interaction between individual and environment results in the two outcomes of interest: the individual's satisfaction and satisfactoriness. In turn, these two outcomes result in a third outcome: *tenure* or length of stay on the job."

586. Emery, F.E., and E.L. Trist. "Sociotechnical Systems." In *Systems Thinking*, edited by F.E. Emery. Harmondsworth, England: Penguin Books, 1969, 398, Bibliography.

Authors present a discussion of "closed" and "open" systems theory followed by a discussion of the environments within and without the enterprise. The main point is that "as the primary task of an enterprise changes, relations with the environment may change with (1) the productive efforts of the enterprise in meeting environmental requirements: (2) changes in the environment that may be induced by the enterprise; and (3) changes independently taking place in the environment."

587. Ford, Robert N. *Why Jobs Die and What To Do About It.* New York: AMACOM, 1979, 220, Bibliography.

In Part I (Job Design and Work Organization) the author tells the reader why jobs get into trouble, gives 22 strat-

egies for increasing the motivational quality of a job,
and proposes a 27-statement prescription for maintaining redesigned jobs. In Part II (About Your Job) he
helps the reader evaluate his own situation and offers
practical suggestions for dealing with unsatisfactory
tasks or work assignments.

588.   ————. "Job Enrichment-Lessons from AT&T." *Harvard
        Business Review*, 51 (January-February 1973), 96-106.

The author, Personnel Director--Work Organization and
Environment Research for AT&T, briefly discusses AT&T's
seven years' experience with job enrichment. He presents
the elements of individual job enrichment and introduces
the "nesting" concept; grouping related jobs which have
already been enriched.

589.   ————. *Motivation Through the Work Itself*. New York:
        American Management Association, 1969, 267.

Summary report of the "work itself" experiments conducted within the Bell System in the mid-1960s. Precipi-
tated by high employee turnover, nineteen separate experiments were initiated to enrich the jobs of selected
employees. The experiments are reported as successful
in achieving the company goals of improved quality of
service, improved (or at least maintained) productivity
levels, decreased turnover, lowered costs and improved
employee satisfaction in job assignments. The report
also contains discussion of the insights gained through
the experiments, a section on "how you too can do it,"
comments on the trials by the author and two appendices
containing supplemental material.

590.   Foulkes, Fred K. *Creating More Meaningful Work*. New
        York: American Management Association, 1969, 210,
        Bibliography.

Focusing on job design, the author "examines selected
conscious attempts to increase the meaningfulness of
work at the nonmanagement level." The programs examined
represent a variety of approaches such as job rotation,
employee participation and involvement, and job improvement (motivation through the work itself).

591.   French, Wendell L., and Cecil H. Bell, Jr. *Organiza-
        tion Development: Behavioral Science Interventions
        For Organization Improvement*. Englewood Cliffs, NJ:
        Prentice-Hall, 1978, 264.

About organization development, "the applied behavioral science discipline that seeks to improve organizations through planned, systematic, long-range efforts focused on the organization's culture and its human and social processes. The means of OD are behavioral science and structural interventions into the ongoing organization. The goals of OD are to make the organization more effective, more viable, and better able to achieve both the goals of the organization as an entity and the goals of the individuals within the organization." This book is one of the best introductions to OD.

592. Gellerman, Saul W. *Management By Motivation*. New York: American Management Association, 1968, 727.

Deals with the motivational levers available to management and explains the "degree of control managers really have over employees, considers their effects, and outlines what appears, on the basis of available behavioral science knowledge, to be a sensible strategy for using them." Examines how this knowledge can be applied to organizational problems, why it is usually not applied and what might be done about this. Reviews motivational theory, considers selection of the appropriate employees and managers and examines the process of individual growth and development. Analyzes the effects of money upon motivation and concludes with an examination of organizational climates and the process of organizational development.

593. Ghropade, J., and T.J. Atchison. "The Concept of Job Analysis: A Review and Some Suggestions." *Public Personnel Management*, 9 (September 1980), 134-144.

The concept of "job analysis has recently been resurrected and is now considered critical in validation of personnel procedures and in promoting effectiveness and efficiency in personnel management." The concept is controversial and "the basic meaning of the term is in dispute. This paper attempts to sort out the areas of controversy and to provide a framework for resolving them."

594. Goldman, Robert B. *A Work Experiment: Six Americans In A Swedish Plant*. New York: The Ford Foundation, 1976, 48.

Six American auto workers from Detroit traveled to Sweden to work in the engine assembly plant of Saab.

The project was designed to record reactions of the workers to work as it is designed in Sweden. The American
workers were concerned with the social aspects of the
job more than the technical content. The report is a
mixture of good and bad reports of individual experiences.

595. Golembiewski, Robert T., and Carl W. Praehl, Jr. "Public
      Sector Applications of Flexible Workhours: A Review
      of Available Experience." *Public Administration Re-
      view*, 40 (January–February 1980), 72–85.

      The literature on flexible workhours (F-T) "reflects
      two themes: hurry up and wait." The authors analyze
      74 applications of F-T "via interpretation of four tabu-
      lar summaries. In order, the tables: (1) present an
      overview of major characteristics of the 32 public
      sector studies; (2) review behavioral effects of F-T
      applications observed in public agencies; (3) summarize
      F-T's major effects on employee attitudes; and (4) pro-
      vide perspective on the major supervisory attitudes re-
      lated to F-T."

596. Grupp, Fred W., and Allan R. Richards. "Job Satisfaction
      Among State Executives in the U.S." *Public Personnel
      Management*, 4 (March–April, 1975), 104–109.

      The results of a questionnaire sent to executives in
      ten states shows that state executives are more satis-
      fied with their jobs than either federal executives or
      executives in private business. Job security, opportunity
      to serve the public, and the challenge they find in their
      work were listed as the attractive aspects of state em-
      ployment. Political interference, lack of self-determi-
      nation, and salary levels were listed as least attrac-
      tive aspects.

597. Guest, Robert H. "Quality of Work Life–Learning From
      Terrytown." *Harvard Business Review*, 57 (July–August
      1979), 76–87.

      The reader is walked through the eight-year process
      of implementing a Quality of Work Life Program in the
      oldest and one of the largest assembly plants in the
      General Motors system.

598. Gyllenhammer, Pehr G. "How Volvo Adapts Work to People."
      Harvard Business Review, 55 (July–August 1977), 102–113.

      Describes the human-scaled work groups within Volvo's
      Kalmar factory in Sweden. The work itself is organized

so that each group is responsible for a particular, identifiable portion of the car. This is the Swedish application of industrial democracy.

599. Hackman, J. Richard. "The Design of Work in the 1980s." *Organizational Dynamics* (Summer 1978), 3-17.

Looks at work in light of the few innovations in job redesign which have been initiated and the larger trend toward fitting people to jobs. He is not optimistic about reversing the trend.

600. ————. "Is Job Enrichment Just a Fad?" *Harvard Business Review*, 53 (September-October 1975), 129-138.

Author lists six attributes of unsuccessful job enrichment projects and five qualities common to successful ones. He asserts that the theory upon which job enrichment is based is sound and that implementation has been faulty.

601. Hackman, J. Richard, and Greg R. Oldham. *Work Redesign.* Reading, MA: Addison-Wesley, 1980, 347.

Central theme is that the quality of the relationship between the worker and his or her job is one of the major influences on organizational productivity. Job characteristics theory provides the framework for the diagnosis and redesign of jobs. The Job Diagnostic Survey, which measures the variables of skill variety, task identity, task significance, autonomy and feedback, is presented and explained. Work redesign is then put into a change/OD context.

602. Hackman, J. Richard, and Mary Dean Lee. *Redesigning Work: A Strategy For Change* (Annotated Bibliography). New York: Work in America Institute, 1979.

Excellent source for anyone embarking on a study of job design.

603. Hackman, J. Richard, and Greg R. Oldham. "Motivation Through the Design of Work: Test of a Theory." *Organizational Behavior and Human Performance*, Vol. 16, 1976, 250-279.

Authors critically review job redesign theories and then present their own "Job Characteristics Model." The model "attempts to specify the objective characteristics of jobs that create conditions for internal work motivation."

604. Hackman, J. Richard, Greg R. Oldham, Robert Janson, and
      Kenneth Purdy. "A New Strategy for Job Enrichment."
      California Management Review, 17 (Summer 1975), 57-71.

      Provides a set of tools for diagnosing existing jobs
      and a map for translating the diagnostic results into
      specific action steps for job redesign.

605. Hackman, J. Richard, and Edward E. Lawler III. "Employee
      Reactions to Job Characteristics." *Journal of Applied
      Psychology* (Monograph), 55 (June 1971), 259-286.

      Report of the research conducted to test the hypothe-
      sis that individuals with strong desires for higher
      order need satisfaction respond much more positively to
      high level jobs than do individuals who have weaker high-
      er order needs. It was found that employees desirous of
      higher order need satisfactions demonstrated a positive
      relationship between the four core dimensions (variety,
      autonomy, task identity, and feedback) and motivation,
      satisfaction, performance and attendance. The subjects
      for this study were 208 employees of a telephone company
      who worked on 13 different jobs.

606. Hall, Douglas T. *Careers in Organizations*. Pacific Pali-
      sades, CA: Goodyear Publishing, 1976.

      Discussion of organizational policies and procedures
      and how they affect individual careers. Stresses indivi-
      dualizing and humanizing the organization.

607. Herzberg, Frederick. *The Managerial Choice*. Homewood,
      IL: Dow Jones-Irwin, 1976, 360, Bibliography.

      Complete Herzberg. Presents his theory and its prac-
      tical applications. Chapter 6 contains questions and
      answers regarding Motivation/Hygiene Theory and job
      enrichment.

608. ─────. "The Wise Old Turk." *Harvard Business Review*,
      52 (September-October 1974), 70-80.

      Presents four approaches to job design and discusses
      the advantages and disadvantages of each. Classifies his
      approach as "Orthodox Job Enrichment" and devotes half
      the article to it. The remaining three approaches to job
      design (sociotechnical systems, participative management
      and industrial democracy) receive a brief review. Sug-
      gests that asking the "Wise Old Turk" about how it was
      years ago may provide the very job design desired.

609. ————. "One More Time: How Do You Motivate Employees?" *Harvard Business Review*, 46 (January-February 1968), 53-62.

Discussion of motivation--what it is and is not. Briefly presents his Motivation/Hygiene Theory and moves on to a description of the characteristics of job enrichment. Included is a guide to the implementation of an individual job enrichment program.

610. ————. *Work and the Nature of Man.* Cleveland, OH: World Publishing, 1966, 203, Bibliography.

Presentation of his Motivation/Hygiene Theory and verification of the theory through duplicative studies. Recommends to industry that they institute a division in the company concerned with motivator needs and outlines the tasks of such a dividion.

611. Herzberg, Frederick, and Alex Zautra. "Orthodox Job Enrichment: Measuring True Quality in Job Satisfaction." *Personnel*, 53 (September-October 1976), 54-68.

Hypothesis 1--employees of Ogden Air Logistics Center (Hill Air Force Base) Utah, would report a positive change in job satisfaction due to the Orthodox Job Enrichment program. Hypothesis 2--emphasis by the employees would be placed on responsibility, advancement and growth. Hypothesis 3--Orthodox Job Enrichment would become institutionalized. Reports a successful OD effort.

612. Hicks, William D., and Richard J. Klimoski. "The Impact of Flexitime on Employee Attitudes." *Academy of Management Journal*, 24 (June 1981), 333-341.

Investigation of "flexitime did not support the traditional flexitime consequences for work satisfaction or leisure satisfaction. However, employees working under a flexitime schedule reported certain other improvements, including easier travel and parking, a smaller amount of interrole conflict, a greater feeling of being in control in the work setting, and more opportunity for leisure activities."

613. Ivancevich, John M., and Michael T. Matteson. *Stress and Work: A Managerial Perspective.* Glenview, IL: Scott, Foresman & Co., 1980, 228, Epilogue, Glossary.

Examines stressors such as role conflict, work overload, personal obsolescence, inflation, marital disharmony and

"how people respond to them, what effects they may have
on health and performance, and what can be done to prevent or neutralize negative stress outcomes."

614. Jason, Robert. "Work Redesign: A Results-Oriented Strat-
     egy That Works." *Academy of Management Journal*, 44
     (Winter 1979), 21-27.

     Suggests that the term "job enrichment" should be bur-
     ied and replaced with "work redesign." Through examples
     from the world of work, the argument is made for jobs
     which involve: (1) completing a whole piece of work; (2)
     receiving feedback from supervisors or clients; and (3)
     dealing with fellow employees in getting the job done.
     Key to accomplishing the above is relinquishing authority
     to the lowest appropriate level.

615. Jauch, Lawrence R., and Uma Sekaran. "Employee Orienta-
     tion Among Professional Employees in Hospitals."
     Journal of Management, 4 (Spring 1978), 43-56.

     Research Questions: "(1) Are employees with more pro-
     fessional identification more likely to have the most
     satisfaction with 'work' itself? (2) Will individuals
     with more organizational loyalty and professional iden-
     tification experience more satisfaction with supervision?
     (3) Will individuals with more peer loyalty experience
     greater satisfaction with coworkers? (4) Will individuals
     with more professional identification and organizational
     loyalty experience greater satisfaction with promotion?
     (5) Do professionals with some particular orientations
     react to satisfaction with pay in distinct patterns?"
     Predictors of job satisfaction were found to be organi-
     zational loyalty, peer loyalty and professional identi-
     fication. Organizational loyalty accounted for the ma-
     jority of job satisfaction.

616. Katz, Ralph. "Job Longevity as a Situational Factor in
     Job Satisfaction." *Administrative Science Quarterly*,
     23 (June 1978), 204-223.

     Explores the relationship between job satisfaction and
     the five task dimensions of task identity, task signifi-
     cance, autonomy and feedback from job at different peri-
     ods of job longevity within the public sector. Job
     satisfaction is directly associated with each of the five
     task characteristics. The strength of the association is
     dependent upon the job itself and job longevity.

617. ————. "Job Enrichment: Some Career Considerations."
Organizational Careers: Some New Perspectives, edited
by John Van Maanen. London: John Wiley, 1977, 133-
147.

Reports on job enrichment data gathered from four
governmental organizations. Longevity measures and
overall work satisfaction were correlated with task
identity, skill variety, autonomy, task significance,
feedback from job, promotional fairness and feedback
from agents. The findings do not support the assump-
tion that employees will always respond positively to
increases in various task dimensions.

618. Keaveny, Timothy J., John H. Jackson, and John A. Fossum.
"Are There Sex Differences in Job Satisfaction." *The
Personnel Administrator*, 23 (March 1978), 55-58.

Findings indicate that "men and women basically do not
differ in the proportion expressing satisfaction with
their jobs."

619. Kerr, Clark, and Jerome R. Rosow. *Work in America: The
Decade Ahead*. New York: Van Nostrand Reinhold, 1979,
280.

Represents the efforts of "more than 300 leaders from
industry, government, labor, communications, and univer-
sities across the country" who attended three national
symposia sponsored by the Work in America Institute and
held in New York, Chicago and San Francisco. This group
identified the "major problem areas and changes in work
in America," wrestled with the issues and this volume is
"the distillation of these debates and discussions, divided into two major areas: The Work Force of the Future
and The Emerging Work Environment.

620. Krausy, Moshe. "A New Approach to Studying Worker Job
Preferences." *Industrial Relations*, 17 (February 1978),
91-95.

Managers and would-be managers were asked to react to
sixty job descriptions and rank their willingness or un-
willingness to join the organization. Each job description contained the following six different reward factors: (1) starting salary; (2) flexibility of work requirements; (3) job security; (4) opportunities for advancement; (5) responsibility and opportunity to participate in decision making; and (6) opportunities for personal growth and development. Findings reveal that se-

curity and salary factors accounted for more than 60
percent of the total variance in organizational choice.
These factors were followed in order by advancement,
flexibility and growth. "It appears that managers sense
psychological pressures to repress the true nature of
their emotions and needs. They often present themselves
as cool, unemotional and nonanxious persons, even when
this is not what they really feel."

621. Lawler, Edward E., III, J. Richard Hackman, and Stanley
      Kaufman. "Effects of Job Redesign: A Field Experiment."
      Journal of Applied Social Psychology, 3 (Nov. 1973),
      49-62.

      Authors sought to enrich two telephone company jobs--
      "directory assistance" and "toll operator." They suc-
      ceeded in enriching these jobs in two of the four core
      dimensions. According to the Hackman-Lawler theory, a
      job must be made high in all four dimensions for in-
      creases in motivation and satisfaction to be realized.
      Results are also reported of "spinoff" effects associated
      with interpersonal relationships.

622. Lawler, Edward E., III. *Motivation in Work Organizations*.
      Monterey, CA: Brooks/Cole Publishing, 1973, 198, Bibli-
      ography.

      Provides the reader with a solid discussion of moti-
      vation theory; the goals people choose and how they de-
      cide to achieve those goals. It also presents research
      results and points the way to pragmatic applications of
      theory.

623. McGregor, Douglas. *The Professional Manager*. New York:
      McGraw-Hill, 1967, 196.

      The four recurring themes are: (1) theory--"assump-
      tions about life and how they influence our worldview";
      (2) the culture of management--an inhospitable milieu
      where the expression of natural human responses is taboo;
      (3) "integration within the framework of a transactional
      concept of power and influence; and (4) the problem of
      managing differences and the ways in which management
      could cope with the necessity of diversity and incon-
      gruities as well as the potentialities for collaboration
      and teamwork."

624. ————. *The Human Side of Enterprise*. New York: McGraw-
      Hill, 1960, 246.

Presentation of now famous Theory X, Theory Y, management assumptions. Author asserts that "the theoretical
assumptions management holds about controlling its human
resources determine the whole character of the enterprise."

625. McNichols, Charles W., Michael J. Stahl, and T. Roger
Manley. "A Validation of Hoppock's Job Satisfaction
Measure." *Academy of Management Journal*, 21 (December
1978), 737-742.

Hoppock's measure consists of four questions related
to various aspects of a person's job satisfaction. The
authors recommend its use.

626. Meyers, M. Scott. "Overcoming Union Opposition to Job
Enrichment." *Harvard Business Review*, 49 (May-June
1971), 37-49.

Unions often impede OD efforts when they view such
efforts as infringing on "what unions see as their pre-
rogative of prescribing the roles and reward systems
of the workers." Author describes the approaches taken
by four companies in "making job enrichment and other
aspects of OD feasible in the unionized work force."

627. Moberg, Dennis J. "Job Enrichment Through Symbol Management." *California Management Review*, 24 (Winter
1981), 24-30.

"Employees perceive their jobs subjectively and their
perceptions are influenced by symbolic messages sent by
those around them. Managers careless about the symbols
they create can adversely affect job perceptions. Of
particular importance are the symbolic messages imbedded
in what managers say, what they do, and where they interact."

628. Newman, John E., and Terry A. Beehr. "Personnel and Organizational Strategies for Handling Job Stress: A
Review of Research and Opinion." *Personnel Psychology*, 32 (Spring 1979), 1-43.

Follow-up article to Beehr and Newman, 1978. The
literature search is relevant to the adaptive responses
facet. Purpose of the paper is to interest (I/O) psy-
chologists in the study of job stress. Stress literature
organized as follows: (1) personal adaptive responses
to stress; (2) organizational strategies for handling

job stress; and (3) strategies by persons and organizations outside the focal organization.

629. Olson, Dan, and Arthur P. Brief. "Review of Research--
      The Impact of Alternative Workweeks." *Personnel Jour-
      nal*, 55 (January-February 1978), 73-77.

      Discussion of the merits and disadvantages of the four-
      day workweek and flexitime. Effects on job satisfac-
      tion have been positive while effects on productivity
      and absenteeism are mixed.

630. Parke, E. Lauch, and Curt Tausky. "The Mythology of Job
      Enrichment: Self-Actualization Revisited." *Personnel
      Journal*, 52 (September-October 1975), 12-21.

      Argues for: (1) holding a person accountable for the
      job he/she does; and (2) rewarding job performance. Job
      enrichment for the sake of helping an employee advance
      up Maslow's scale is unrealistic.

631. Patten, Thomas H., Jr. "Job Evaluation and Job Enlarge-
      ment: A Collision Course." *Human Resource Management*,
      16 (Winter 1977), 2-8.

      Discussion of the problems surrounding job enrichment
      since it is traditionally viewed as a challenge to per-
      sonnel work and to concepts of job descriptions and job
      evaluation.

632. Prescott, Donald L. "Variation in the Scheduling of
      Work: A Look at Some of the Models." *The Bureaucrat*,
      9 (Summer 1980), 58-64.

      Five work-hour models are discussed: "the standard
      workweek (the rational-legal), the extended workweek
      (human resources), staggered work hours (scientific),
      flexitime (human relations), and the compressed work-
      week (systems)." As indicated, each work-hour model sub-
      sumes a specific management theory.

633. Rainey, Glenn W., and Lawrence Wolf. "Flextime: Short-
      term Benefits; Long-term ...?" *Public Administration
      Review*, 41 (January-February 1981), 52-63.

      Report of an experiment at the U.S. Social Security
      administration, in which "flextime elicited generally
      favorable subjective evaluations, but objective indica-
      tors of performance and employee commitment produced
      mixed results and there were tentative signs of declin-

ing supervisor/employee rapport. Several observations, including an unexpected rise in leave usage, suggested that employees valued flextime principally for rewards obtained away from the work site. The analysis suggests several points of caution to guide future research: (1) flextime may augment the intrinsic rewards of work already enjoyed by white collar employees while reemphasizing the relative attractiveness of domestic life for blue collar employees; (2) the gains observed in prior research may reflect a 'Hawthorne' effect and be short lived, and as enthusiasm for flextime wanes, the alienating effects of problems not remedied by flextime might reasonably be expected to reassert themselves with redoubled force; (3) therefore, future research must be extended to encompass the effects of the entire work setting as well as employees' domestic interests; and (4) managers who rely on poorly conceived field research to test flextime must be prepared to encounter unanticipated problems in the long-term."

634. Rainey, Glenn W., and Lawrence Wolf. "The Organizationally Dysfunctional Consequences of Flexible Work Hours: A General Overview." *Public Personnel Management*, 11 (No. 2, 1982), 165-175.

"Summarizes the evidence concerning unanticipated consequences of the adoption of variable work hours, tentatively identifies potential causes, specifies a series of dysfunctional results which may be experienced by organizations that adopt variable work hours, and suggests some means by which organizations might minimize or avoid these dysfunctional outcomes."

635. Rawson, G.E., and R.L. Smith. "A Look at Job Satisfaction in the Public Sector Through the Need-Satisfaction Theory." *Midwest Review of Public Administration*, 12 (September 1978), 155-163.

The measurement and use of job satisfaction "as an indicator of the quality of the work situation in America" has been given increasing attention in recent years. "Motivation and organization development through job satisfaction may be one of the most easily implemented management strategies in the public sector." The authors examine data gathered from a 1975 survey of state employees and find "that the determinants of job satisfaction lie in both the job and the work environment." However, much work must be done before the need-satisfaction theory can be operationalized in "organizational and individual development programs."

636. Reitz, H. Joseph, and Linda N. Jewell. "Sex, Locus of Control, and Job Involvement: A Six-Country Investigation." *Academy of Management Journal*, 22 (March 1979), 72-80.

Three hypotheses were tested: (1) "There is a significant relationship between locus of control and job involvement: internals are more involved than externals; (2) the relationship between locus of control and job involvement for males differs from the relationship between IE and JI for females; and (3) job characteristics moderate the IE-JI relationship: the relationship is stronger for high skill than for low skill jobs." Findings indicate that: (1) Hypothesis one is supported. Internals scored higher on job involvement than did externals. A discussion of male and female differences is presented; (2) Hypothesis two is supported; and (3) Hypothesis three is not supported by the research.

637. Roberts, Karlene H., and Frederick Savage. "Twenty Questions: Utilizing Job Satisfaction Measures." *California Management Review*, 15 (Spring 1973), 82-89.

The authors have designed twenty questions which they feel are effective in determining whether a job satisfaction survey should be conducted within an organization. "The 'Twenty Questions' strategy will merely force consideration of the costs and benefits associated with job satisfaction surveys and provide the groundwork for selecting instruments."

638. Rosow, Jerome M., editor. *The Worker and the Job: Coping with Change*. Englewood Cliffs, NJ: Prentice-Hall, 1974, 208.

The forty-third American Assembly considered the issue of job satisfaction. This volume contains a collection of essays arising from that assembly. The issue seems to be the out-of-step work place that is not changing as rapidly as the worker and the environment and is dealt with conceptually as well as from a pragmatic point of view.

639. Rouleau, Eugene J., and Burton F. Krain. "Using Job Analysis to Design Selection Procedures." *Public Personnel Management*, 4 (September-October 1975), 300-304.

The many facets of job analysis are explored from the perspective of experienced job analysis practitioners.

The adequacy and sufficiency of job analysis information
is questioned in light of the possible pitfalls that
may befall such a study. A table is presented to relate
various job analytic techniques to sample sizes, cost and
complexity of occupations. Limitations as to the uses
to job analysis information are also presented."

640. Rush, Harold M.F. *Job Design For Motivation: Experi-*
ments in Job Enlargement and Job Enrichment. New
York: The Conference Board, 1971.

Presents an overview of job design theories, some
strategies for implementation and describes seven job
design projects that were judged successful.

641. Saari, J.T., and J. Lahtela. "Job Enrichment--Cause of
Increased Accidents." *Industrial Engineering*, 10
(October 1978), 42-45.

Findings indicate that high accident frequency jobs
were enlarged and enriched in a "natural" way rather than
through active planning. The solution appears to be to:
(1) enlarge and enrich jobs through planned activity; and
(2) train workers in the enlarged/enriched aspects of the
job as well as they were trained in the original task.

642. Sauer, William I., Jr., and C. Michael York. "Sex Differences in Job Satisfaction: A Reexamination." *Per-*
sonnel Psychology, 31 (Autumn 1978), 537.

In the past there have been a number of studies which
report men are more satisfied with their jobs than women.
Other studies assert the opposite. Still others say
there is no difference. This study demonstrates that
there are a number of variables which modify the sex-
job satisfaction relationship.

643. Sheppard, Harold L., and Neal Q. Herrick. *Where Have*
All the Robots Gone? New York: The Free Press, 1972,
222, Bibliography.

Where have all the workers gone who are willing to en-
dure boring, soul-killing tasks for the weekly pay check?
This book reports the results of three national surveys
of working class men and women. The findings illustrate
a deepening discontent. The authors are optimistic and
see change as a possibility.

644. Sheppard, Jon M. "Job Enrichment--Some Problems With Con-
      tingency Models." *Personnel Journal*, 53 (December
      1974), 886-889.

      Points out flaws in contingency models and warns pro-
      job enrichers as well as con-job enrichment advocates to
      move cautiously. One answer does not fit all situations.

645. Singleton, W.T. *Man-Machine Systems*. Baltimore: Pen-
      guin Books Inc., 1974, 162, Glossary, References.

      Examines "the design of work from a systems viewpoint.
      The systems in question have men and machines as their
      components, and it is the integration of these components
      which provides the focus. Concerned with the allocation
      of function between man and machine author emphasizes
      how this should be seen as a matter of delegation from
      the former to the latter. Deals with the analysis of
      work-tasks, skills, and errors, and moves on to ques-
      tions of selection and training. Scene is set for an
      examination of the complex interfaces between operators
      and their machines."

646. Smith, Howard R. "The Uphill Struggle for Job Enrich-
      ment." *California Management Review*, 23 (Summer 1981),
      33-38.

      "Why do we see substantially more lip service to the
      idea of job enrichment than enrichment innovations cal-
      culated to 'buy' more or better work? Three things may
      be involved. There is a scarcity of job richness, and
      more for workers could mean less for first-level bosses,
      who already enjoy little enrichment. Also, the job
      enrichment 'bargain' may not seem nearly as inviting
      to potential enrichees as management writers and mana-
      gers have led themselves to believe. Finally, we may be
      implementing the most promising job enrichment possibili-
      ties first--and moving thereby toward greater and greater
      cost-benefit difficulties."

647. Smith, Russ. "Job Redesign in the Public Sector: The
      Track Record." *Review of Public Personnel Administra-
      tion*, 2 (Fall 1981), 63-83.

      Examines the use of "job redesign techniques in the
      public sector. The psychological basis of job redesign
      is briefly reviewed, focusing on motivation theories.
      Several cases are reviewed illustrating the application
      of different techniques, and the utility of job redesign

in the public sector is assessed, concluding with a call for more rigorous research. An Appendix lists twenty-one cases of various job redesign efforts in the public sector."

648. Staines, Graham L., and Robert E. Quinn. "American Workers Evaluate the Quality of Their Jobs." *Monthly Labor Review*, 102 (January 1979), 3-12.

Report of the 1977 survey designed to measure the quality of employment in America. The 1977 data are compared with survey data collected in 1969 and 1973. A downward trend in job satisfaction is noted; there is an increase in willingness of employees to seek a different employer; and there is a life satisfaction decline. The authors offer an explanation for these survey results. Work related problems are: (1) earnings, (2) income, and (3) fringe benefits. Labor unions are discussed briefly.

649. Stenson, John E., and Thomas W. Johnson. "Tasks, Individual Differences, and Job Satisfaction." *Industrial Relations*, 16 (October 1977), 315-322.

Explores the "influence of individual differences on worker response to job characteristics by examining the moderating effect of need for achievement and need for affiliation on relationships between task characteristics and worker satisfaction." The task characteristics measured were task repetitiveness, task autonomy, and task structure. The findings indicate that: (1) task repetitiveness should be reduced or eliminated where possible; (2) repetitive jobs should, at least, be enlarged horizontally; (3) job enrichment programs that reduce job structure and repetitiveness and increase job autonomy would have a positive effect. Where possible, firms should match low achievers and low need affiliators with structured, simplified jobs.

650. Strauss, George. "Job Satisfaction, Motivation, and Job Redesign." In *Organizational Behavior: Research and Issues*, edited by George Strauss, Raymond E. Miles, Charles C. Snow, and Arnold S. Tennenbaum. Madison, WI: Industrial Relations Research Association, 1974, 220, Bibliography.

Provides background on worker discontent and offers a definition of job satisfaction. Studies are cited and results reported. Discusses the role of work in life, proposes forms of adjustment and discusses the process of adjustment.

651. Susman, Gerald I. *Autonomy At Work*. New York: Praeger,
      1976, 210, Bibliography.

      Analyzes present working conditions and forces for
      improving the quality of work life. Proposes design of
      socio-technical systems.

652. ————. "Job Enlargement: Effects of Culture on Worker
      Responses." *Industrial Relations*, 12 (February 1973),
      1-15.

      Tests the hypothesis that rural workers respond favor-
      ably to job enlargement while urban workers do not.
      Job enlargement is defined as "the process of allowing
      individual workers to determine their own pace (within
      limits), to serve as their own inspectors by giving them
      responsibility for quality control, to repair their own
      mistakes, to be responsible for their own machine set-
      up." The results do not confirm the hypothesis. "It
      appears that rural and urban birth or residence is too
      crude a distinction in the American context to expect
      opposite responses to occur."

653. Terkel, Studs. *Working: People Talk About What They Do
      All Day and How They Feel About What They Do*. New
      York: Avon Books, 1974, 762.

      A collection of interviews with all kinds of workers.
      Mr. Terkel travelled the U.S. for three years, talked to
      working people and sets forth in this book their feel-
      ings about what they do. It reveals pride and despair,
      passion and pathos, and truth about how it is to work in
      America in the 1970s.

654. Turner, Arthur N., and Paul R. Lawrence. *Industrial Jobs
      and The Worker*. Boston: Harvard University Graduate
      School of Business Administration, 1965.

      Report of three years of research in eleven industries.
      The research was designed to "develop and implement a
      method of measuring job attributes [such as the amount
      of variety, autonomy, responsibility and interactions
      with others] that would help predict workers' response
      to their jobs across a wide range of differing technolo-
      gies.

655. Vough, Clair F. *Tapping the Human Resource: A Strategy
      For Productivity*. New York: AMACOM, 1975, 212, Bibli-
      ography.

The author, formerly Vice President of the Office Products Division of IBM, is convinced that real job satisfaction and productivity result when a person has "total responsibility in a vertically organized job with the person's name on it." He uses his IBM experience to present a concrete and practical discussion of job responsibility, accountability, motivation, pay, and promotion and the interactions that increase productivity.

656. Walton, Richard E. "Work Innovations in the United States." *Harvard Business Review*, 57 (July-August 1979), 88-98.

Summary article about work innovations. The author presents his three-level conception of work improvement and discusses the interrelationship among techniques, outcomes, and culture. He concludes that work innovation projects that give equal weight to quality of working life and improved productivity are more likely to be successful than projects that stress one over the other.

657. Warr, Peter, and Toby Wall. *Work and Well-Being*. Harmondsworth, England: Penguin Books, 1975.

Study of Quality of Working Life through the examination of job satisfaction and mental health of the individual employee. Among the findings: "jobs which offer variety and require the individual to exercise discretion over his work activities lead to enhanced well-being and mental health."

658. Weaver, Charles N. "Job Satisfaction as a Component of Happiness Among Males and Females." *Personnel Psychology*, 31 (Winter 1978), 831-840.

Job satisfaction may not be of central importance to the overall happiness of most workers. Work and the work place are not always central life interests.

659. White, Bernard J. "Innovations in Job Design: The Union Perspective." *Journal of Contemporary Business*, 6 (Spring 1977), 23-25.

Presents: "(1) summary and evaluation of the criticisms directed at unions by certain advocates of the job dissatisfaction thesis and proponents of innovative job design; (2) some lessons from cooperative ventures and union response to management initiated innovations; and (3) a number of predictions concerning likely future directions of union response to these issues."

660. Wild, Ray. "Dimensions and Stages of Job Design." *Per-sonnel Management*, 6 (December 1974), 32-34 and 37.

Presents a job design life cycle and illustrates its development from industry job design programs.

661. *Work in America*. Report of a Special Task Force to the Secretary of Health, Education and Welfare, James O'Toole, Chairman. Cambridge, MA: The MIT Press, 1973, 186, Appendices, Bibliography.

Report addresses the ramifications of work, or lack of it, upon the American social system. It discusses the functions of work, the problems of blue- and white-collar workers, and the physical and mental costs paid by workers in poorly designed jobs. The "keystone" of the report is the chapter on the redesign of jobs. Recommendations, which appear throughout the text, include upgrading occupational status; more human supervision; increased emphasis on work teams; and creation of more challenging and responsible jobs. For those whose jobs are mundane, those who wish to make a career change and those desiring more training, the report recommends worker self-renewal programs. The issue of a federal policy advocating full employment (job creation) and the economic effects of such a policy are discussed.

CHAPTER 11

PUBLIC PERSONNEL TEXTS AND READERS

662. Bopp, William, and Paul Whisenand. *Police Personnel Administration*. Second edition. Boston: Allyn and Bacon, 1980, 341, Appendices.

663. Cayer, N. Joseph. *Managing Human Resources: An Introduction To Public Personnel Administration*. New York: St. Martin's Press, 1980, 226, Bibliography.

664. ————. *Public Personnel Administration in the United States*. New York: St. Martin's Press, 1975, 161, Bibliographical Note.

665. Crouch, Winston W., editor. *Local Government Personnel Administration*. Washington, DC: ICMA, 1976, 295, Bibliography, List of Contributors.

666. Famularo, Joseph J., editor. *Handbook of Modern Personnel Administration*. New York: McGraw-Hill, 1972, 81, Readings.

667. Golembiewski, Robert T., and Michael Cohen, editors. *People in Public Service: A Reader in Public Personnel Administration,* second edition. Itasca, IL: F.E. Peacock Publishers, 1976, 593.

668. Klingner, Donald E. *Public Personnel Management: Contexts and Strategies*. Englewood Cliffs, NJ: Prentice-Hall, 1980, 459.

669. Klingner, Donald E., editor. *Public Personnel Management: Readings in Contexts and Strategies*. Palo Alto, CA: Mayfield Publishing, 1981, 409.

670. Lee, Robert D. *Public Personnel Systems*. Baltimore: University Park Press, 1979, 424.

671. Levine, Marvin J., editor. *Public Personnel Management:*
     Readings, Cases, and Contingency Plans. Salt Lake
     City: Brighton Publishing, 1980.

672. Macy, John. *Public Service: The Human Side of Govern-*
     ment. New York: Harper and Row, 1971, 294.

673. Mosher, William E., and J. Donald Kingsley. *Public Per-*
     sonnel Administration. New York: Harper & Brothers,
     1936.

674. Nigro, Felix A. *Public Personnel Administration.* New
     York: Henry Holt & Co., 1959, 424, Selected Bibli-
     ography, Appendices.

675. Patten, Thomas H. Jr., editor. *Classics of Personnel*
     Management. Oak Park, IL: Moore Publishing, 1979,
     625.

676. Shafritz, Jay M., editor. *The Public Personnel World:*
     Readings on the Professional Practice. Chicago, IL:
     IPMA, 1977, 339, Appendices.

677. Shafritz, Jay M., editor. *A New World: Readings on Mod-*
     ern Public Personnel Management. Chicago, IL: IPMA,
     1975, 291.

678. Shafritz, Jay M., Albert C. Hyde, and David H. Rosenbloom.
     Personnel Management in Government: Politics and Pro-
     cess. Second edition. New York: Marcel Dekker, 1981,
     420, Bibliography.

679. Stahl, O. Glenn. *Public Personnel Administration.*
     Seventh edition. New York: Harper and Row, 1976,
     512, Bibliography.

680. ————. *The Personnel Job of Government Managers.*
     Chicago: IPMA, 1971, 176.

681. Stahl, O. Glenn, and Richard A. Staufenberger, editors.
     Police Personnel Administration. North Scituate, MA:
     Duxbury Press, 1974.

682. Thompson, Frank J. *Classics of Public Personnel Policy.*
     Oak Park, IL: Moore Publishing, 1979, 363, Appendix.

683. Torpey, William G. *Public Personnel Management.* New
     York: D. Van Nostrand Co., 1953, 380, Questions and
     Problems, Appendix.

684. Warner, W. Lloyd, et al. *The American Federal Executive*. New Haven, CT: Yale University Press, 1963, 405.

AUTHOR INDEX

Abdel-Halim, Ahmed 570
*Abood v. Detroit Board of
   Education* 181
Abramson, Joan 69
Adams, Harold W. 341
Adelsberg, Henri van 480
Adkins, John I., Jr. 143
Alber, A. 571
Albrecht, Maryann H. 103
Aldag, Ramon J. 572
Allan, Peter 208, 481
Ammons, David N. 342
Andersen, David F. 220
Anderson, Charles L. 542
Annoni, Anthony J. 235
Anthony, William P. 70
Argyle, Nolan J. 1
Arnett v. Kennedy 182
Arvey, Richard D. 295
Ashenfelter, Orley 257
Asher, Janet 71
Asher, Jules 71
Atchison, T. J. 593
Atwood, Jay F. 258

Backhouse, Constance 72, 73,
   74
Bakaly, C. G. 75
Balk, Walter L. 343, 344, 345,
   356
Ban, Carolyn 2
Barnes, Lewis B. 564
Barney, Jay B. 539
Bartlett, C. J. 430
Baruch, Ismar 259
Beaulieu, Rod 482

Beehr, Terry A. 573, 628
Beer, Michael 483, 484
Bell, Cecil H. 591
Bellone, Carl J. 3, 76
Benford, Robert J. 431
Berg, Ivar 574
Berliner, William M. 440
Bernardin, H. John 485
Bernstein, Marver H. 4
Berwitz, Clement J. 77
Beyer, Janice M. 486
Biles, George E. 209
Birchall, David 575
Bishop, Joan Fiss 78
Bishop v. Wood 183
Bittker, Boris 79
Blakely, Robert T., III 210
Blodgett, Timothy B. 87
Blumberg, Paul 576
Blumrosen, Alfred W. 296
Board of Regents v. Roth 184
Bocher, Rita B. 80
Bolton, Elizabeth B. 81
Bopp, William 662
Bowen, Marshall 70
Bowey, Angela 211
Branti v. Finkel 185
Brief, Arthur P. 572, 629
Brim-Donohoe, Lue Rachelle 432
Brinkerhoff, Derick W. 487
Brown, F. Gerald 433
Brown, Marsha D. 82
Brown, Robert W. 488
*Brown v. General Services Ad-
   ministration* 186
Brumback, Gary B. 489

201

Hackman, J. Richard 599, 600,
601, 602, 603, 604, 605,
621
Haire, Mason 226
Hall, Chester G., Jr. 23
Hall, Douglas T. 606
Hall, Francine S. 103
Hall, Grace 104
Hall, Thomas E. 227
Hamilton, Edward K. 366
Hanson, Bob 244
Hariton, Theodore 310
Harmon, Michael M. 105
Harris, Patricia A. 106
Harrison, Jared F. 367
Hart, David K. 107
Hart, Gary L. 311
Harty, Harry P. 368, 369
Harvey, Donald 24, 371
Hatvany, Nina 370
Hayes, Frederick O'R. 371
Hayward, Nancy S. 372, 373
Heclo, Hugh 25
Hellriegel, Don 108
Henderson, Richard 270, 271,
503
Heneman, Herbert G., III 228,
332, 552
Hennigan Patrick J. 346
Herbert, Adam W. 109
Herrick, Neal Q. 643
Herzberg, Frederick 607, 608,
609, 610, 611
Heyel, Carl 504
Hicks, William D. 612
Higginson, Margaret V. 238
Hoffman, Carl 110
Holley, William H. 497, 498,
505
Holmberg, Steven R. 209
Holmen, Milton G. 312
Hoogenboom, Ari 26
Hopkins, Anne. H. 506
Horton, Raymond D. 374
Huddleston, Mark W. 27
Huett, Dennis L. 313
Humphreys, Luther Wade 81
Hunsaker, K. A. 111
Hunt, Deryl G. 112

Hunter, L. C. 394
Huse, Edgar F. 450, 507
Hyde, Albert C. 229, 451, 461,
508, 678

Ingle, Henry T. 509
Ingraham, Patricia 11
Issac, Stephen 314
Ivancevich, John M. 230, 613

Jackson, Carlos 90
Jackson, John H. 618
Jacobson, Beverly 231
Jakus, Larry 30
James, Jennifer 113
Janson, Robert 604
Jason, Robert 614
Jauch, Lawrence R. 615
Jensen, Ollie A. 272
Jerdee, Thomas H. 154
Jewell, Linda N. 636
Johnson, Harriet McBryde 114
Johnson, Thomas W. 649
Jongeward, Dorothy 115
Josephson, Matthew 28
Judge, Noreen A. 147
Judson, Arnold S. 375

Kahn, Robert L. 315
Kaholas, Harvey 223
Kanter, Rosabeth Moss 487
Kaper, Robert 58
Kaplan, L. B. 579
Karnig, A. K. 116
Karper, Mark D. 273
Katz, Ralph 616, 617
Katzell, Raymond A. 376, 377
Kaufman, Hubert 510
Kaufman, Stanley 621
Kay, Emanuel 529
Kearney, William J. 511
Keaveny, Timothy J. 618
Keevey, Richard F. 378
Keller, R. L. 265
Keller, Robert T. 95
Kelley v. Johnson 193
Kelly, Michael J. 316
Kelso, William 117
Kenrick, John W. 379, 380